'This guide lives up to my high expectations and the authors' wisdom continues to guide my practice and challenge what I understand about autism. In my opinion, this is an essential resource for not only the person affected but also the people in their lives.'

– from the Foreword by Kirsty Dempster-Rivett, MSocSci PGDip Psych (Clin.)

'Finally, a much needed contribution to the literature on autism and mental health. Incredibly readable, this is a self-help book for adults across the spectrum to understand, manage and improve their mental health. A practical resource, dense with information and strategies, it covers many aspects of mental health, all of which are woven into the rich tapestry of the author's personal experience. The stories shared give this book another dimension by providing valuable insights into supporting those with Autism Spectrum Condition (ASC), making it an essential companion for families, friends and mental health professionals.'

– Gillian Chappé de Léonval, Family Support Advisor, Autism Asperger ACT

'For individuals with autism and mental health conditions, this self-help book empowers the reader with the information necessary to improve their lives. This book also needs to be read by neurotypicals for the exceptional insight into the autistic mind. I especially liked the thorough information regarding the importance of pets as therapy. This is a MUST READ!'

– Anita Lesko, BSN, RN, MS, CRNA, Certified Registered Nurse Anesthetist, Autism Advocate, Author, Speaker, Diagnosed with Asperger's at age 50

by the same authors

The Autism Spectrum Guide to Sexuality and Relationships
Understand Yourself and Make Choices that are Right for You
Emma Goodall
ISBN 978 1 84905 705 9
eISBN 978 1 78450 226 3

The Wonderful World of Work
A Workbook for Asperteens
Jeanette Purkis
Illustrated by Andrew Hore
ISBN 978 1 84905 499 7
eISBN 978 0 85700 923 4

Finding a Different Kind of Normal
Misadventures with Asperger Syndrome
Jeanette Purkis
Foreword by Donna Williams
ISBN 978 1 84310 416 2
eISBN 978 1 84642 469 4

of related interest

The Autism Spectrum and Depression
Nick Dubin
Foreword by Tony Attwood
ISBN 978 1 84905 814 8
eISBN 978 0 85700 242 6

Mindful Living with Asperger's Syndrome
Everyday Mindfulness Practices to Help You Tune in to the Present Moment
Chris Mitchell
ISBN 978 1 84905 434 8
eISBN 978 0 85700 867 1

Meditation for Aspies
Everyday Techniques to Help People with Asperger
Syndrome Take Control and Improve their Lives
Ulrike Domenika Bolls
Translated by Rowan Sewell
ISBN 978 1 84905 386 0
eISBN 978 0 85700 756 8

Aspies on Mental Health
Speaking for Ourselves
Edited by Luke Beardon and Dean Worton
ISBN 978 1 84905 152 1
eISBN 978 0 85700 287 7

The Guide to Good Mental Health on the Autism Spectrum

**Jeanette Purkis,
Dr Emma Goodall
and Dr Jane Nugent**

*Forewords by Dr Wenn Lawson
and Kirsty Dempster-Rivett*

Jessica Kingsley *Publishers*
London and Philadelphia

First published in 2016
by Jessica Kingsley Publishers
73 Collier Street
London N1 9BE, UK
and
400 Market Street, Suite 400
Philadelphia, PA 19106, USA

www.jkp.com

Library of Congress Cataloging in Publication Data
Names: Purkis, Jeanette, 1974- | Goodall, Emma, 1971- | Nugent, Jane.
Title: The guide to good mental health on the autism spectrum / Jeanette
    Purkis, Emma Goodall, and Jane Nugent.
Description: London ; Philadelphia : Jessica Kingsley Publishers, 2016. |
    Includes bibliographical references and index.
Identifiers: LCCN 2015038780 | ISBN 9781849056700 (alk. paper)
Subjects: LCSH: Autism spectrum disorders. | Autism. | Mental illness. |
    Comorbidity. | Mental health.
Classification: LCC RC553.A88 P85 2016 | DDC 616.85/882--
dc23 LC record available at http://lccn.loc.gov/2015038780

British Library Cataloguing in Publication Data
A CIP catalogue record for this book is available from the British Library

ISBN 978 1 84905 670 0
eISBN 978 1 78450 195 2

Printed and bound by CPI Group (UK) Ltd, Croydon CR0 4YY

CONTENTS

FOREWORD
Wenn Lawson

'People are born with their autism but…how it is expressed depends on their genes and their environment.' These words suggest a powerful concept at work amongst the autistic population that is often overlooked. Because our brains, as autistic people, are wired differently to the general population our responses to general issues can cause marked difficulties that can be mis-read and mis-treated. Neural diversity is true for all of us and all brains are wired differently, but as autistics we are different again.

It's not unusual for an autistic adult (especially women) to be either misdiagnosed with schizophrenia, personality disorders, depression and other mental health issues, because their autism isn't recognised, or appropriately diagnosed, but without understanding the impact autism has upon how the brain interprets daily life. Either way, individuals are strapped to mental health services. However, such services, without understanding autism, may only add to the individual's woes. So often mental health issues are poorly understood in any population, but if you add autism into the mix things are heightened and/or under-exposed. Firstly, appropriate assessment and diagnosis of an autism spectrum condition (ASC), where they exist, and then any possible mental health issue, need to be separately identified. Then, professional support informed of both scenarios (ASCs and mental health issues) can be offered with a possibility of making a real difference.

This book not only outlines the various mental health issues that anyone might live with; it goes much further, because it takes the knowledge of the issue but then adds autism too. The autistic population, being traditionally labelled as a population that lacks empathy, is devoid of imagination and lacks common sense, is at even higher risk of suicide and/or falling in with the wrong crowd, leading to issues with the criminal justice system. Our prisons have far too many inmates who would qualify for a diagnosis of ASC but have 'slipped through the net'.

When we begin to appreciate how ASC impacts upon individual's thinking and belief patterns we can also begin to understand how best to support them. Take a typical scenario from one autistic person's daily life:

'I know I must do some shopping today. I know I must do the washing. There are weeds growing in my garden today. Inside, my head is popping. If I rush into the day and go at it without stopping, I'll crash when only half way done; days go by without coping.

The beer sits in the fridge and is ready now for drinking. Just one or two, or more should do, to help me stop from sinking. After four or five, and I'm still alive, I crawl into bed without thinking.

Tomorrow is another day; a repeat of the day before. I'll wake up in the morning and my head will feel sore. My body will lack energy and my mood will be low. I know I should be 'up and at it', but the weeds continue to grow.

If only I could make a start and finish something, but how? If only I could understand what other people know. Why is life so demanding? Why is it that I fail? My autism impacts how I think, but society does as well.'

Autism influences perceptions and belief systems in a number of ways. If the individual is an introvert, naturally slow to make decisions, and finds it difficult to process facial and bodily information (body language) they easily misperceive the intentions of others as well as not understanding themselves. Very easily, misperceptions and false beliefs build up and take hold of the landscape one is living in. It's not just seeing life through a larger or smaller window, it's a larger or smaller window that has opaque glass in it too. This difficulty can be the way to unlock an answer. When the cloudiness and tarnish is removed from the window, clarity is allowed to emerge.

The authors of this book have taken this understanding and applied it to their knowledge and experience of both autism and a variety of mental health issues. The words in this book may help to take out the distortions that are paved into the core of belief systems, everyday choices and established misconceptions that negatively impact upon mental health.

Therefore, this book is more than just another resource tool for those of us living with ASC. It is a guide book for all those bumps in the road that offer a variety of options and confuse us or catch us unawares. It takes our mental health threats and draws a map to aid navigation around or through these. Its clear and concise explanations, plus practical application, make it a must have for anyone living and supporting ASC individuals.

Wenn Lawson

FOREWORD
Kirsty Dempster-Rivett

When I was training, the texts and articles written about the experience of living on the spectrum were largely written by 'experts' and often only about *what can be done to or for* the person. However, my friends and clients on the spectrum were people who passionately wanted to be active participants and drivers of their lives. Therefore, it is wonderful to finally have a resource available that provides information to empower people to be their own experts in understanding and managing their mental health and wellbeing.

There are many different mental health conditions that we as human beings can experience over our lifetime. Some of these occur during times of increased stress and/or are related to genetic vulnerabilities or biochemical changes. For others, feelings of sadness and anxiety can result from living in a world that does not readily understand or accommodate the needs of people with autism. When someone has autism, his or her experience and interaction with the world is different. Therefore it is logical that the expression of mental illness will have unique aspects that need to be considered.

This book provides the education needed to aid accurate identification of mental health conditions for people on the spectrum. This is essential to reduce the chance that thoughts and behaviours are not incorrectly attributed to autism alone or missed entirely. For example, withdrawal from others or agitation may be attributed to having autism, but may actually be symptoms of depression. A literal interpretation of 'do you hear voices' might be misconstrued as being indicative of psychosis.

A particular strength is the wide range of practical strategies targeted for the styles of thinking for people on the spectrum.

This ensures that the journey towards wellbeing can be tailored to an individual's strengths and can be adjusted as and when required. It is also an honest account that does not shy away from the challenging realities of managing the complexities of living with both. The coverage of the role of medication is one of the most thorough analyses I have seen and leaves the reader highly informed of the pros and cons of the options available.

The inclusion of real life experiences highlights the strategies that have worked well for people on the spectrum and, of course, those options that have not been helpful and in some cases harmful. Hopefully the honest insights provided will save people from years of confusion and suffering that have previously been the experience of others. This in turn reduces the sense of isolation and is in direct contradiction to the stigma and discrimination often surrounding mental illness and autism. It is not often that a book deftly manages to both challenge assumptions at the same time offer hope as achieved here.

I have admired these authors for sometime and have been very impressed with their educative approach to the topics addressed in this book. This guide lives up to my high expectations, and their wisdom continues to guide my practice and challenge what I understand about autism. In my opinion, this is an essential resource for not only the person affected but also the people in their lives, including mental health clinicians.

Kirsty Dempster-Rivett
MSocSci PGDip Psych (Clin.)

PREFACE

The Guide to Good Mental Health on the Autism Spectrum is a resource to help build mental health and wellbeing for adults who identify as being on the autism spectrum, their families and clinicians. It focuses on understanding and managing mental health conditions and symptoms in people on the autism spectrum, and presents information on a number of experiences around mental health that people on the autism spectrum commonly experience, outlining a range of strategies to address difficulties as well as explaining what these experiences are like and how they may present.

The book is written from a strong self-advocacy and recovery perspective, and focuses on empowering and enabling people to improve their lives and to live well with autism and mental health conditions. It contains useful guidance and easy-to-access information on the causes, outcomes and ways to address a number of issues faced by many people on the autism spectrum. It starts from the premise that people on the autism spectrum are the experts in living their own life. The book is essentially a self-help resource or a 'how-to' guide aimed at providing people on the spectrum with strategies to make life easier and to help them to achieve greater mental health and wellbeing. Information in the book is targeted specifically at people on the autism spectrum and their particular needs and experiences.

While much of the literature around mental health is aimed at assisting non-autistic people with mental health issues, these often present differently in people on the autism spectrum, who may struggle to access assistance and may respond differently to interventions that are more often effective for non-autistic people.

The book will be useful for people with autism and mental health difficulties (diagnosed or otherwise) of all ages and genders, and will also be a useful tool for their families as well as clinicians and professionals in the mental health field who work with autistic people. It provides an insight into autistic perspectives on mental health and wellbeing as well as key issues in diagnosis processes and prescribing for adults on the autism spectrum. It contains information on effective communication strategies for clinicians to use when working with people on the autism spectrum and explains why these might be needed. This is of particular value in relation to mental state examinations, symptom evaluation and discussions around medication.

Outline of the book

The book includes:

- descriptions of mental health symptoms and conditions commonly experienced by those on the autism spectrum

- treatments and strategies to address the symptoms and issues

- information on accessing appropriate treatment and support

- information on how people on the autism spectrum may differ from more 'typical' people experiencing mental health issues

- strategies on maintaining health and wellbeing

- peer mentoring advice from a lived experience perspective

- psychopharmacological information around medications and brain chemistry

- personal accounts

- a lengthy list of mental illness and autism resources available in most English-speaking countries.

The book is set out in the following chapters:

Diagnosis – this includes information on the neurobiological basis for mental illness conditions and autism, issues around diagnostic 'labelling', diagnosis for people with autism and co-morbid mental health conditions, understanding the diagnostic classifications and criteria (*Diagnostic and Statistical Manual of Mental Disorders*, 5th edition (DSM-5) and *International Classification of Diseases*, 10th revision (ICD-10)), considerations around seeking an autism spectrum diagnosis and peer mentoring advice around diagnosis.

Anxiety disorders – this examines anxiety, the prevalence of anxiety and anxiety disorders among people on the autism spectrum and specific issues faced by this group. It also includes information on the different types of anxiety disorders and peer mentoring advice around managing anxiety.

Depression – this looks at what depression is, specific issues faced by people with autism and co-morbid depression, and ways to identify and effectively treat depressive symptoms and disorders. It also includes some information on diagnostic assessments for depression in people on the autism spectrum and skills for clinicians, as well as peer mentoring advice on living well with depression.

Self-harm – this looks at reasons for self-harm in individuals on the autism spectrum and strategies to understand and address both the symptoms and their underlying causes as well as peer mentoring advice.

Suicidal thoughts – this looks at the prevalence and reasons for suicidality among people with autism, risk factors and early warning signs and protective factors, how to access help and peer mentoring advice.

Psychosis – this looks at what psychosis is, how it can be misdiagnosed in people on the autism spectrum, dispels myths about psychosis, provides advice on accessing help and looks at medication and strategies for living well with a psychotic illness.

Communication problems – looks at the differences in communication styles between autistic and neurotypical people,[1] with a focus on how communication issues can exacerbate mental

---

1   'Neurotypical' is a word used to describe people who do not have a diagnosis of an autism spectrum condition.

illness issues and make it harder for people on the autism spectrum to access appropriate help from mental health professionals. Some strategies are provided to help overcome this.

Stigma and discrimination – this looks at reasons for, prevalence of, and impact of stigma and discrimination – at different life stages – and how individuals and clinicians can work to address it. It focuses on specific issues relating to stigma, such as cultural impacts and the different ways in which people on the autism spectrum respond to stigma and discrimination.

Family incidence of autism and mental illness – this looks at the prevalence and patterns of mental illness and autism in families, providing guidance around holistic strategies to support the entire family as well as information on issues faced by family carers who may also have autism and/or mental illness.

Strategies to aid sleep – this looks at what 'good sleep' is and the importance of getting the right amount and quality of sleep. It also looks at why people with a diagnosis of autism and/or mental illness may have issues with sleep, including factors directly related to autism and mental illness, and different therapies or strategies that might assist to improve sleep.

The value of pets – this looks at the benefits of pet ownership and why pets can be helpful as therapy and support for people with autism and mental health issues. It provides practical information around deciding whether or not to get a pet, and on how to access different therapy pet programmes in the main English-speaking countries.

Mindfulness – this looks at what mindfulness is and how mindfulness practice can assist with anxiety, intrusive thoughts, trauma, shame/self-hatred, depression and other mental illness and autism-related issues. It provides practical advice on some different mindfulness practice methods.

Psychotherapy – this looks at how, why and when talk therapy can be effective to assist people with autism and mental illness. It provides information on a selection of the main psychotherapy practices used, and how and why they may benefit different people.

Medication – this looks at specific issues around psychiatric medications for people with autism. It also provides advice on some more practical issues around taking medication and psychopharmacological information on how medications work.

Crisis measures – this looks at psychological crises and meltdowns, and offers practical steps to understand and address crises, such as distraction, seeking help and accessing mental illness crisis services. It focuses on specific issues people on the autism spectrum face around crises and meltdowns, and strategies to address difficulties through accessing the right services and strategies.

Self-esteem and self-confidence – this looks at why people with autism face issues with self-esteem and self-confidence, and provides strategies to address these and how to build a positive self-image. It includes some helpful peer mentioning information around self-esteem and confidence.

Resilience – this looks at what resilience is and strategies to build and support it. It focuses on specific issues around resilience for people on the autism spectrum and the impact of resilience and independence on mental health and wellbeing.

Summary of strategies to maintain mental health – this is a quick reference chapter so that the reader can find possible strategies easily, whenever needed.

Resources – the section provides a list of organisations, web-based resources and books that include further or more specialised information about the chapter contents.

Introduction

THE NEUROBIOLOGY OF AUTISM

The central nervous system comprises the brain and spinal cord, which collect sensory information from multiple sources, and then integrate and interpret the various stimuli. For example, sight is the sensory information gathered by photoreceptors in the eyes, which travels via neuronal pathways to the visual cortex in the occipital lobe in the brain, whereas vision is the result of the brain's interpretation of various sensory inputs. If, for example, you are seated in a library late at night working with classmates on a term paper, and 'out the corner of your eye', that is, in your peripheral vision, you detect movement. Your brain takes that information, integrates it along with other sensory information, and determines that it is a friend carrying photocopying etc. However, if you are sitting at home alone late at night and something is detected by your peripheral photoreceptors, the brain takes the stimulus, integrates it with information such as 'you're supposed to be alone in the house' and is likely to interpret the same stimulus as a threat, resulting in provocation of the sympathetic flight/fight response. While the 'sight' experience is essentially the same in both scenarios, the 'vision' experience is not. The sensory experience is interpreted by the brain based on previous experiences, bias, emotional state etc.

From an anatomical and biochemical perspective, the brain is simply a fatty, gelatinous mass, containing cells known as neurones that, via highly specialised interconnecting electrical pathways and chemical messengers, communicate with the external world. In the modern world we are highly reliant on electricity to provide light, heat and many other functions that we consider to be necessities. The electrical wires within a house are covered by a plastic insulating sheath that stops the electrical current dissipating before it reaches its target (e.g. a light bulb). These pathways are static and at times malfunction, requiring the change of a light bulb and/or a fuse. Sometimes an electrical fault may even cause a fire. In the body's central nervous system, electrical impulses are called 'action potentials' and are transmitted quickly and efficiently along neuronal axons covered with myelin sheaths which – like the plastic around electrical wires – ensure the electrical current remains concentrated and focused. Given the complexity of the nervous system (both peripheral and central) and its ability to adapt, what is surprising is that it doesn't 'malfunction' more frequently. These malfunctions in the electrical wiring of the brain can be associated with issues such as mental illness symptoms.

Like physical health, mental health is a continuum that ranges from wellness through to serious illness. In both physical and mental health, illness can be of short or long (chronic) duration or episodic, and can impact the individual mildly, variably or seriously. Living well strategies presented in this book aim to minimise the impact of mental illness for the individual, whether the illness is chronic, episodic or of short duration.

Factors such as genetics, an individual's support network, stressors (including sleep deprivation) and coping strategies determine where an individual sits on the continuum of mental health at any given time. For example, a person may exhibit symptoms of depression with anxiety when their genetic vulnerability has been exposed through increased psychosocial stressors (such as a relationship break-up), inadequate or maladaptive coping strategies (e.g. excessive alcohol intake and/or use of other substances of abuse). Other factors that are likely to exacerbate psychological distress include inadequate social and/or emotional supports.

Autism is generally not viewed as or included within the category of mental illness, even though the diagnostic criteria are in the *Diagnostic and Statistical Manual of Mental Disorders* (DSM) written by the American Psychiatric Association (APA). Instead, we know that the autism spectrum conditions are neurological conditions and are classified under the area of neurodevelopment. Evidence suggests that there is a genetic loading to autism (explored further in Chapter 1, on diagnosis). However, the manifestation of atypical development and behaviours is considered a complex interplay between multiple potential genetic vulnerabilities and environmental factors. What this means is that current evidence suggests that people are born with their autism, but that how it is expressed depends on their genes and their environment.

Although the signs and symptoms that result in a diagnosis of autism have significant inter-individual variation, it is the commonalities in regards to an individual's autistic behaviours coupled with emotional and/or sensory differences that has given rise to the collective diagnostic term of 'autistic spectrum disorder'.[1]

People on the autism spectrum may have any of a number of mental health diagnoses co-occurring with their autism. They may access mental health services such as psychologists, psychiatrists, in-patient treatments and other residential mental health services and medications. Psychotropic medications such as selective serotonin re-uptake inhibitors (SSRIs), anti-psychotics and neurostimulants are commonplace in the management of any accompanying mental health issues, which are commonly referred to by mental health professionals as 'co-morbid psychopathologies'. These mental health issues can include hyperactivity, depression and anxiety, or they can lead to challenging behaviours such as agitation, aggression and irritability. While co-morbid mental illness conditions occur quite commonly in people on the autism spectrum, it can be hard for autistic people to access appropriate and effective treatment that takes into account their needs as autistic people and the impact of their autism on their mental health.

While medications are often effective in assisting people with mental illness conditions, it can be hard to find a good 'fit' – psychiatric medications are like a pair of shoes, that is, 'one size does not fit all'. This applies to the type of medication as well as the dose.

---

1   The terms 'autism', 'autism spectrum' and 'autistic spectrum' are used interchangeably in this book. People with a diagnosis of a condition on the autism spectrum are described as 'autistic people', 'autistic individuals', 'people with autism' or 'people on the autism spectrum'.

For some people it can take months to find the right dose of the right medication to provide relief from or the ability to manage mental illness symptoms; for others it is much quicker. It is important to note that there is a role for medication in the management of all mental health conditions, but that for some people this role is brief and infrequent, whereas for other people it may be lifelong. Medication is not the only treatment for mental health conditions, however, and there are a number of other approaches that can be of assistance, such as mindfulness, appropriate psychotherapy and building personal insight and resilience (see the chapters later in this book).

It is important to note that a co-morbid mental illness is not, at least in practical terms, a separate, compartmentalised entity from autism. It is not possible to treat the mental illness in isolation from understanding how autism impacts the person; the two are inexorably linked. It is worth understanding how each process works on the other and seeing the two conditions as being interrelated. Each person with autism has their own unique set of symptoms, thinking styles and psychology that are impacted by a combination of autism, environmental factors (e.g. personal history), biological factors, brain chemistry and mental illness presentation. As such, to treat people with autism and a co-morbid mental illness, it is essential that clinicians understand the person's unique pathology, their personality and presentation of their illness, and that they have a good understanding of autism and how it affects the individual. Treatments should always aim to support the individual to live well in a way that minimises their distress, stress and anxiety.

Elements of autism can sometimes appear to be symptoms of a mental illness process, and sometimes symptoms of a mental illness can appear to be resulting from autism. This can make it very hard for clinicians to know whether a person's symptoms are resulting from their autism, from a mental health issue or a combination of the two. It can also be difficult for people with autism and mental health challenges to describe their symptoms clearly when talking to their doctor. In addition, they may have limited insight or self-awareness. This book provides information to increase understanding of autism and how it interacts with mental health considerations to benefit both individuals on the autism spectrum and clinicians.

1

DIAGNOSIS

Neurobiological basis of autism and mental illness

As described in the Introduction, signals in the brain can malfunction and not reach their intended destination, potentially resulting in mental illness symptoms. Historically, clinicians and academics have viewed the loss or damage of neurons as irreparable. This was particularly the case in regards to major head and/or spinal injuries, where the ability of nerves to completely regenerate was seen as limited at best. But it is now accepted that neuronal pathways are capable of plasticity, that is, neuronal networks can increase and decrease synaptic connections as required (Doidge 2007, 2015). This means that if the part of the brain that is damaged was the part used for a particular function, it is possible for a person to relearn that function by training a different part of their brain. The science behind this is still in its infancy, however, and as of yet there are no simple systems in place for people to, for example, train their brain to not be anxious or to interpret language literally.

If you view the brain as an incredibly complex, large fatty organ with trillions of neuronal connections, then you can see how, via electrical impulses (action potentials) and chemicals (neurotransmitters), the brain is capable of not only receiving, processing and storing information, but also of interacting with the external world, including other individuals, through these electrical impulses and chemicals.

Neurodiversity is the idea that brain-based differences are part of the natural variation of humanity and should be accepted as such. The autism spectrum is now known to be such a neurodiversity. The neurobiology of people on the autism spectrum is most likely the product of a complex interplay between multiple genes, epigenetic factors[1] and the environment.

Neuroscientists have found that the brains of people on the autism spectrum differ from those of neurotypical people in terms of the level of electrical activity and areas of activation in their brains in response to stimuli. However, there are also differences across different autistic people. This suggests that there are different types of autism, rather than one type that differs only in terms of severity. This viewpoint seems to be one accepted by adults on the autism spectrum as being valid and, indeed, fairly obvious to their community. Various neuroscientists have found that areas of 'autistic brains' are hyperactive and/or underactive, and that there are a number of phenotypes of autism.[2] Observable behaviours form the basis of the diagnostic process for the autism spectrum, as the known neurological differences are not yet understood well enough to be used in any diagnostic processes.

Some aspects of autism, such as difficulty with reading the facial expressions of others, seem to have a neurobiological basis. In the case of facial expressions, neurotypical people process these in the area of the brain known as the fusiform gyrus, while people with autism have been shown to process facial expressions using the same parts of their brains as are used for processing objects (Pierce *et al.* 2001).

Some neurobiological differences have a hereditary/genetic basis, which appears to be the case for the autism spectrum, while others may be acquired in life through injury or illness, such as following on from meningitis. For example, the identical twin of a person with schizophrenia has around a 50 per cent chance of developing schizophrenia themselves. Although this demonstrates a significant degree of inheritance, it also shows that the underlying psychopathology for some mental health conditions (such as schizophrenia) is due to a complex interplay between multiple genes

---

1   Epigenetics is the word used to describe the cellular and physiological variations expressed within a person, where these differences are caused by external or environmental factors switching individual genes on and/or off, therefore affecting how cells read/express genes.

2   Phenotypes are the observable characteristics or traits, such as development, biochemical and/or physiological properties, behaviour and products of behaviour such as anxiety.

and environmental factors. This is also likely to be the case with other mental illnesses such as depression and anxiety.

The interplay between environment and genetics may also account for some of the differences in the way autism manifests in different people.

Psychiatric 'labelling', autism and co-morbid mental illness

Psychiatry is based on the notion of diagnostic labels, agreed on by eminent clinicians and codified in such publications at the DSM-5 and ICD-10. Diagnostic labels are essentially based on a taxonomy (classification system) of medicine and mental health that places people into diagnostic categories based on symptoms and presentation. Diagnoses are not hard and fast and may change over time. Notably, the criteria for Asperger's syndrome (and indeed, its diagnosis) were recently replaced with a diagnosis of autistic spectrum disorder in the DSM-5.

Sometimes social attitudes impact on the description of mental illness – homosexuality was famously removed as a category of mental illness when DSM-IV replaced the earlier version in response to attitudes around sexual preference and gender identification changing in Western society.

Autism and mental health conditions are seen within psychiatric taxonomies as being deviations from a standard or 'norm' of mental functioning. It is important to realise that a psychiatric 'label' or diagnosis is only useful when it provides some benefit to the individual. For example, if a diagnosis enables access to subsidised treatment such as medicines or psychological therapy, then it is of benefit. 'Labels' may also provide the person with explanations for how they feel, the behaviours they exhibit and/or why they struggle to connect with others. Diagnoses are also important when accessing psychological, speech language therapy and educational supports, etc.

LAURA'S STORY: Diagnosis, a pathway for understanding

I was diagnosed with Asperger's syndrome in my forties. Until then I just thought I had culture shock all my life and problems understanding people around me because of this. Once I got my diagnosis, my life made much more sense, and I realised that I didn't have culture shock, I just had a completely different understanding of the world to most people. Meeting other adults on the autism spectrum has been so positive, because I finally have a peer group, a community that understands me and that I also understand. Now if I am really anxious, I can take a moment to think about what is making me anxious and what to do about it; before I would just spiral into a meltdown really quickly, with no understanding of why.

Some of the literature regarding the autism spectrum suggests that people on the spectrum are uninterested in others, and even actively avoid making social connections. However, it is more likely that, as part of the condition, autistic people struggle to read social cues and demonstrate restricted facial expressions, which may be misinterpreted as a lack of caring or interest. Their verbal response and facial expressions may also appear incongruent with a given social situation, producing further miscommunication, misunderstanding and greater social isolation from peers. This may then exacerbate feelings of loneliness and social disconnection. In turn, the individual may express maladaptive behaviours associated with frustration and resentment, causing further isolation.

Another misconception many non-autistic people – including clinicians – may have is that individuals on the spectrum are severely disabled and incapable of participating fully in activities such as work, education or leisure. Health professionals have historically viewed autism as primarily a disorder of language, which may be why Asperger's (although considered similar to autism) was a separate diagnosis under DSM-IV. A diagnosis of Asperger's was previously given when the person met all the same criteria as autism, but they had not experienced a delay in or loss of language acquisition. The newly released DSM-5, however, has combined pervasive developmental disorder (PDD) and Asperger's as part of the autistic spectrum.

While there are benefits to this reclassification, there are also disadvantages. People who may have met the criteria for Asperger's under DSM-IV may no longer reach the 'threshold' for diagnosis under DSM-5. One of the reasons for this is that to be diagnosed with autism spectrum disorder the person must be 'clinically significantly impaired', which can be interpreted by some diagnosticians as excluding anyone who is in paid employment or a long-term committed relationship. The concept of 'significant impairment' can be seen as being quite subjective and hard to define. This may result in confusion among clinicians, and potential inconsistency in diagnosing people as being on the autism spectrum.

'Co-morbid' is the term used by health professionals for any health condition that exists alongside another one in the same person, for example, a person with autism and a co-morbidity of depression. Someone could not previously be diagnosed with autism if they had a co-morbid mental health condition or physical health condition. This is why many adults with Down's syndrome who are also autistic did not get a diagnosis of autism even though they demonstrated the characteristics required for a diagnosis. This is no longer the case, and as there is more understanding of the autism spectrum, there is a growing awareness of the large numbers of common co-morbidities.

Issues around psychiatric 'labelling'

Autism and mental illness diagnoses can have more loaded meaning than physical health diagnoses. For example, people don't generally use the term 'diabetic' to denote a personality type or a set of behaviours, but they often use terms such as 'schizophrenic', 'obsessive-compulsive' or 'depressive' to mean a lot more than just the diagnosis itself. In fact, just as there is no one autistic personality, there is no personality type for schizophrenia, obsessive-compulsive disorder (OCD) or depression. People with those conditions are as varied in how they think, feel and act as people with a physical illness such as diabetes or heart disease.

There is currently no definitive diagnostic test for any of the mental illness conditions. Diagnosis is usually made by a psychiatrist observing the person, asking them questions, and talking to their family or support people. Any diagnosis is therefore subject to the opinions and understanding of the individual psychiatrist making the decisions about what diagnosis to give. To complicate matters further, a relatively large percentage of people with a mental illness do not fall neatly within any diagnostic label.

JENNY'S STORY: Labels or symptoms

I have been diagnosed with a large number of mental illnesses during my lifetime and was considered by many psychiatrists hard to 'place' diagnostically. This led to a lot of confusion and questions. For years, I wanted to have a clear-cut 'label' which described my experience, but this did not seem to be possible. Recently, I have been under the care of a psychiatrist who is unconcerned with 'labels' and prefers to treat symptoms. I feel a lot more comfortable with this approach.

Coming up with an accurate diagnosis can be quite difficult. Autism can further complicate matters as people with autism and a co-morbid mental illness often present differently to non-autistic people who have the same mental health diagnosis. A co-morbid mental illness is not a separate entity from autism. It is not possible to treat the mental illness in isolation from autism, as the two act on one another in a dynamic way. The way that people on the autism spectrum can interpret and respond to diagnostic questions may complicate the diagnostic process for clinicians who are unfamiliar with these adults.

Some typical difficulties with the diagnostic process occur as soon as people on the autism spectrum are asked to fill in a screening questionnaire or diagnostic assessment tool. These often have tick boxes or ratings for each question that need to be ticked to differentiate if a symptom or behaviour is common or uncommon, using words such as 'never', 'sometimes', 'rarely', 'often' or 'always'. These concepts are often interpreted literally, so an adult on the autism spectrum may tick 'sometimes' rather than 'never' if they did/experienced that behaviour once in their lifetime. 'Always' would be taken literally too, and definitions of 'sometimes' and 'often' can cause anxiety and stress as the person attempts to complete the form accurately. Clinicians will often then receive a form with notes written all over it that seek to clarify the answers provided.

Women and girls on the autism spectrum who have a co-morbid mental illness may struggle with obtaining an appropriate diagnosis, both for their mental health condition and their autism, given that some clinicians have a more limited understanding of how autism generally presents in women than they do for their male clients. People with autism and a co-morbid mental illness may receive a number of different diagnoses over the course of their lifetime. In some cases the presentation of mental illness in an individual with autism changes over time, so that each time they see a psychiatrist – sometimes a number of different psychiatrists over the course of many years – they will appear to have a different mental illness. It can then be frustrating for a person on the autism spectrum to be given a number of different psychiatric 'labels' over time.

Seeking an autism diagnosis as an adult

For adults who think they may be on the autism spectrum it can be important to have an accurate diagnostic evaluation in order to access appropriate support services or funding, or simply to gain a greater understanding of themselves. Some people may already have been (mis)diagnosed with a mental illness – common misdiagnoses are schizophrenia for males who are on the autism spectrum and borderline personality disorder for women. However, some males will have schizophrenia as well as being on the autism spectrum, just as some women with borderline personality disorder will also be on the autism spectrum.

Most health systems worldwide have processes in place to assess, evaluate and diagnose autistic children. However, it can be difficult and expensive to find and go through a diagnostic process as an adult. If you think that you may need such support services or funding, ensure that the person who does your diagnosis is recognised by the relevant government authorities. For example, in some countries two professionals from different but specified occupations must both give a diagnosis via a multidisciplinary process. In other places a psychologist working alone is sufficient. If you do not think that you need support services or funding but still want an official diagnosis, you may need to find a private psychologist or psychiatrist who specialises in assessing adults for autism.

Clinicians use two main manuals to diagnose autism – DSM-5, published by the APA, and ICD-10-Clinical Modification (CM).

DSM-5 autism spectrum diagnostic criteria

The criteria for autistic spectrum disorder in DSM-5 are as follows:

A. Persistent deficits in social communication and interaction across multiple contexts, as manifested by all of the following (currently or by history):

    1. Deficits in social-emotional reciprocity.

    2. Deficits in non-verbal communication behaviours used for social interaction.

    3. Deficits in developing, maintaining and understanding relationships.

    Current severity specified, based on social communication impairments and restricted, repetitive patterns of behaviour.

B. Restrictive, repetitive patterns of behaviour, interests or activities, as manifested by at least two of the following, currently or by history:

    1. Stereotyped or repetitive motor movements, use of objects, or speech.

    2. Insistence on sameness, inflexible adherence to routines, or ritualised patterns of verbal or non-verbal behaviour.

    3. Highly restricted, fixated interests that are abnormal in intensity or focus.

    4. Hyper- or hypo-reactivity to sensory input or unusual interest in sensory aspects of the environment.

    Current severity specified, based on social communication impairments and restricted, repetitive patterns of behaviour.

C. Symptoms must be present in the early developmental period (but may not become fully manifest until social demands exceed limited capacities, or may be masked by learned strategies in later life).

D. Symptoms cause clinically significant impairment in social, occupational or other important areas of current functioning.

E. These disturbances are not better explained by intellectual disability (intellectual developmental disorder) or global developmental delay.

Individuals with a well-established diagnosis of autistic disorder, Asperger's disorder, or pervasive developmental disorder not otherwise specified (PDD-NOS) should be given the diagnosis of autism spectrum disorder. Individuals who have marked deficits in social communication, but whose symptoms do not otherwise meet criteria for autism spectrum disorder, should be evaluated for social (pragmatic) communication disorder (adapted from CDC no date).

The 'severity' level of the symptoms described above must be considered and recorded by the clinician as part of the evaluation process:

- Level 1 is 'requiring support'.

- Level 2 is 'requiring substantial support'.

- Level 3 is 'requiring very substantial support'.

ICD-10-CM diagnostic definitions

Autism and Asperger's are still separated in the 2015 ICD-10-CM (US version), which became the US insurance coding book on 1 October 2015. Both autism and Asperger's are classified as PDDs, which are defined as being characterised by impaired communication and socialisation skills. The impairments are incongruent with the individual's developmental level or mental age, and they may or may not be associated with general medical or genetic conditions. Listed below are the ICD-10-CM diagnostic criteria for autism and Asperger's (ICD10Data.com no date).

Autism: 2015 ICD-10-CM diagnosis code F84.0

Clinical information:

- A disorder beginning in childhood. It is marked by the presence of markedly abnormal or impaired development in social interaction and communication and a markedly restricted repertoire of activity and interest. Manifestations of the disorder vary greatly depending on the developmental level and chronological age of the individual (from DSM-IV).

- A disorder characterised by marked impairments in social interaction and communication accompanied by a pattern of repetitive, stereotyped behaviours and activities. Developmental delays in social interaction and language surface prior to age three.

- Autism is a disorder that is usually diagnosed in early childhood. The main signs and symptoms of autism involve communication, social interactions and repetitive behaviours. Children with autism might have problems talking with someone, or they might not look someone in the eye when they talk to them. They may spend a lot of time putting things in order before they can pay attention, or they may say the same sentence again and again to calm themselves down. They often seem to be in their 'own world'. Because people with autism can have very different features or symptoms, healthcare providers think of autism as a 'spectrum' disorder. Asperger's syndrome is a milder version of the disorder. The cause of autism is not known. Autism lasts throughout a person's lifetime. There is no cure, but treatment can help. Treatments include behaviour and communication therapies and medicines to control symptoms. It is important to start treatment as early as possible (National Institute of Child Health and Human Development (NICHD)).

- Disorder beginning in childhood marked by the presence of markedly abnormal or impaired development in social interaction and communication and a markedly restricted repertoire of activity and interest; manifestations of the disorder vary greatly depending on the developmental level and chronological age of the individual.

- Type of autism characterised by very early detection (<30 months), social coldness, grossly impaired communication and bizarre motor responses.

Asperger's: 2015 ICD-10-CM diagnosis code F84.5

Clinical information:

- A childhood disorder predominately affecting boys and similar to autism (autistic disorder). It is characterised by severe, sustained, clinically significant impairment of social interaction, and restricted repetitive and stereotyped patterns of behaviour. In contrast to autism, there are no clinically significant delays in language or cognitive development (from DSM-IV).

- A disorder most often diagnosed in the paediatric years in which the individual displays marked impairment in social interaction and a repetitive, stereotyped pattern of behaviour. The individual, however, displays no delay in language or cognitive development, which differentiates Asperger's syndrome from autism.

- Asperger's syndrome is an autism spectrum disorder. It is milder than autism but shares some of its symptoms. It is more common in boys than girls. An obsessive interest in a single subject is a major symptom of Asperger's. Some children with Asperger's have become experts on dinosaurs, makes and models of cars, even objects as seemingly odd as vacuum cleaners. Their expertise, high level of vocabulary and formal speech patterns make them seem like 'little professors'. Children with Asperger's have trouble reading social cues and recognising other people's feelings. They may have strange movements or mannerisms. All of these make it difficult for them to make friends. Problems with motor skills are also common in children with Asperger's. They may be late learning to ride a bike or catch a ball, for example.

Treatment focuses on the three main symptoms: poor communication skills, obsessive or repetitive routines, and physical clumsiness.

- A neuropsychiatric disorder whose major manifestation is an inability to interact socially; other features include poor verbal and motor skills, single-mindedness and social withdrawal.

- This syndrome or disorder is usually first diagnosed in childhood, characterised by severe and sustained impairment in social interactions and restricted, repetitive patterns of behaviours, interests and activities.

Considering seeking a diagnosis

Before spending time and money finding out if you are on the autism spectrum, it may be helpful to use some free online screening tools that indicate the likelihood of you being on the spectrum or not. There are a number of such tools for adults, and these can help you to get an idea of whether it is worth paying for a diagnostic assessment. The best known is the RDOS,[3] a series of questions that you are meant to answer quickly, and the result is displayed as a sort of colourful spider web that indicates if you have specific traits of Asperger's syndrome or traits that are 'neurotypical'. While it has been extensively researched and validated as a screening tool, it is worth noting that results often vary from test to test, even when the same person is taking the test at the same time of day but a few weeks apart. Another well-known quiz that is evidence-based and that has research validity is the University of Cambridge's autism spectrum quotient, known as the 'autism quotient' (AQ).[4]

You may also like to do online quizzes on alexithymia,[5] prosopagnosia ('face blindness') and emotional recognition. You could take the results from these to a formal assessment to give the clinician an idea of who you are. If you choose to do this, it is important to also note how you took the quiz; for example, did you complete it quickly

3   See http://rdos.net/eng/Aspie-quiz.php.
4   See http://aq.server8.org/.
5   Emotional blindness, or the difficulty in recognising and naming emotions – the person is aware of emotions but cannot distinguish between them.

without thinking too much, or did you agonise over each response for a few minutes? With the facial and emotional recognition quizzes, did you guess, or did you have some idea? Did you find the process interesting or frustrating or something else?

If the RDOS and AQ indicate that you are unlikely to be on the autism spectrum, you may choose not to spend money on a professional evaluation. If they indicate that you are highly likely to be on the spectrum, you may also choose not to pursue a formal diagnosis, instead being content with 'self-diagnosis'. Whether or not to go down the path of formal diagnosis is an individual choice, with benefits and issues associated with each option. However, having a clear autism spectrum diagnosis can be very helpful if you also have a mental health diagnosis, as autism may mean that the presentation and treatment of mental illness can be quite different from the typical presentation.

The diagnostic process should consist of most or all of the following steps, although this can vary. First, there needs to be some indication that you may be on the autism spectrum, which could come from yourself, or from observations by family, friends or colleagues. This could then be discussed with your family, GP, mental health professional, friends, or yourself, to ascertain if there is some agreement that autism might be the explanation. At this point you may want to do some of the free online screening tests and then ask for a referral to either a private psychologist or a diagnosing service provider (see the Resources section at the end of the book for more information). This will then lead into diagnostic interviews and possible observations. There is usually a financial cost, and this may vary across different clinicians. When the clinician completes their evaluation of interviews and observations, they will give feedback including whether or not you meet the diagnostic criteria for autism spectrum condition. This process may take up to a week and may incur further cost.

Once you have clarification, it is up to you what you do with your diagnosis, although it will certainly be of use to any mental health professionals you see. In addition, it can be helpful to give your main healthcare provider, such as your GP, a copy of the diagnostic report as autism is linked to a number of health issues that they may need to investigate to see if these are relevant to you.

Many people who have received a diagnosis of autism/Asperger's as an adult have talked about their post-diagnosis journey. This can often involve anger at not being diagnosed earlier, and sadness about the years of being misunderstood and possible missed opportunities. Other people are so excited about having a diagnosis that they feel 'explains' who they are and how they relate to the world that they go through a period of intense research and growing self-awareness.

If a diagnosis is presented as a 'bad thing', this can have a negative impact on the person receiving it. This is the case no matter what the diagnosis is for. For example, if one person is told "It's great that we now know you have anxiety, because we can start to support you more effectively," and another person is told "I'm so sorry to let you know that you have an anxiety disorder," it is likely that the second person will find the news more upsetting than the first. If people are given a diagnosis in a negative manner, they may believe that having the diagnosis is equal to *being* the diagnosis, and that they will be in a sorry and miserable state for the rest of their lives. Presenting the diagnosis as an aide to understanding themselves and their interaction with others is far more helpful.

Psychiatric diagnoses

It is important to note that a psychiatric diagnosis is only beneficial if it helps the individual (and/or significant people in their life) to access treatments and resources, or as part of a journey of self-discovery, self-awareness and self-acceptance. It may also help identify 'vulnerabilities' that negatively impact on the person's quality of life and level of functioning as defined by themselves and/or significant people in their life. A psychiatric diagnosis should enable the implementation of support and strategies to improve the person's social functioning and quality of life. It is also an opportunity to reframe thinking – taking perceived weaknesses and threats and creating instead strengths and potential opportunities.

A 'one size fits all' approach to psychiatric labels is problematic at many levels, as is evidenced with labels such as 'intellectual impairment'. In some countries, such as New Zealand and Australia, to access resources including admission to specialty units, the person needs to have met criteria such as an intellectual quotient (IQ) of less than 70. However, some individuals with an IQ of less than 70 may have a relatively 'higher' level of ability to manage their lives while others with a 'higher' IQ score may have a greater level of disability.

Health professionals working with adults who they think may be on the autism spectrum – even if they do not yet have a formal diagnosis – should be aware of the framing of assessment questions to suit the communication style of the client. Where answers appear pedantic, this can indicate an attempt to give as honest and complete an answer as possible. Questions that require responses in a format such as 'all the time', 'some of the time', 'occasionally' and 'never' can be difficult for people with autism, who may become stuck trying to define 'all' (did one exception three years ago mean it is some, not all?), 'some' and 'occasionally' (exactly how frequently?). In addition, if the clinician does not allow enough time for processing (as many people on the autism spectrum have auditory processing disorders), the risk is that answers will be provided that have no relation to the question at all.

JOHN'S STORY: Confusing questions

When my specialist asked me if I got a rash after a hot bath, as part of his assessment of my physical health, I said 'no'. When I got home and talked to my wife about it, she reminded me that I get a rash after my shower every morning. I just hadn't understood what the implied questions were, I just responded to the actual question. I can't get a rash after a hot bath, because we don't even have a bath in our house! One of the other questions I got all confused about and just said 'no' even though now I think about it, I probably meant 'yes'. I wish doctors and nurses would say what they mean or explain what information they need and why. That would really help me to give accurate responses.

Other considerations for diagnostic assessments are the understanding and expressive skills of the individual. Some people with autism who are non-verbal have excellent auditory processing skills and can express themselves fluently through text or alternative communication systems. In contrast, some adults with autism who sound fluent may struggle to comprehend complex sentences or instructions and not volunteer this information. It is useful to check comprehension of complex sentences by asking the person to complete a series of tasks prior to commencing a diagnostic assessment. An example of this would be to ask the person to 'Pick up the pen, write your name in the corner, then draw a person and give the paper back to me.' This should be said at normal speed. If the person is known to be unable to write, they might be asked to pick a series of objects up and place each of them in a different place.

Peer mentoring advice

- A diagnosis does not describe the kind of person you are. It is simply a description of a condition or set of symptoms. Your diagnosis cannot determine whether you are a moral or immoral person, whether you are loving and compassionate, or whether you are a good parent. It is simply a description of your illness or health condition.

- If a psychiatrist or other professional gives you a diagnosis, don't think of it as being 'final'. You have every right to disagree with it or to seek further explanation or a second opinion.

- A diagnosis doesn't really say a lot about you or your experiences; it is more a label for the convenience of clinicians. However, it can sometimes help to meet up with other people with the same or a similar diagnosis as you may share some things in common. This is true for both autism and the range of different mental health conditions. You may benefit from talking with other people with autism or other people with a similar mental health condition, or both.

- Many autistic adults are self-diagnosed, and it is often the case that adult women with autism are self-diagnosed. This may be due to clinicians not understanding the particular qualities that women and girls with autism have, and it thus being difficult for them to acquire an official diagnosis. Unfortunately, even when a person's self-diagnosis is accurate, doctors and other clinicians do not set much store by diagnoses that do not come from an official channel such as a GP or psychologist. So self-diagnosed people may find it difficult to convince clinicians that they have autism, and it will be almost impossible for them to access support or funding for issues related to autism. If you are self-diagnosing, it may be preferable to seek out a psychologist or psychiatrist who specialises in diagnosing and treating people from your demographic (e.g. women with Asperger's syndrome). You could search the internet for a suitable clinician, or word of mouth is also a good place to find out information on suitable specialists. Even if you are completely convinced that you have a particular diagnosis, it may feel better – and makes accessing services exponentially easier – to have an official 'piece of paper'.

- Many people on the autism spectrum feel that autism is part of their character. They see the diagnosis as defining them in some way, and as an integral part of who they are. Some people with a mental illness diagnosis also identify strongly with their identity as a person with mental illness. Think about how you feel about your autism diagnosis and your mental health diagnosis – whether you identify with one and not the other. It may help you gain insight and understanding of yourself to consider these sorts of things.

- Use a diagnosis to your own advantage. It may help you to access useful services and programmes that people without a diagnosis cannot.

2

ANXIETY DISORDERS

What is anxiety?

Everyone experiences anxiety at certain times in their life. Anxiety is an evolutionary necessity and is the word used to describe the freeze, fight or flight response of humans to perceived danger or significant events. These responses are regulated by our sympathetic nervous system. When we are anxious, it affects our thoughts, behaviours and our physical body. Once the danger has passed, we begin to relax as the parasympathetic nervous system takes over to decrease our heart rate, relax the pupils and stop hyperventilation. The sympathetic and parasympathetic nervous systems cannot operate at the same time, however, so if you are in a heightened state of anxiety much of the time, you cannot be relaxed at the same time. Anxiety is as much a part of being human as feeling sad, irritated, confused or happy, or all the other emotions. 'Nothing in the affairs of men (sic) is worthy of great anxiety. (Plato, nd). While a degree of anxiety is normal and even healthy – particularly in risky situations or circumstances where a considered response is required – it can also become an overwhelming and damaging thing. This is because of the physiological effects of anxiety, such as the slowing of the digestive system – if a person's digestive system is continually being slowed down, they will most likely suffer from constipation, which is painful and distressing for most people.

The following image illustrates the effect and usefulness of anxiety in a dangerous situation.

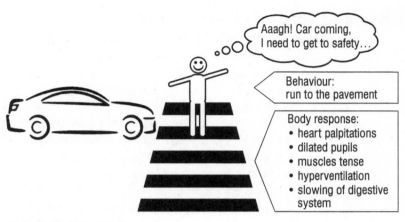

Fight or flight response

Some people are more worried than others or are anxious for much or all of the time or experience severe anxiety. Most people with autism fall under this category. For people on the autism spectrum, anxiety can be particularly debilitating due to the cycle of being worried about being anxious, which leads to anxiety. When people are anxious too frequently or in response to situations that are not really dangerous, this is problematic and can be labelled as an anxiety disorder. Panic attacks can happen when some people are highly anxious over a sustained period of time. These are acute periods of severe anxiety that can be mistaken by the people experiencing them as heart attacks, as the heart may feel as if it is pounding really hard. People cannot die from a panic attack and panic attacks are not due to and do not cause heart problems. However, if you are unsure if you are experiencing a panic attack or a heart attack, it is best to be safe and go to an emergency room or GP surgery to be checked over.

Some people with autism do not realise that they have chronic anxiety as they have either not noticed or recognised the symptoms as anxiety. This seems to be because the anxiety and accompanying symptoms have existed as long as the person can remember, so it feels as if it this is just their 'normal state of being'.

TYSON'S STORY: Learning to control anxiety

My psychologist got me to fill in this questionnaire, and then she said my answers showed I had severe anxiety. I had no idea what she was talking about; I didn't think I had anxiety at all. When she explained to me that my hyperventilating and my heart palpitations were signs of anxiety, I was amazed. I never knew that's what it was, I thought I was really unfit or had heart problems. Now I know I have anxiety I can try and manage it through meditation and mindfulness. When it gets really bad and causes a meltdown, I do take medication. I was really anti-medication, but then when I took it during a particularly bad meltdown, I was amazed. This tiny pill stopped my distress completely, and I was able to calm down and get on with my day. Normally a big meltdown would leave me distressed and frustrated for days.

If you are not sure whether or not you have anxiety, ask your GP, psychologist or psychiatrist to give you an anxiety screen. This is a questionnaire with tick boxes, which takes two to five minutes to complete. It can be very helpful if you have alexithymia (the inability to identify and describe your own emotions; alexithymia is thought to affect approximately ten per cent of people – see Taylor, Bagby and Parker 1999). As Tyson's story shows, it is imperative to be able to recognise and understand your anxiety in order to be able to decrease and manage it.

Anxiety can be either generalised or related to specific things, such as social anxiety. For people with autism, it is unclear if their anxiety is an inherent part of their autism or a co-occurring phenomenon (Kerns and Kendall 2012). What *is* known is that a large percentage of people with autism have clinically significant anxiety, although the exact figure is hard to ascertain because traditional measures of anxiety may misinterpret autistic behaviours as anxiety, or underestimate anxiety by misconstruing it as typical autistic experience. In their meta-analysis of research into the prevalence of anxiety disorders in people with autism, including children, Kerns and Kendall (2012) suggest that anxiety is a core component of autism, but that it may manifest differently in different people with autism, in the same way that autism manifests differently in different people.

People with autism are more likely to experience an anxiety disorder than the general population. An anxiety disorder is a medical condition characterised by persistent, excessive worry. It doesn't just mean that someone is anxious from time to time and is not simply being stressed about a particular worrying event; it involves experiencing anxiety so distressing that it interferes with a person's ability to carry out or take pleasure in their day-to-day life (SANE Australia no date).

Anxiety disorders are the most commonly reported mental illness. Research suggests that between 25 and 84 per cent of people with an autism spectrum condition have a co-existing anxiety disorder (Baron 2006), although, as mentioned, it is unknown whether these are true anxiety disorders or the expression of anxiety that is innate to autism.

Anxiety disorders include things such as generalised anxiety disorder (GAD), phobias (including social phobia), OCD and panic disorder. Repetitive behaviours, difficulty in managing changes to routines and perfectionism are autistic traits that have been found to be related to high anxiety levels in people with autism (Rodgers *et al.* 2012).

Anxiety, like all mental illness processes, is not just about psychological issues, or issues with how a person thinks; there are also biomedical and genetic factors at play with a number of genes implicated in anxiety; even caffeine-induced anxiety has a genetic component.

What does anxiety look/feel like?

Anxiety can manifest as psychological and physical symptoms. Social anxiety in people with autism is common and is often characterised by a difficulty in making and keeping friends, being comfortable around other people, socialising and working with others in a team environment (Bejerot, Eriksson and Mörtberg 2014). Both social and generalised anxiety can present the same psychological symptoms of anxiety. These can all be present at the same time, or a person may only experience a few. The symptoms are as follows:

- impatience
- difficulty concentrating

- catastrophising (thinking about the worst possible outcome)

- disrupted sleep

- depression

- avoidance

- becoming preoccupied with or obsessive about one topic.

Some of the physical symptoms of anxiety include:

- thirsty/dry mouth

- digestive upsets

- frequent urination

- racing heart

- muscle aches

- headaches

- dizziness

- pins and needles

- muscle tremors.

Anxiety and the autism spectrum

The high rate of anxiety disorders among people on the autism spectrum may be due in part to the issues that people with autism spectrum conditions have to contend with in being part of the 'neurotypical' world. On a daily basis, autistic people have to make sense of a world that is extremely hard to decipher, deal with sensory overload (and worry about potential sensory overload), and navigate an often hostile and incomprehensible social world. All of these experiences can contribute significantly to a person's anxiety levels. In addition, the autistic traits of perfectionism, preference for structure/routine and repetitive behaviours can all add to the levels of anxiety.

In trying to make sense of the world, people with autism often want to imagine the outcomes of events or situations that involve them.

This may start from the position of trying to make the world less stressful by creating a picture or map of the future so that change or new experiences don't seem quite so daunting. Depending on how the thought processes are structured, however, rather than making life easier, this may lead to catastrophising (or worrying about the worst-case scenario) as people imagine in great detail all the terrible things that may happen. Catastrophising is not usually about likely or even possible events, but can be related to social paranoia – not understanding how non-autistic people operate, so creating an unlikely, negative future that revolves around misunderstanding the motivations of others. An example of this would be someone worrying that they are going to lose their job because they might have seen their manager in a meeting with the door closed, despite the fact that there is no process of redundancies or lay-offs going on in the workplace and they have done nothing wrong at work that might warrant their dismissal. Instead of allowing yourself to ruminate on negative thoughts, try to diminish any anxiety by engaging in a SWOT (strengths, weaknesses, opportunities and threats) analysis, as outlined in Chapter 17 on resilience, or by practising mindfulness as a way to accept and move through the situation.

The autistic thinking style can be very rigid; that is, people with autism usually think very definitively about things. This is often described as 'black-and-white' thinking. Autistic thinking is also usually very logical, rather than emotive. This is not to say that people with autism do not have emotions, as they do. It is more that when a decision is required, a person with autism is most likely to make a practical and logical decision rather than an emotion-based decision.

Autistic thinking can also be hyper-focused and repetitive, described as being 'like a broken record'. In other words, people with autism may fixate on thoughts that go around and around in their head.

All three styles of autistic thinking are usually present in people with autism and may increase or decrease anxiety, depending on how they are used. The table below details how these thinking styles can be helpful or problematic in relation to anxiety in someone with autism.

Thinking styles

Autistic thinking style	How this can be problematic	How this can be helpful	Strategies to increase the helpfulness of this style
Logical	Can lead to misunderstandings when others do not share your logic Can lead to other people assuming you are unsympathetic or have no empathy	Creates a sense of control and/or order Helpful in evaluating options	Try to understand that in some situations an emotive response is socially expected and that logical responses can sometimes upset and/or hurt people
Rigid (black and white)	Cannot see the myriad possible outcomes of a situation; instead tend to focus on the worst possible outcome Assume people either like or dislike you, when they may do neither Judge things/people/situations very quickly before getting to understand the full picture	Creates a sense of control and/or order	Focus on the best possible realistic outcome Realise that people can feel neutral too Try to find out more about a thing/person/situation before deciding on your attitude to that/them
Fixated (repetitive thoughts)	Often leads to difficulties falling asleep Can increase anxiety and/or distress due to negative focus	Can occasionally lead to clarity and/or insight into oneself/others/situations	Try to balance negative thoughts with positive thoughts Try to end each day by thinking about something that went well or something that made you happy

If your repetitive, fixated thoughts become very intrusive and are affecting your state of mind and quality of life, talk to your GP or a mental health professional about this. They can support you so that you can have a better quality of life.

Adapting to change

Change is another factor in anxiety for people on the autism spectrum. While most people find some changes challenging, people with autism can be adversely affected by any change, even things that most people would consider positive changes, such as getting married or buying a new car, or minor changes such as shoes or clothing wearing out over time. Autistic people often have a set routine that helps them to feel more in control of their life. Changes or interruptions to a routine can be highly anxiety-provoking. One of the reasons for this is that many adults with autism have become routine-dependent as they were brought up with strict routines, where any changes were clearly signalled well in advance. Although this was done because professionals initially thought it would benefit children with autism and help them to make sense of the world, it has been found to be disabling for people with autism in the long run – because the world is not routine, daily life is not able to be routine. External events intrude into and interrupt the routines that may have been created. People who have grown up with these strict routines therefore struggle to have coping strategies or resilience for managing change.

Interestingly, there are a number of people with autism who were brought up with little or no adherence to routine, and for many of these adults, change itself is routine. These adults with autism understand that even though things change, it is okay, and it is not the end of the world as they know it. For other adults with autism, it is the fear that change will bring about a catastrophic event or end to the world as they know it that leads to crippling anxiety. When change is self-instigated, the person with autism can remain in control as they are aware of the change, the rationale for the change and the likely outcomes (Goodall 2013).

If you are anxious about changes, try setting up some small changes yourself. When you do this, you will be able to maintain control and this will help minimise anxiety. The more you are able to use self-instigated change as a strategy, the better you will be at developing more adapting and coping skills that are helpful for changes imposed on you externally.

LYNNE'S STORY: Adapting to change

My parents moved all the time when I was growing up. By the time I was 18, I had lived in 18 homes in a number of different countries. As a consequence, moving is normal for me, and I see change as routine. I am horrified when people tell me they have lived in the same house all their lives. At the same time, I have no understanding of why people think moving countries is any more problematic than moving down the street. In both cases, you have to pack up all your stuff, and it gets moved from one house to the next. It is just a lot more expensive to move abroad. Admittedly, I do still have routines and I don't like them to be interrupted or changed, but at the same time, I really understand that things do change, because most things are out of my control, like earthquakes, volcanic eruptions, the global recession etc.

If you do not already have coping strategies for change, it may be wise to develop some. This could involve identifying which changes cause you the most anxiety, and deciding how to approach this. You may choose to write or draw a list of pros and cons around a particular change, to decide if it is something you want to do. This technique only really works on changes that involve a decision you need to make, such as enrolling in a course at university or joining a particular club. It won't work so well on changes or new situations you can't avoid. For these, you could use some strategies, like a SWOT analysis, to reframe your thinking about the change in a more positive way, and plan how to approach the change. Otherwise, you could speak to a counsellor or psychologist to help you with any upcoming changes. You could also make up or role-play some scenarios about the change to help prepare you for the actual event. Ask a trusted friend, autism or mental health worker or family member to help with this if you want to gain a more objective and rounded view of what might help you to get through the change. They can also challenge any paranoia or catastrophising you may be engaging in if you tell them what your concerns are around the change. You could also try to learn some of the skills or knowledge that you will need in the changed situations (e.g. if you are starting a new job). Sometimes just having a conversation and talking through the change will lessen your anxiety.

Sensory sensitivities

The way people with autism experience the world is quite different to other people. Sensory input that doesn't bother others can be painful or joyous. Additionally, the physical and emotional reactions of people with autism to sensory input are affected by a number of variables:

- physical wellbeing

- mental wellbeing

- level of tiredness

- hunger/thirst

- combinations of sensory input

- temperature

- air pressure

- task demands (what a person is doing)

- communication demands (how much a person is being required to communicate)

- mental associations/memories.

MICHAEL'S STORY: A time for music

I love listening to loud music; it really helps me calm down or makes me happy, just depending. But if I am not feeling well, or it is really cold in my apartment, I just can't abide music on loud. Then it gives me a huge headache and makes me really, really angry. I can't explain why, and it took me about a year of my family asking why music made me angry sometimes but happy at other times, when it is the same album that I listen to over and over, so it couldn't be the song or anything. Now that I know this, if I am not well, or it's cold, my family know not to put my Iron Maiden album on, but otherwise to put it on real loud!

When people with autism have sensory aversions – sensory input that they intensely dislike and try to avoid – these can generate a lot of anxiety, not just for the individual with autism, but also for the other people around them. Unfortunately, for many, but not all, people with autism, if people around them are anxious, they feel that anxiety, and become anxious themselves. This can make it difficult to manage sensory-driven anxiety, unless everyone involved agrees on the same plan of action. For example, if people try to avoid particular smells, such as bleach, they are likely to try and avoid places where this smell could be, such as a public toilet. If someone is out and needs to go to the toilet, they will probably just try to wait until they get home or can find a toilet that they think should be okay. This situation might make the person anxious, in case when they go in the toilet area it does smell of bleach and this may provoke a meltdown. The people with the person may get really anxious about them possibly having a meltdown, which will, in turn, probably make the person more anxious, and so more likely to have a meltdown.

There are a number of strategies that would be useful in this situation, but all of them require the agreement of the people with the person. These other people just need to agree to *not* get anxious themselves, which may not be possible, especially if they are on the autistic spectrum too. However, if they are aware of and can support the person with any new strategies, by, for example, going into the public toilet before the person to check it, and sprinkling some essential oil to mask any smell of bleach, they are less likely to become anxious. This will, in turn, help the person to successfully implement their chosen strategies.

For some people with autism, feeling hungry or thirsty can increase their anxiety significantly. If you are one of these people, always have a snack or non-alcoholic drink with you. You can then eat or drink regularly to prevent that heightened state of anxiety.

If you are not sure what sensory triggers increase your anxiety, you could ask your family/friends/professional support, or you could keep an anxiety journal. This should help you to identify your triggers, but it will only work if you know how to recognise your own anxiety. The following table shows how to set out an anxiety journal, followed by an example:

Anxiety journal

Date	Time	What happened	What was happening before	Possible trigger

Example of an anxiety journal

Date	Time	What happened	What was happening before	Possible trigger
3/1/15	8.09	My heart started beating fast, and I was hyperventilating	Joe turned the air conditioner on, because he said it was really hot. Alarm clock went off	Cold air Alarm clock
3/1/15	9.17	Heart beating fast, muscles tensed up	The doorbell rang when I was eating my breakfast	Doorbell Interruption to eating
3/1/15	11.29	Heart beating fast, I jumped in the air, hyperventilating	Ambulance went past the house	Siren
3/1/15	11.52	Jumped out of my chair, heart beating fast	Doorbell rang again when I was playing an online game	Doorbell Interruption to game

If this journal continued for a week or so, the writer would be able to see if there were particular triggers for their anxiety. Based on these entries, the triggers seem to be loud, sudden noises and/or cold air and/or being interrupted. For those who struggle with writing, either draw or type this or ask someone else to do the writing.

Once you know what your sensory anxiety triggers are (or at least have made a start on identifying at least one of them), you can work out some strategies to decrease the problems. Either try to minimise the triggers – for example, getting a quieter doorbell or door knocker – or work with a professional to desensitise yourself to your triggers.

People and communication

There are a number of difficulties for people with autism that relate to being around other people and communicating. One of the common issues is a fear of rejection, or worry about people not understanding them and responding unkindly or even meanly. People with autism tend to worry not just about being hurt by other people, but also about unintentionally hurting others. Additionally, there can be anxiety around looking stupid or not knowing what to do or say around other people. This can be the case anywhere in life, at home, in the supermarket, at the doctors, or even with family.

It is a natural part of autism to have less well-developed social skills, but this doesn't mean that people with autism are stupid or that they seem stupid to other people. In addition, many social skills are quite proscribed and can be learned. For example, it is quite easy to learn to say, sign or type 'thank you' whenever someone gives you something, even it is their job to do so. Using 'please' and 'thank you' appropriately can be very useful, as often other people will look more favourably on people they view as polite.

For situations where you do not know how to respond, it is okay to ask someone else what you should have said or done, so that you know for next time. Either ask a peer mentor, a trusted friend or family member or a support worker. The more situations you learn how to respond to, the less anxious you will be about interacting with other people.

However, there are some people who are just mean or unkind. It is okay to avoid these people where possible. If they are at work, discuss any issues with your manager. If the person being unkind is your manager, if they have a boss, you could try talking to them. It can be difficult to resolve workplace issues, and so if work is making you very anxious and/or depressed, it is probably a good idea to seek professional help and/or to look for a new job.

It may be helpful to join a club or group that is focused on your area of interest, or join a social group for people on the autism spectrum. These will provide you with a way to interact with people that is less anxiety-provoking than other situations. The key to being able to interact comfortably is to first be comfortable in yourself. If you are going to a club/group that focuses on your area of interest, you are more likely to be excited than nervous, and you will be able to talk about a familiar and interesting topic instead of worrying about struggling with social chit-chat.

ROB'S STORY: Joining a group

I don't much like other people, they are so complicated and mostly boring beyond belief. But I found a gaming group, where I could talk about my models and get painting tips from them. That was pretty cool, none of this 'what do I say to their inane questions?', because there was no pointless talk; it was all focused on the models.

LYNNE'S STORY: Like-minded people

I work in a people job, and I just don't want to socialise at all after work, I just want to relax and be quiet. I knew some people that ran an Aspie social group, so I thought I'd try it just to see what they did. One of my online friends had asked me if they sat around rocking together! You know, they didn't, but I know some groups who do. Going there opened up my world so much – I could stim and fidget or tic and no one minded; in fact, they were all so relaxed with us all just being us, Autie and Aspie, all just being. I was so at home I joined a self-advocacy group too, and then it just grew, and I know so many people on the spectrum now. If I don't get to hang out with them for a while I miss it. I still get anxious going out with people who are not on the spectrum, but I am much more comfortable in myself now, and I don't worry so much about whether they will see me tic or stim.

If you are anxious about particular social interactions or worry that you can't do something because of communication issues, plan it out in advance, or do a practice role-play with someone (or even with yourself in a mirror). You could buy a book that explains the social rules that most people operate in but are not taught at school or at home (e.g. Myles, Trautman and Schelvan 2004).

Professional support

Anxiety disorders that are diagnosed by a medical professional often require specialist treatment from a psychiatrist or psychologist. While the strategies discussed in this chapter may assist you with an anxiety disorder, you may also need to seek help from a health professional or service. For example, phobias (including social phobia) are generally treated using different techniques from panic disorder or OCD.

Many adults with autism have suggested that peer mentoring has made a significant impact on their ability to manage their anxiety. Some of the techniques that professionals may suggest that you engage in to learn to manage anxiety are mindfulness, wellbeing therapy, acceptance and commitment therapy (ACT) or cognitive behaviour therapy (CBT) (see Chapter 13). Some will benefit from taking prescribed medication to help them manage their anxiety. This section briefly introduces each type of anxiety disorder and likely treatment.

In order for health and mental health professionals to work out if someone has a particular kind of anxiety disorder, they will need to ask some questions and/or ask the person to complete some written (or read aloud) questions. The reason they need to find out which kind of anxiety is to tailor treatment, to try to ensure any support is as effective as possible. Unfortunately, for people with autism, it can be difficult to respond to some of these questions and evaluations, and some of this difficulty can be due to difficulty processing the questions or due to the literal interpretation of the question. For example, when trying to find out about anxiety, doctors may ask what worries a patient. For a patient with autism, this question can be too big to answer, as they may be unable to work out where to start.

If you have autism and are planning to seek an assessment, it could help if you wrote down before you go all the things you are worried about, things that you are afraid of, what happens to you physically and mentally when you are worried/afraid, and how often you are worried/afraid. This doesn't have to be completely accurate, as the GP just needs an overall picture. You might say most of the time, or every evening or about 75 per cent of the time. You don't need to say the exact number of hours and minutes that you felt something or get anxious about being accurate about every detail.

Generalised anxiety disorder (GAD)

Diagnostic criteria for GAD (DSM-5) are excessive worry and difficulty controlling worry for at least three or more of the last six months of the following symptoms:

- restlessness

- irritability

- sleep disturbance

- easily fatigued

- difficulty concentrating

- muscle tension.

Individuals with GAD often experience:

- trembling/shakiness

- muscle aches

- sweating/nausea/diarrhoea

- irritable bowel

- headaches.

Symptoms must cause a significant impairment in functioning. These symptoms must not be due to another axis I illness (acute clinical symptoms such as major depressive episodes, schizophrenic episodes and panic attacks), medical illness or substance (drug of abuse or medication). GAD is where a person is highly anxious in the long term, which is described as chronic anxiety that decreases a person's quality of life. It can be hard for people with autism and GAD to understand that life could be more enjoyable if their anxiety was treated, especially if they have had these symptoms all their lives. Meta-analyses of research have indicated that GAD is one of the hardest types of anxiety to treat successfully, but a number of treatments are effective (Hayes-Skelton, Roemer and Orsillo 2013). Where people with GAD are supported to develop a broader, kinder and expanded way of responding to their internal thoughts, they have been shown to have an improved quality of life.

For those with GAD, this means that instead of focusing on one negative potential outcome of an event and then continuing to focus thoughts on that one bad thing, they could help decrease their anxiety by accepting that they are initially worried about that one bad thing, but that actually there are other possible much better outcomes too.

When people are able to do this, they will have developed new skills that will reduce the need to always avoid certain people/places/ experiences. Hayes-Skelton *et al.* (2013, p.762) found that 'empathic validation, self-monitoring, formal and informal mindfulness exercises, encouragement of acceptance through psycho-education and experiential exercises, and writing and behavioural exercises that apply these skills to personally meaningful activities' can all help to decrease GAD and improve quality of life.

One interesting finding for people with autism is that a decrease in negativity about change can be one of the most helpful strategies for people with GAD. This means that if people can develop an acceptance and awareness of change without becoming too upset or worried, over time their quality of life is likely to continue to improve.

Panic disorder

Diagnostic criteria for panic disorder (DSM-5) are recurrent and unexpected panic attacks. You will have experienced the following symptoms for at least one month:

- persistent concern about having another attack

- significant maladaptive change in behaviour related to attacks.

Panic attacks are an abrupt surge in symptoms, including:

- palpitations

- sweating

- trembling/shaking

- shortness of breath/choking

- chest pain

- nausea

- dizziness

- chills/heat sensations

- feeling of tingling or pricking of skin

- loss of sense of reality

- fear of losing control

- fear of dying.

Symptoms must cause a significant impairment in functioning. These symptoms must not be due to a medical illness or substance (drug of abuse or medication).

Obsessive-compulsive disorder (OCD)

Diagnostic criteria (DSM-5) of OCD requires the presence of obsessions or compulsions that are time consuming (e.g. >1 hour/day total) or that cause major distress or impairment in functioning for the individual. Research indicates that OCD has a lifetime prevalence of 2 per cent, is highly disabling, strongly heritable, and has a neuro-biologic basis, but is highly influenced by environmental factors (Gorman and Abi-Jaoude 2014). It is considered to be on a spectrum that encompasses hoarding disorder, body dysmorphic disorder, skin-picking disorder and hair-pulling disorder. People with OCD have varying degrees of insight into the irrationality of their OCD symptoms, from some to no insight.

Obsessions are often unwanted and consist of recurrent thoughts, images or urges. Compulsions are repetitive actions undertaken to relieve the anxiety associated with obsessions or because of adherence to rigid rules. Examples of OCD activities are constant cleaning, incessant checking or ordering or counting. People with OCD are often concerned about harm to self or others if their compulsions are not completed.

Many more people have traits of OCD than actually have clinical OCD. For example, most people with autism order or check things compulsively, but this doesn't mean that these people with autism have OCD. For people with OCD, their need to do certain things over and over can and often does become the single most important thing in their life, and significant distress and fear can accompany this need. Research suggests that OCD symptoms occur in over 25 per cent of adults, and developmentally appropriate rituals are common in children (Gorman and Abi-Jaoude 2014).

Social anxiety disorder or social phobia (SAD)

All people have some social anxieties and fears, and these can be helpful and adaptive (e.g. keeping one aware in uncertain social situations). However, they can also be disabling (e.g. being unable to start or keep close friendships even though the person is lonely and wants to have friends). Unpleasant emotional states and maladaptive behaviours associated with social situations can be significant, life-affecting problems for many (Hofmann 2014). Diagnostic criteria (DSM-5) state that a person who has SAD is fearful or anxious about or avoidant of social interactions and situations that involve the possibility of being scrutinised in a manner that significantly impairs their life. From this, it could be extrapolated that most people with autism have SAD as people with autism often feel that every social interaction involves the possibility of being judged or evaluated. Deciding not to worry what people think in every interaction is a good starting point to manage SAD. The techniques described in this chapter will all be useful in dealing with SAD.

Anxiety can be one of the most challenging and destructive symptoms that people on the autism spectrum have to deal with. It can lead to people feeling unable to do things that others take for granted, such as getting a job, raising a family, going on holiday, buying a house or socialising, to name but a few. People on the autism spectrum need strategies for dealing with anxiety, as it can be such a significant part of their life. Learning strategies to address anxiety and learning to manage its impact can make life much easier and improve the quality of a person's life considerably.

Peer mentoring advice

- Anxiety disorders are among the most common of mental ill health complaints. This means that you are not alone, and that many other people experience similar feelings, including non-autistic people.

- People with autism tend to be more prone to anxiety than others. Talking to another person with autism might be a good place to start in dealing with anxiety, as they are more likely to understand what you are going through. Sometimes talking to a good friend, sympathetic relative or partner can help you work through your anxiety as well. If you don't know many other people on the spectrum, you might benefit from getting involved in autism advocacy groups on social media or support or friendship groups run by your local autism organisation.

- Like any mental illness or negative facet of life, an attitude of acceptance and willingness to live well with anxiety will often be more beneficial to you than an attitude of regret, of wishing you didn't have anxiety, or refusing to try to learn new ways to manage your anxiety.

- Develop a 'kit' of relaxation techniques that you can use when you are anxious. There's a huge range of relaxation techniques people use: going for a walk, playing with pets, listening to soothing music, doing a painting or craft, writing, having a cup of tea or a positive sensory experience. Choose a few techniques that work for you, and when you are anxious, get out your 'kit' and use one or more of the techniques that you find helpful.

- Some people find writing down their thoughts and experiences can be very helpful in addressing anxiety. You may want to keep an anxiety journal and write in it when you are having difficulties with anxiety. You could also use your journal to jot down solutions and strategies you think of or just to record your thoughts. For some, just the act of writing can help reduce anxiety, so writing your thoughts and observations (not necessarily around anxiety or autism), poems or stories can help too.

- For some people, drawing, painting or cartooning their thoughts or experiences is more useful than writing. This is often the case for people who struggle with literacy or who have negative associations with trying to express themselves through the written word.

- If your anxiety is about a specific topic (e.g. worrying that you will lose your job), it often helps to get another person to provide an objective view of the situation you are stressed about and to reassure you as to whether it is something you need to worry about at all.

- Try using CBT techniques to reframe your negative, anxious thoughts. Many people on the autism spectrum significantly benefit from using these techniques to address things such as anxiety and depression. You will usually need to see a clinical psychologist or other mental health professional to help you with CBT techniques. (There is more information about CBT later in this book – see Chapter 13.)

- You may need to try a few different strategies and therapies until you find the ones that work for you. A psychological technique that some people find beneficial (such as CBT) may be less helpful for you, but by all means try some of the different strategies and therapies until you find one that works. Each person's 'kit' of strategies to address anxiety will be slightly different.

- Some things that are highly worthwhile – such as learning to drive – may be anxiety-provoking in the short term but very rewarding in the long term. If possible, try to do worthwhile things that are stressful, and as you do them, remind yourself of the positives and the expected outcomes.

- It can be good to expose yourself to minor challenges and things that might be difficult, as this helps you to build resilience.

- Think of anxiety as a physical symptom as well as a psychological or mental one. You may then find that some relaxation and meditation techniques, for example, deep breathing or mindfulness, which work on both mental and physical factors, are very helpful to alleviate anxiety. (There is more information on mindfulness later on in this book, in Chapter 12.)

- Physical exercise can be an excellent strategy to address anxiety. You don't need to join a gym or sports team; you can go for a brisk walk or run or do some exercise at home – either with home gym equipment or just using your body (e.g. climbing stairs or doing jumping jacks or crunches). Exercise is a great way of maintaining mental health and works well to help address depression and anxiety and improve your sense of wellbeing. It is also good to exercise due to its long-term physical health benefits. If you dislike exercise, you may still be able to harness the mental health benefits of exercise through a more gentle form, such as yoga or swimming, or more fun methods such as bouncing on a trampoline.

- Some medication can be helpful. If you wish to pursue this option, talk to your psychiatrist or GP about medications that can help to safely alleviate anxiety symptoms. (For more information, see Chapter 14 on medication, and also the section on specific anxiety disorders.)

JAMES' STORY: Learning to tackle anxiety

I am 38 and have Asperger's syndrome. I also have quite severe phobias of dogs and bees. For years, I often wouldn't leave the house because I was terrified I would be attacked by dogs, but I also am afraid to drive, so I don't have my license. If I had to go to the shops or anything, I need to take the bus, and even though the walk to the bus stop takes about five minutes, every time I walked to the stop I was in high alert for dogs and bees. In summer it was even worse. It was so bad that I couldn't work. Most of the time I would just sit at home, unless my dad came over, and then he would take me out. I relied on my dad for pretty much everything – shopping, company, driving places.

All this stopped in 2011. I got assigned a case manager from the local autism centre, Suzanne. Suzanne was a psychologist. I was pretty embarrassed about my phobia – I mean most people used to think I was weird when I told them – but I plucked up the courage and came out with it. Suzanne was really great. It took a while, but we worked on a few techniques to help get me out of the house and feel more safe and confident. Mostly we worked on reframing my thoughts about going out so that instead of being terrified of things that might not happen, I focused on how good and independent I would be if I overcame the fear. We did exposure therapy too – I got to the point where I could pat a dog. I can still do that now. It really helped.

So now I can walk down to the bus stop any time I like, even when it's dark in winter. I'm working five hours a week at the autism centre too.

- You are in control of your own mind – what you focus on, what you spend time thinking about and what you do. Try not to let anxiety take control. Be firm and confident that you are in control.

- There are groups that assist people with mental health issues such as anxiety. These include self-help groups and '12-step' mental health programmes where all the participants have similar issues. Some people on the autism spectrum respond well to groups like these. Examples of some of these groups are included in the Resources section at the end of this book.

- Anxiety is not all bad; a certain amount of anxiety is natural. It is part of our human nature, a remnant of the time when we had to kill mammoths, and so forth. Having no anxiety whatsoever would be a very bad thing. You would not look when crossing the road, you'd drive without care, you'd pat venomous snakes and you might even break the law, not worrying about the consequences. Sometimes you can use a degree of anxiety to your own advantage, such as being careful with money, and considering what you say to friends and colleagues.

- Learning to live with your anxiety and understand ways of lessening its impact can make a huge difference in your life. Remember that you are in control!

Over the last few years the idea of neuroplasticity has gained traction. This idea suggests that people can rewire their own brains to develop new skills and attitudes (Doidge 2010). One of the core theories is that by visualising changes in the way we respond to a situation, we can rewire our brains so that our responses actually change and over time become learned or automatic responses. For example, if someone is anxious about missing their bus stop and getting lost, they can start by interrupting that negative thought before they become fixated on it, and instead visualise or imagine themself getting off the bus at the right stop and easily finding their destination. Then they can think about how good it feels to be getting off at the right stop and finding their way. They would engage in this visualisation and follow up thoughts every time they started to feel anxious about the bus. Over time, they should find that there are longer and longer periods where they are not having anxious thoughts about the bus, and eventually that they are rarely anxious about the bus.

Doidge (2015) has recently discovered that although this visualisation technique works for a number of people, it is not as useful for others. For these other people, he recommends the use of sound, touch and/or vibrations as neurological distractors that can override the brain's current response and replace it with listening and/or feeling. This gives validity to the common strategy of listening to music while walking or dancing as a distractor to anxiety, and hope that over time these strategies will lead to a decrease in anxiety.

Dr Stephen Shore has suggested that people with autism can live well and decrease some of their anxiety through effective self-advocacy, where a person with autism asks people to make specific accommodations, while explaining how these accommodations will help. This type of self-advocacy is equally useful in residential accommodation settings as in the workplace. People do not need to disclose their autism or mental illness when using this type of self-advocacy as they are being very proactive and specific in asking for support and/or accommodations that they know will benefit them. An example of this would be for someone to ask their supervisor at work if they can sit at the end of the row, not in the middle, as this will help them to focus better on their work, as the fluorescent light in the middle gives them headaches.

LYNNE'S STORY: Overcoming anxiety

One of the most helpful tips I have ever been given was to not worry about things that are out of my control, and if I am worried about things I can do something about, I need to stop worrying and do something about it! Of course, I am still anxious, but not nearly so anxious as some of my Aspie friends who worry about everything. What is the point in worrying about whether or not the bus will come on time? It either will or it won't, nothing I can do will have any impact either way. One of the interesting things for me is that I realised how much anxiety, stress, worry and sleepless nights were had for NO REASON. I can't prevent a nuclear war or create a ceasefire so why worry about it? I was just making myself ill for no reason. And instead of worrying if I would run out of cereal, I learned to buy two boxes, so I always had a spare one, then I didn't need to worry. It is great how tiny little shifts in the way we Aspies think can change things so much.

3

DEPRESSION

What is depression?

Euthymia originated from the Greek word used to describe the 'wellbeing of the soul' but is now a clinical term used to describe an individual whose mood is relatively stable, generally within a positive range, but, most importantly, they do not appear depressed or elevated. Mood, rather than being static, has a range of 'normal' variants or fluctuations including the subjective feeling of sadness that is also part of the 'normal' human experience. However, when sadness is the predominant emotion, which becomes pervasive, entrenched and is eventually coupled with clusters of other negative self-ruminations and experiences such as guilt, despair, hopelessness and social dislocation, it is no longer a normal variant but is indicative of depression, particularly when those negative emotions insidiously serve to erode an individual's self-esteem and self-confidence. This negative self-talk is often accompanied by more destructive thought, such as 'I (or others) would be better off if I were dead'.

Historically, we have erroneously believed that depressive symptoms had to be present 'all day and every day' for at least around six months for a person to meet the diagnostic criteria for depression, but we now realise that depressed people can still laugh at times and appear future-focused, while still experiencing clinically significant depressive symptoms. 'A lot of people don't realise that depression is an illness. I don't wish it on anyone, but if they would know how it feels, I swear they would think twice before they just shrug it.' (Davis, nd). Although we generally consider depression to be a disorder primarily of the mind, it is also frequently associated with physical conditions such as changes to appetite with subsequent fluctuations in weight and insomnia, or conversely somnolence. Moreover, individuals with depression can also experience an exacerbation of pain symptoms (both acute and chronic). Sometimes (especially in the elderly or child/adolescence) non-specific physical co-morbidities include nausea, constipation and headaches, etc. Some individuals with severe depression can even present with significant psychomotor retardation (i.e. catatonia) to the point where they are physically incapable of performing even the most basic self-care.

Other non-specific manifestations of depression can include monotone and monosyllabic speech that is sometimes coupled with latency of verbal responses. Neurocognitive changes, including impaired memory and poor concentration (to name but a few), are also commonplace.

Variation in mood/feelings is integral to being human, but if the troughs in mood become too low or negative emotions predominate, 'depression' is likely. These experiences and symptoms of depression may occur for both neurotypical people and people with autism alike. However, people with autism may find it harder to realise that they are experiencing symptoms of depression. Keeping a diary or journal can help people to identify when they are just sad for a few days versus clinically depressed.

The monoamine theory of depression

> Disease, then, is something an organ has; illness is something a man has.
>
> Eric J. Cassell, 1978

Disease, by definition, generally has an identifiable biological precipitant – for example, bacterial meningitis, which is directly due to infection of the meninges by bacteria, has a potential for cure. But should the meningitis – despite 'curative' medical intervention – result in permanent brain injury, damaging visual pathways, and producing blindness, it is highly likely that the individual will experience 'illness' as a result of negative emotions including grief, anger, anxiety and distress, associated with the sudden loss of sight arising from the original disease process. Furthermore, not all diseases are curable, but an illness (which strongly correlates with emotions) closely associated with the disease can respond to non-curative treatments and even a placebo – that is, the disease is 'cured', but symptoms of the illness persist (sometimes the illness is refractory, or non-responsive to treatments).

At times, the medical model of psychopathology has viewed individuals from a reductionist perspective (i.e. people are merely the 'sum of their parts'). So the monoamine hypothesis of depression suggests that insufficient serotonin, noradrenaline and/or dopamine biochemically underpin depression (previously referred to as 'endogenous depression'). Contrary to this, a traumatic/tragic event in an individual's life that appeared to precipitate the depression resulted in the diagnosis of 'exogenous depression'. However, as illustrated in the mental wellness continuum diagram below, in depression, like any other illness (including physical illness such as diabetes), there are precipitants and vulnerabilities that may be exacerbated or precipitated by events in a person's life; depression is not necessarily caused by any individual event, and this is supported by the fact that not everyone exposed to a significant stressor/trauma will experience depression.

Depression can be treated using many different treatment modalities/strategies, including medication, different forms of psychotherapy, peer support and mindfulness or meditation techniques – and often a combination of these things. There is also a type of depression, called treatment-resistant depression, that is uncommon and is not helped by any of the usual treatments. However, this type of depression can be successfully treated with electro-convulsive therapy (ECT). ECT is carried out very differently now than in years gone by, and people who have had ECT for chronic treatment-resistant depression report symptom alleviation and improvement in their quality of life.

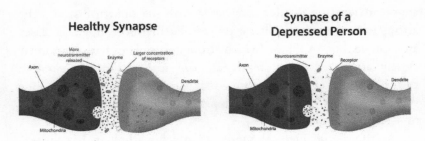

The mental wellness continuum – the monoamine theory of depression

People with autism spectrum conditions and depression

People on the autism spectrum are susceptible to depression, and this co-morbidity is quite a common experience. Research shows that adolescents and young people with autism spectrum conditions are more likely to experience depression than those without (Ghaziuddin 2002), although the prevalence of depression and autism co-occurring in any age group has not yet been definitively established. Much work has been done in this area, however, and some studies show the prevalence of depression in people with autism spectrum conditions as being as high as 65 per cent (Clissold 2012).

Depression for people on the autism spectrum can be a response to their awareness of 'difference' from the non-autistic world as they grow older. A sense of 'not fitting in' is common among both children and adults on the spectrum. However, this in itself is unlikely to lead to depression, and can be countered by meeting other people on the spectrum or joining groups that are focused on their special interest, as special interest groups are often more accepting than other groupings of people such as school classes or workplaces. Trauma and/or bullying can also lead to or impact depression, as can issues around obtaining a correct autism diagnosis as well as inherited factors or a genetic predisposition to depression.

Other issues that may exacerbate or precipitate depression among people on the autism spectrum include loneliness and isolation, grief or loss, sexual frustration, feelings of failure or high levels of anxiety. For a person who has high levels of anxiety, it is important to be proactive in getting support for this and implementing strategies to manage the anxiety, as this may be able to help prevent depression.

Interestingly, it has been found that optimising levels of vitamin D, EPA (eicosapentaenoic acid) and DHA (docosahexaenoic acid) (omega-3 fatty acids) can boost serotonin synthesis, serotonin release and potentiate its activity (respectively) within the central nervous system, improving symptoms associated with neurocognitive disorders such as attention deficit hyperactivity disorder (ADHD), and depression (Patrick and Ames 2015). The three forms of omega-3 are: α-linolenic acid (ALA) (found in plant oils including flaxseed and hemp oil), EPA and DHA (derived from 'animal fats' including fish and krill oils).

Prostaglandins are important chemical mediators in the 'inflammatory response', and prostaglandin E2 appears to be associated with inhibition of serotonin release from presynaptic nerve terminals so, given EPA's inhibition of E2, it is hypothesised to improve depressive symptoms while DHA is believed to potentiate the effects of serotonin at postsynaptic serotonin receptors. The biologically active form of vitamin D (e.g. cholecalciferol) is, by definition, more of a steroid hormone than an actual vitamin, in part because much of it is derived predominantly from exposure to sunlight, with very little being acquired from the typical Western-style diet. However, oily fish such as salmon and supplements such as cod liver oil can sufficiently augment vitamin D produced from sun exposure.

Vitamin D is important in calcium regulation, and so deficiency is associated with bone demineralisation, including rickets and osteomalacia (which is also associated with chronic musculoskeletal pain). Hence supplementary vitamin D is used for bone protection and is believed to reduce the risk of fractures in osteoporosis. Individuals with increased skin pigment (and potentially those wearing sunscreen) are frequently deficient in vitamin D despite the amount of sun exposure in more temperate climates. This deficiency is at least in part due to melanin impeding the UVB (ultraviolet shortwave) dermal conversion of vitamin D. Vitamin D as a hormone appears to play an important role in the synthesis of serotonin, and so its supplementation in individuals with low vitamin D is hypothesised to improve symptoms in cognitive and mood disorders (although the evidence is conflicting, and supplementation without conclusive proof of deficiency is controversial, with the risk of toxicity – albeit rare – outweighing postulated benefits).

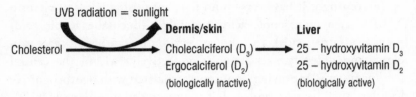

The benefits of sunlight

Depression can sometimes go undiagnosed or misdiagnosed in a person on the autism spectrum as they can present differently when seeking support. Many report being incorrectly diagnosed with schizophrenia or psychotic illnesses or personality disorders. These misdiagnoses can have a number of unintended and negative consequences, such as people feeling invalidated and discriminated against, unnecessary hospitalisation, or ineffective medication therapies. For some, it can be quite a journey to an appropriate and beneficial diagnosis. One reason that depression can go unnoticed or misdiagnosed in people on the autism spectrum is that they may be less likely to express emotions as visibly or clearly as neurotypical people. This means that they may appear to others to have a 'flat' mood, whether depressed or not.

Many people with autism find it hard to be aware of their physical or mental state. This can mean that some do not report depression, even when they are extremely depressed, because they themselves cannot articulate that they are experiencing feelings of low mood and depression. This can compound misdiagnosis or under-diagnosis of depression in people on the autism spectrum, and is a significant concern as people who need urgent help may not be able to identify that anything is wrong. This is why keeping a diary or journal can be helpful. If you notice, for example, that for six weeks you have not washed or cleaned your home, which you used to do previously, this could be a symptom that you can share with your GP or treating clinician.

Assessments for depression – Kessler Psychological Distress Scale (K10)

There are some relatively objective instruments that can be used by clinicians to assess whether a person is depressed. Such instruments may be able to pick up depressive feelings or disorders in people on the autism spectrum that may otherwise go undiagnosed. One such instrument is the Kessler Psychological Distress Scale (K10), which is used by medical practitioners to measure depression and psychological distress. Conducting the K10 involves asking the following ten questions and giving a score for each from the scale:

1. None of the time. 2. A little of the time. 3. Some of the time. 4. Most of the time. 5. All of the time.

Questions:

1. During the last 30 days, about how often did you feel tired out for no good reason?

2. During the last 30 days, about how often did you feel nervous?

3. During the last 30 days, about how often did you feel so nervous that nothing could calm you down?

4. During the last 30 days, about how often did you feel hopeless?

5. During the last 30 days, about how often did you feel restless or fidgety?

6. During the last 30 days, about how often did you feel so restless you could not sit still?

7. During the last 30 days, about how often did you feel depressed?

8. During the last 30 days, about how often did you feel that everything was an effort?

9. During the last 30 days, about how often did you feel so sad that nothing could cheer you up?

10. During the last 30 days, about how often did you feel worthless?

This scale is a measure of psychological distress. The numbers generated from the person's ten responses are added up, and the total score is considered the level of the K10. Final scores are between 10 and 50.

People who:

- score under 20 are likely to be well

- score 20–24 are likely to have a mild mental disorder

- score 25–29 are likely to have a moderate mental disorder

- score 30 and over are likely to have a severe mental disorder.

The K10 can be used as a diagnostic tool or also as a tool to measure a person's progress over a period of time. It can be used to determine whether a person on the autism spectrum is experiencing depression and to what extent. However, it is important to be aware of any communication issues around questionnaires such as the K10 in use with people with autism to avoid any false or misleading results. People on the spectrum should be given the time and opportunity to ask any questions or to raise issues around the scale, and then work through these to ensure that the clinician's understanding of the responses and the autistic person's are matched, and that both parties are 'on the same page' about what the questions and responses (numeric values) mean.

It is particularly important to clarify the meaning of 'for no good reason', 'hopeless' and 'worthless', as a person on the autism spectrum may respond one way because they felt there was a tiny glimmer of hope that their pet would snuggle with them, or something that rules out hopeless and worthless because of their literal interpretation of language. The intent behind the questions needs to be stressed rather than the wording where the wording is problematic for someone on the autism spectrum (Andrews and Slade 2001).

Skills for clinicians in treating depression

Clinicians treating people with autism and depression may have an improved outcome if they know the circumstances of the individual well, particularly their communication style, preferences around social interaction, personal history, interests and goals. Many people on the autism spectrum will prefer to be treated by a psychiatrist or psychologist with a good understanding of autism, and evidence suggests that better treatment outcomes will be achieved (Attwood 1998; Wing 1986). Clinicians with no experience of working with people with autism may unintentionally cause harm or damage due to making incorrect assumptions around autistic people based on their experiences in treating non-autistic people. A productive, open and honest relationship between client, carers/family and clinician, where the clinician is prepared to listen to concerns and develop an understanding of autism, is the ideal treatment environment.

Where the person with autism uses a different form of communication from speech, the treating clinician must let the person use their chosen/preferred communication method, even if they are unfamiliar with it – it is important for the person with autism to be able to communicate their responses, and if they are not able to use their preferred method, they may become so stressed that they are unable to communicate at all or in any meaningful manner. If the person with autism uses PECS (Picture Exchange Communication System), however, it is important to check that their PECS has all the possible responses so that the person is not left unable to respond.

Treatment of depression for people with autism needs to encompass and incorporate an understanding not only of their depression, but also the impact of issues related to autism and how their experience of autism might influence the presentation of depression. This may include an understanding of the person's relationships with others, environments they operate in (such as their school, university, family or workplace), their interests and sensitivities. Sensory sensitivities can be affected by depression, and in turn affect suggested treatment options.

Treatment for depression can include more conventional interventions such as medication or psychotherapy, but also needs to consider practical and other issues related to autism that may impact on the person's health and wellbeing. These include things such as improving interpersonal relationships, addressing toxic or negative environments (such as a school or work environment where bullying is not addressed), sensory issues, poor self-esteem or anxieties around specific activities or situations. Exercise is often suggested and is known to have a positive effect on a person's wellbeing, although for some people on the autism spectrum, exercise is something that they struggle with and may need support to integrate successfully into their day-to-day life.

Peer mentoring advice

- It is sometimes hard for people on the autism spectrum to realise that they are experiencing depression. Some common warning signs include that they lose interest in things they usually enjoy, feel sad a lot or all of the time, find it hard to feel anything, stop looking after themselves (hygiene, cooking, etc.), think about death and dying a lot, or feel hopeless about the future. If you are experiencing these things, seek help. Talk to a GP, a psychiatrist, a psychologist or a trusted friend or family member. Tell them everything you are going through, and how it is making you feel. Also, if family members, friends or your partner express concern about your mental state, even if you are not aware that there is a problem, listen to them and talk through their concerns. They may pick up that you are depressed even if you have not. You could ask them to go to see a GP or psychologist with you to explain why they have concerns. If you do this, you do not have to have them present for the whole time.

- A useful weapon in your arsenal against mental illness and/or depression is self-awareness. This means that you understand what you are going through, and can view it relatively objectively. Some people with autism struggle with self-awareness, and this can be even more difficult in the context of mental illness. A lot of 'neurotypical' (it's all relative) people struggle with self-awareness around mental health issues. Among people with autism the difficulties with self-awareness can be due to their self-image and their perceptions of self and others and how they relate to and are treated by others. However, people with autism are not innately incapable of developing a useful awareness and understanding of themselves and their mental health. How to develop self-awareness and insight are discussed at greater length later in this book (see Chapter 16).

- People with depression are deserving of sympathy and understanding, just like people with any other health condition are, but in the past, depression, like other mental illnesses, was often considered shameful. However, it is now becoming more acceptable to discuss depression in the public sphere. This is likely to have a positive impact that may result in people with depression feeling more able to talk openly about their condition. There is no reason for you to feel guilty or ashamed about your depression. It is an illness like other illnesses. You did not cause it, and you should not feel ashamed or embarrassed about discussing it with others. It is part of the many and varied elements that makes you who you are along with your autism and your life experiences. If people react negatively to your disclosure of depression, it may be because they do not understand what depression is, and they may be afraid of the unknown.

- Sometimes clinicians, friends and family members do not understand that a person with autism is depressed. There may not seem to be much difference between their depressed state and their 'usual' state. If you think you are depressed and nobody seems to believe you and denies your suspicions, persevere. Again, this is where keeping a journal of your feelings and daily activities and showing it to your psychiatrist or psychologist can be useful. If you can, try to think about the differences in feelings, perceptions and behaviours between your depressed self and your non-depressed self, and note them down. Explain to clinicians how you usually feel and how things are different for you at the moment. If you have previously been treated for depression, you might like to note what is similar now to when you were last depressed.

It is okay to shop around for a psychiatrist or psychologist too. If you are not being 'heard' by your current clinician or treating team, seek a second (or third or fourth) opinion. It can be hard to get treatment, and you may feel overwhelmed or ignored. Finding an 'ally' in your mental health journey will help you feel less alone. This could be your partner (if you have one), parents, sibling, autism worker or close friend. They can provide moral support, and can also assist by talking to your GP, if you want them to. It can be hard talking about your illness or issues to another person, but having their support can be invaluable. 'Taking the plunge' and asking for help can be a great first step to feeling better.

- Talking to a telephone counselling service such as Lifeline can assist people experiencing depression (see the Resources section at the end of the book). When you call a telephone counselling service, talk about how you feel or difficult situations you are dealing with. Many people – those with autism and neurotypical people alike – may find talking to a telephone counsellor helpful as they can be honest and talk about feelings or issues they may feel unable to with someone they know. Telephone counsellors are anonymous and will not ask your name. Most are volunteers and some are more experienced and have more training than others, so be aware that some of them will understand about autism and how it might affect people, but not all of them will. In my experience, however, telephone crisis counsellors are often willing to learn about things they haven't experienced – like autism – and are not judgemental. You just might need to explain your situation to help them understand what you are going through and how your autism might be impacting on your mental health. The service is confidential, so nothing you say will be recorded or go beyond the conversation you have with the counsellor. The only exception to this is if you tell the counsellor that you are planning to commit suicide. In this case, they have a duty of care to help keep you safe, so they may call the ambulance for you, or a mental health service you may be connected with.

- Some people on the autism spectrum, particularly more introverted people, find it hard to talk on the phone. Thankfully there are a number of online depression and mental health resources, ranging from services where you can chat in real time with a counsellor via the internet to courses like MoodGym where you can complete an online program to improve your mental health and coping skills. There is more information, and examples of these services, in the Resources section at the end of this book.

- People can live a good life with depression. Many of the treatments are very effective. Each person responds differently, but for most people, things such as psychotherapy or medication make a big difference to their quality of life. However, it is important to be aware that not all treatments for depression work for all people. In fact, psychological and psychiatric treatment is sometimes a bit 'hit and miss' or 'trial and error'. Doctors do not know precisely what will work to help you feel better, so it may take some time for an effective medication to be found. Some people have depression that does not respond to medication therapy; others have periods of being mentally healthy and periods of being unwell. If you have depression that does not respond well to treatment, a good strategy you can use is to adjust your attitude about your illness. How you approach your mental health can make a huge difference to how well you deal with your mental health and engage with life. If you feel that everything is hopeless and you'll never get better and that the world is against you, chances are that this will become true. Conversely, if you accept that you have a health problem that is difficult to manage but that you can be strong and do the best you can to stay healthy, this will also be true. You are essentially in charge of your own approach to life and this is an enormous power. Try to focus on – and add to – the positive things in your life, if you can. Although this sounds counterintuitive when thinking about depression, what we are talking about is long-term mental illness, whether that is depression or another mental illness. Over the years of your illness you can choose to accept that you have a mental illness and still engage positively with the world around you.

- Sometimes talking to someone else who has depression – especially a fellow autistic person – can be very helpful as they may understand where you are coming from and what you are experiencing better than others. It's also much easier to tackle something like depression if you have a friend who understands and with whom you can confide, a 'partner in crime', so to speak. If you do not have any autistic friends or any with depression, you may want to join an online group if you have access to the internet. Many people on the autism spectrum find their online friends are a great source of support in difficult times and a source of fun at others.

- You might want to keep a diary or journal. This can be a way to express your feelings confidentially. You could also keep a gratitude journal listing three positive events or thoughts for each day. This is a way of reframing your negative experiences and thoughts in a positive way. The very act of identifying good things when you are having a hard time helps you to turn your thinking around. Identifying positives in your life is a way of latching on to positivity and focusing on the good things you actually have – and all of us have good things in our life. We just need to look a bit harder for them sometimes. Reframing your thinking in this manner can help to retrain your brain to see things positively, and thus work to alleviate your low mood.

- Reframing your negative thoughts as positive ones is part of the psychotherapy model known as CBT. A psychologist who practices CBT can help you to start using the technique and reframing your thoughts. Many people with autism spectrum conditions have been assisted to deal with their depression using CBT techniques. There is more information on CBT and other psychotherapy models in Chapter 13. ACT is a form of CBT that is being used by a growing number of therapists.

- There is a huge range of medications that are used to treat depression. These are discussed later in this book, in Chapter 14.

JENNY'S PERSPECTIVE: Distraction strategies

I am 40 years old. I have an autism spectrum condition and a mood disorder.

I have found that a good way of tackling depression on a day-to-day basis is a strategy called 'opposite action'. When we are depressed, our natural inclination may be to get into bed, pull the covers over our head and hope that this will somehow make us feel better and the world will leave us alone. We certainly don't feel like doing anything strenuous or mentally taxing. I find that if you do get into bed and do nothing, chances are the depression and any associated negative thoughts will actually get stronger. In my experience, the best thing to keep depression at bay is to do the opposite of what we feel like doing. If I have a low mood or feel overwhelmed, I ignore my wish to do nothing and challenge it. I clean my house, go to work, or bake a cake. I think that the best things to do are mildly physically taxing or moderately mentally challenging things. Whenever you have that feeling that you want to withdraw and wallow, find yourself something engaging to do. You will almost certainly feel better – maybe not cured, but better. Life is difficult at the best of times, so setting achievable goals coupled with distraction strategies are essential for promoting and maintaining good mental health.

- Some people make ill-considered comments such as 'Oh, so you just have depression?' or 'Build a bridge and get over it!' These are highly unhelpful statements and betray the ignorance of the person who says them. Depression is not something you can decide not to have. It may require years of therapy or a lifetime of medication treatment to manage depression symptoms. Always be aware that depression is a serious issue and not something to dismiss or ignore. It is better to have supportive comments around the things that you are managing to do despite feeling so awful.

- People may also dismiss the mental health concerns of people on the autism spectrum as being unimportant or an inevitable manifestation of autism and something not really worthy of intervention or even sympathy. However, for people on the autism spectrum who have depression, their autism is one thing and their depression another – even if some of the issues around autism impact on depression and vice versa. Depression is just as, and sometimes more, serious in people on the autism spectrum as it is for people generally. For an autistic person with depression, developing a strong sense of self-worth can be a great way of countering negative or ignorant comments from others. Even if you don't feel strong or confident, try and 'fake it 'til you make it', as they say. To do this, think about things that others have said or might say about depression that you find invalidating or rude. Then, practising with a friend, family member or partner, develop a repertoire of confident responses or retorts. Practice scenarios or role-play around appropriate responses to comments about depression and other mental health issues. You could also direct people to online resources about depression such as beyondblue (see the Resources section at the end of the book).

- A good tool for tackling depression is liking and valuing yourself. Remind yourself that you're a great person who deserves respect – or whatever positive affirmation you like. Some people like to do this in front of a mirror. You can also ask friends, family members and people you trust to tell you things that they like about you (although be very selective, and make sure that the people you ask really are friends, as somebody who doesn't like you might say something unpleasant and this will undo your good work). You could even ask them to make a video or photomontage about your good qualities, if they are technologically inclined, or you could make one yourself. If this sounds too hard, make lists of the things that you have lots of knowledge about.

Once you have a list you can see that you have achievements – gathering knowledge and insight into those topics. This can be a starting point for your positive affirmations.

- Like all mental illness symptoms, depression can be managed so that you can live as well as possible. You will almost certainly see some change or improvement in your mood over time. Try to remind yourself of this if you become depressed again. Some people find that it helps alleviate their depression symptoms to surround themselves with mementos of when they were well or not depressed. Try making a space in your house for things like photos of yourself in happy situations or of your children, pets, family – anyone who you love or like to be around – books or art you like or anything else that helps remind you of happy times to help lift your mood, and reminds you that you have had better times in the past. This approach can help reinforce the idea in your mind that episodes of depression are only temporary.

Predisposing risk factors for depression (and other psychopathologies):

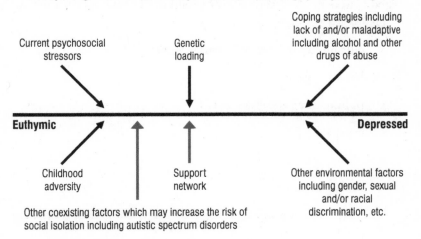

Predisposing risk factors for depression

4

SELF-HARM

Self-harm is a complicated phenomenon that is fairly common throughout society for a wide variety of reasons, including, but not limited to, feeling numb, trauma, a need for punishment of self or others. People with autism, and especially children, may intentionally self-harm or engage in self-injurious behaviour due to sensory or emotional overload or other issues. Self-harm is also a common occurrence among people with a lived experience of mental illness. Sometimes the reasons people with autism self-harm are different from those of people with mental illness. However, people with autism and a co-morbid mental illness may self-harm for reasons related to autism, mental illness, or a kind of dynamic mix of the two.

Deliberate self-harm includes such actions as:

- cutting, scratching or burning oneself

- head-banging

- pulling one's own hair out

- eye-gouging

- biting oneself

- hitting oneself

- deliberately engaging in dangerous activities (such as driving recklessly)

- starving or bingeing on food

- taking overdoses of medication

- abusing drugs or alcohol, including prescription medication (some refer to this as self-medicating).

People may engage in deliberate self-harm as a maladaptive way of coping with distressing feelings or experiences. Self-harm is not the same as suicidal actions – while people who self-harm may also attempt suicide, there is a distinct difference between the two things.

Reasons for self-harm include:

- compulsive behaviours

- a perceived need to punish oneself

- impulsive or intrusive thoughts directing the person to harm themselves

- hallucinations (voices, commands etc.) telling the person to harm themselves

- self-hatred

- feeling detached from reality (self-harm as a way to feel something).

For people with autism, there are some additional causes or triggers for self-harm, which include:

- sensory overload

- communication difficulties

- physical pain

- frustration around communication

- seizures or epilepsy

- as a manifestation of an obsessive thought

- overwhelming emotions.

It is important to understand that self-harm can have serious consequences for self-esteem, physical wellbeing, self-worth and relationships with others. Self-harm is something that people should ideally be supported and encouraged to move beyond and to stop undertaking. This may require psychotherapy, but it is also important for the person to build support networks of people such as family, friends or peer supporters and mentors.

Overcoming self-harm often requires a two-pronged approach – addressing the underlying reasons for the behaviour and also developing strategies to stop or de-escalate the behaviour when the urge arises. In other words, new strategies need to be learned to replace the self-harming. This is the case regardless of why someone is self-harming. Unfortunately, self-harming behaviour can stimulate reward pathways in the brain, and even though the person may want to stop these behaviours, it has become addictive due to physiological reinforcement. For these people naloxone (similar to morphine) may be used to treat the addiction pathways and to aid in the treatment to prevent further self-harming.

Self-harming behaviour in people with autism can be extreme and very dangerous. People with autism spectrum conditions who self-harm as children may outgrow the behaviour, but it can return in adulthood in times of severe stress or trauma, unless help to manage emotionally/mentally is sought during those times. The therapies and strategies that work for individuals with only a mental illness diagnosis can also be effective for people with autism and mental illness. However, it is important for clinicians assisting people with autism and mental illness who self-harm, to have a good understanding both of the circumstances and presentation of the individual they are treating, and autism more generally.

Addressing self-harm requires a programme of therapy or interventions targeted to the individual rather than a 'one size fits all' approach. For example, non-verbal adults with autism who are engaging in biting themselves may be expressing muscle pain, or they may be deliberately self-harming, and it is important to understand why in order to treat them effectively.

Children with autism who self-harm should be referred to specialist services to gain support for themselves and their families. This support will hopefully identify triggers for the self-harm and possible replacement behaviours. Once replacement behaviours have been identified, they will need to be explicitly taught and scaffolded for the child. This method can also work for adults with autism. Initially, the person with autism will need to be prompted to use the new strategies, especially when they are not aware of their mood change or build-up of factors that trigger their feelings of need or compulsion to self-harm.

It is possible for people who engage in self-harm to recover and bring the behaviour to a halt. Even those who are most severely affected and undertake the most extreme self-injurious behaviour can go on to live well without engaging in self-harming behaviour. There are many therapies and treatments that can help people regain their health and move on from self-harm.

A large part of the recovery process involves attitudinal changes that tend to build momentum once a person commits to them, especially if they have the support of family and/or friends and/or mental health support services. There are, however, a number of unhelpful attitudes around self-harm, and probably the most pervasive of these is the idea that people who self-harm are doing it to 'get attention'. This attitude breeds prejudice and misunderstanding, and can represent a barrier to recovery for people who self-harm. The advocacy group selfharmUK describes how the concept of self-harm as 'attention-seeking' behaviour is problematic and damaging for those who experience self-harm:

> This is a major difficulty experienced by many people who self-harm. Being perceived as 'attention-seeking' is painful and far from the truth. If attention-seeking really was the biggest motivation for someone struggling with self-harm, it's a long way from being the most effective way to go about getting it. Self-harm may be a way of someone communicating that they are emotionally distressed or finding life difficult to manage, but there are a huge number of ways to 'get attention' that don't involve inflicting pain on oneself or hurting those around us. Self-harm is about expression, not attention.
>
> Even if it were about attention, what is so awful for that person that hurting themselves has become the best way to be noticed? Perhaps we need to stop seeing 'attention-seeking' as being something negative, and actually accept that every one of us needs and enjoys attention of some kind or another at times. Attention is about connecting with others and feeling as though we matter – this isn't negative in itself.
>
> (selfharmUK no date, a)

A significant issue for autistic people who self-harm is that of misdiagnosis by medical professionals. People who self-harm, especially adults, may attract an incorrect or unhelpful explanation for their actions from health professionals, such as a diagnosis of borderline personality disorder. Misdiagnosis can lead to inappropriate treatment, invalidation and anger, which in turn may exacerbate the self-harm and its underlying causes.

There may occasionally be an increase in self-harm for some people when new medications are introduced. This may be due to an increase in impulsivity or physical side effects. SSRI medications, such as fluoxetine and citalopram, need to be started on a very low dose and titrated up (increased slowly). If high dosages are prescribed too quickly, this can result in a surge in serotonin in the central nervous system, which can lead to increased agitation, anxiety and hyper-arousal as well as feeling physically uncomfortable, which can lead to increased self-harming behaviours as the person tries to deal with these physical symptoms.

It can take up to six weeks to titrate up the dosage of an SSRI medication to the therapeutic level for an individual. People with autism can be hyper- or hypo-sensitive to medications and may require much lower or higher doses of medications than neurotypical people. This sensitivity is not uniform, and people can be hyper-sensitive to one drug and hypo-sensitive to another.

There is one documented case where a non-verbal adult increased his self-harm – biting – and to try and manage this, his clinical team increased his methotrimeprazine dosage, which is usually a helpful medication. However, in this case he developed an extremely rare side effect called neuroleptic malignant syndrome, which caused rhabdomyolysis, an extremely painful breakdown of the muscles in the body. This led to acute renal failure as clinicians were unable to ascertain why he was biting himself more, and they continued to slowly increase the dosage, which was started off at an extremely low level. Sadly, renal failure led to this man's death.

It is very important to ensure that non-verbal adults (with or without autism) have access to visuals that could enable them to explain that their body or body parts are hurting during evaluations of self-harming behaviour. For example, an infected ear can cause head-banging. New incidences of self-harming must also be assessed as if they are not related to previous incidences, and physical causes again ruled out before considering psychiatric causes.

Peer mentoring advice

- People self-harm for genuine reasons. Despite this, there remains a stigma about self-harm with some people expressing a variety of judgmental opinions about self-harm and the people who engage in it. It is a good thing to address self-harm and to move beyond it, but people judging you or blaming you may increase your stress or feelings of unworthiness. Remind yourself that the behaviour does not make you a bad person, or an attention-seeker, or less worthy than others, whatever people might say. Self-harm is usually a response to events, feelings or situations you experience. It is a sign of an illness in the same way that a tumour is the sign of cancer or a fever is a sign of malaria. It is your mind's way of coping with the issues you are facing. Be kind to yourself when trying to deal with self-harm.

- It is possible for everyone to learn to live without needing to self-harm, but for some it can be a lengthy and difficult journey. The longer someone harms, the harder it can be to break the pattern of behaviour.

- You may feel that you can never overcome thoughts and acts of self-harm when you are caught up in it, but there are a number of effective strategies and therapies (see selfharmUK no date, b).

- A good strategy to help you stop self-harming is to remove the underlying reason for the behaviour, and the first step is learning why you self-harm. This can be tricky to do by yourself, and it is often preferable to enlist the help of a mental health professional such as a psychologist or counsellor. If you identify that you self-harm because you find certain situations emotionally overwhelming, at the same time as you work on addressing emotional regulation with your mental health worker, plan how to avoid those situations on days where you feel it would be too much. If you identify that your self-harming behaviour is a result of traumatic issues from your past, do some work on 'making peace' with your past issues. Addressing the underlying causes is often an effective way for people to say goodbye to self-harm, and to build self-respect and self-care.

- Self-harm can often feel like a sudden impulse or urge, and might not last longer than a few minutes. Here are some strategies to help you get past that urge when it arises, bearing in mind that it is not always helpful to focus on complete abstinence or stopping self-harming behaviour in one sudden step. Instead, build new strategies for dealing with situations that may trigger self-harm, and this can gradually take the place of self harm:

  » Try to de-escalate the impact of the self-harm (i.e. start to reduce the physical damage to yourself and set a goal of minimising the impact). For example, instead of hitting yourself, hit a punch bag or pillow. Instead of biting yourself, bite a piece of latex rubber with the same texture as the body part that you bite; instead of cutting yourself, rub ice or salt grains onto your skin, or wear elastic/rubber band bracelets and ping these forcefully.

  » If possible, start to get in touch with your emotions and learn to identify how you are feeling when the urge to self-harm occurs. This can help you to seek help or leave the situation before the urge to self-harm occurs. This is something you will probably need to do with a counsellor or other mental health worker. This can be very difficult for some people with autism, and you may need to trust other people to let you know when they think that you are entering into the state of mind where you may begin to self-harm. It can be very useful to ask this trusted person (or people) to remind you not only when to use your replacement strategies, but also what these strategies are, until these new strategies become habitualised. Some people with autism like to have reminder cards that they carry around with them or keep visible in their homes at all times. A reminder card usually consists of a brief statement such as: 'When I am distressed I can listen to music on my iPod. Listening to music on my iPod helps me to feel better.' For those who struggle to identify emotions, their card may be quite different and detail physical signals. For example: 'When my skin gets tight on my face I need to keep still, breathe deeply and then go for a walk. Going for a walk is healthy and helps me to live well.'

» Know what triggers your self-harm and reduce the risks. Knowing what kinds of situations are likely to end up in self-harming behaviour can help you plan to reduce the risks. For example, if spending time with certain people is emotionally overwhelming and you have noticed that seeing them often results in difficult emotions and/or self-harm, avoid spending time with them, especially when you are feeling vulnerable. It is okay to avoid certain people, even if those people are members of your family. If you identify someone in your workplace as the issue, however, it is very difficult to avoid them, and in this case you need to seek support for yourself and discuss the problem with a manager. If you are entitled to sick leave, discuss how that leave could be used to help you mange at work or apply for other jobs.

» Learn some strategies to take care of and comfort yourself when you are feeling overwhelmed. Try out different things to see what you find most helpful. Some thoughts include having a bath, stim toys that you enjoy, pleasant sensory experiences, cuddles with your pet, listening to music that you like. Find whatever works for you. There are now stim toys that look like jewellery and can be chewed or fidgeted with. Some people with autism have reported that these are very helpful in preventing emotions becoming overwhelming. Have some strategies that can be used anywhere as some are not practical in all circumstances. For example, if having a bath is the best way you can feel better, it is not going to be useful in the middle of your working day! In this case you might use your second-best strategy.

» Try to distract yourself and not act on the urge to self-harm for short periods of time initially. It is not necessary to try and completely stop self-harming instantly; it will take time. Be kind and supportive of your desire to change and learn new ways of living well. Distraction techniques can include anything that you find engaging and to which you can devote your whole attention. Some people find television helpful, others like using social media (although be aware that this can present issues with triggering if you have a negative interaction with a contact or see something disturbing or if most of your social media 'friends' are engaging in self-harm). Distraction is basically any activity you can do to engage your mind and 'put off' the thoughts of self-harm until they have dissipated. Find whichever distraction works for you.

• Self-harm and suicide are distinct entities. People can deliberately self-harm without having any intention of ending their life. However, self-harm can be an indicator that somebody is having thoughts of suicide. Self-harm should always be taken seriously.

• Always seek help for self-harm, even if the harm is not outwardly visible to others. Treat any physical injuries first, and ensure you are safe before getting to work on the underlying psychological issues.

• When getting help for self-harm or other mental health symptoms, it is a good idea to see a GP, psychiatrist, psychologist or counsellor who specialises in treating adults with autism spectrum conditions before seeing a general psychiatrist or psychologist. Autism specialists are likely to know more about the reasons people on the spectrum self-harm and how to help you move past it. It can do more harm than good to see a professional who doesn't know much about treating people on the autism spectrum, as they may misread the reasons why you self-harm, and could give you unhelpful or even damaging treatment. If you do not like or trust the first person you seek help from, it is okay to ask to see someone else instead. Keep trying until you find someone who is able to help you.

- If you move to a new city or town, you will almost certainly need to see new mental health workers. This can cause 'continuity'-type issues in regard to your treatment. It is important to make sure that you get consistent care based on a shared understanding of your psychiatric history, personality and unique mental health challenges. When giving your 'history' in the initial consultation with a new mental health worker, tell them that you have self-harmed in the past and how it might be related to your autism, if you can. Ask to take your treatment records with you when you move from one practitioner to another, and your treatment provider should supply a summary of your mental health history and current mental health plan.

- Ask a friend, family member or professional who knows you to advocate on your behalf and inform your treating clinicians who may not understand the reasons for your self-harm or who are not aware of autism and how it impacts you. You can take this support person with you to medical/mental health appointments. If you do this, you will need to give consent to the doctors and nurses to talk to your support person because of the privacy laws and issues around confidentiality.

- If possible, have at least one person – a sympathetic or understanding clinician, a family member, partner or friend – that you can confide in about your self-harm. This person can be an advocate for you if you are in a potentially disempowering situation, such as a psychiatric hospital. If you do not personally know anyone, you may find someone to talk to on a telephone helpline or an online advocacy or support service. These could be in the area of autism or mental health. Contacts are provided in the Resources section at the end of this book.

- Sometimes people who engage in self-harm have a circle of friends who also engage in self-harm. This is particularly common among young people and teenagers, as approximately 10 per cent of 12- to 17-year-olds have self-harmed at some stage (headspace no date). You may find yourself being the confidant for all your friends, where they tell you their issues and describe their self-harm in detail. This is an exceptionally difficult position for anyone to be in, but especially for somebody on the autism spectrum who may struggle with enforcing boundaries and being able to monitor their level of emotional discomfort. Some tips in this situation for friends of people who self-harm include:

  » Don't promise to keep a friend or anyone else's 'secret' around self-harm or suicidal behaviour. In some countries and some circumstances you have a legal obligation to report this and/or to seek help for them. This is usually the case where the person is under 18. Keeping people's self-harm secrets will probably serve to make you stressed around possible disclosure. You might feel that all the responsibility for your friend rests with you and that if they self-harm, or worse still, die by suicide, that it was 'your fault'. Your friend may say that if you tell anyone, they will kill themselves. In this situation, tell someone, and realise that it is not your fault if they do end their own life.

  » Try not to use blaming or angry language, but explain to your friends that you yourself are struggling, and that their reliance on you is making your life harder. Perhaps suggest that they talk to a mental health professional or counselling service, such as Lifeline or the Samaritans. Pass on the details of a mental health worker or counsellor you have used who has helped you (if you know of one), or refer them to one of the places listed in the Resources section at the end of this book.

» Focus on positive things in conversations with your self-harming friends. Instead of comparing 'war stories' about self-harm, try to do things that are affirming and steer the conversation to more constructive topics, such as activities you and your friends enjoy. However, if your friends glorify self-harming and try to compete to see who can do the most harm to themselves, you probably need to distance yourself from them. Encouraging others to self-harm is not something that friends do; it is neither kind nor caring. In this situation, it is okay to tell your friends that you need to spend time apart from them. You many even want to block them so that they cannot contact you on social media or by phone.

- If possible, get rid of objects in your house that you use to self-harm, such as razor blades, cigarette lighters etc. Then, if you want to use such items for self-harm, you will need to make a conscious decision and effort to buy those items and associate that with self-harm. This puts a barrier between you and the means of self-harm. You could put stim toys in the places where you normally keep objects that you use to self-harm, so that, for example, when you go to get your cigarette lighter, you find a small hard squeezy toy that you can pinch and squeeze as a distractor.

- If you have an issue with frequent self-harm and you don't self harm for a set period of time – a day, a week, a month, whatever you feel is a valid achievement – reward yourself in some small way. You might want to buy a new game, or make a special cup of hot chocolate or go to the cinema. Whatever you do, make it something special that you enjoy and that makes you feel good. Be proud of your achievement. If you can stop for a short period, you can stop for a longer period. If you relapse, try to identify what it was that was different leading up to the self-harm than the times you did not self-harm recently.

- Dialectical behaviour therapy (DBT) can be very helpful in addressing self-harm. It is a skills-based therapy programme where people can learn how to manage their emotions and deal with crisis situations. It is often run in small groups, so you may like to look up groups in your local area. A psychologist can deliver it in a one-on-one setting, if that's what you prefer.

- Often the best person to help you overcome self-harm is somebody who has experienced self-harm themselves and overcome it, especially someone else on the autism spectrum. There are mental health recovery groups, such as Grow, which provide peer support (see the Resources section at the end of this book).

- Most of the time, the more you resist the urge to self-harm, the weaker that urge will get. If you continue resisting the urge, your resolve will grow stronger and you will be less likely to self-harm in the future.

- Many people find self-harm challenging and confronting. This is because self-harm *is* challenging and confronting! If you don't want to talk to others – including, in some cases, strangers – about your experiences of self-harm, and explain why and how it happened, consider covering up any scars or obvious physical injuries. People can be very curious and quite intrusive with their questions about how someone got a scar or physical injuries.

- Like having a tattoo of your ex-partner's name, self-harm often leaves marks that you will probably regret in the future. You can use this knowledge as a protective factor. Instead of feeling guilty and hating yourself for making those scars, try instead to use them to remind you of where you have come from, the fact that you have survived, and that you can use your experiences of recovery and healing to help others.

- The thing that will banish self-harm quicker than anything is loving, valuing and respecting yourself. To achieve this, try to surround yourself with people who like and respect you. Challenge any negative self-talk – be it your internal monologue about yourself or how you speak about yourself to others. Celebrate your successes. Make a list of all the good things about yourself and all the things you have achieved – they don't have to be anything earth-shattering. Sometimes just getting out of bed each morning is an achievement. You may have to make a bit of an effort and it may take a long time, but if you start to love, like and respect yourself, self-harm will most likely be something you say goodbye to.

- For some people, having a pet to take care of can help prevent self-harming, as pets can interact with a being who loves them unconditionally. And having to take care of the pet can provide a distraction and build self-care skills too. Dogs can help forge new contacts with people in your local community, as people will often talk to someone who is walking a dog or sitting in a park playing with a dog. This can help you to feel more confident as a person and feel less judged.

5

SUICIDAL THOUGHTS

Suicidal thoughts are surprisingly common, with up to a third of people having thought about suicide at some point in their life. This is even more prevalent among people on the autism spectrum. In a recent study, two-thirds of a group of adults diagnosed with Asperger's syndrome said they had thought about committing suicide at some point, and 35 per cent had made specific plans or actually made an attempt. Cassidy *et al.* (2014) found that for the people with Asperger's in their study, having depression was the biggest risk factor for suicidality. However, people with autism/Asperger's may not realise that they are depressed, and this may not be picked up on traditional types of depression screens.

It is important to note that not everyone who ever thinks about suicide will go on to attempt it. There is a complex relationship between self-harm and suicide. However, it is wrong to assume that people who self-harm are trying to kill themselves. Usually, self-harm is a coping mechanism, not a suicide attempt. Some people use self-harm as a way to try to cope and not to try to end their life. Sadly, sometimes people injure themselves more seriously than they were intending, and this can put their life at risk. In addition, research has found that young people who self-harm are also at a much higher lifetime risk of attempting suicide than those who don't self-harm, even if they are not suicidal at the time. And there is a higher risk associated with having close family members who have committed suicide. This doesn't mean people will always attempt suicide, but that their risk of attempting to do so is higher. It is important to encourage anyone who is self-harming to seek help from a health professional to address any underlying emotional or mental health problems (e.g. depression or anxiety).

Suicidal thoughts can be described in mental health settings as suicidal ideation. The term 'suicidal ideation' refers to thoughts that life isn't worth living. These can range in depth and breadth from brief thoughts that life is actually not worth living, through to clear plans for committing suicide to a constant preoccupation with ending one's life. Most people who experience suicidal ideation will not go on to kill themselves; however, most who do attempt or complete suicide have had suicidal thoughts. This is why it is important to seek help if you have suicidal thoughts.

There are a number of risk factors that are correlated with attempting suicide. The more risk factors, the higher a person's risk that they will go from just thinking about suicide to trying or completing suicide. These factors include:

- a previous suicide attempt

- mental health and/or substance use disorders

- physical illness: terminal, painful or debilitating illness

- family history of suicide, alcoholism and/or other psychiatric disorders

- history of abuse: sexual, physical or emotional

- social isolation and/or living alone

- bereavement in childhood

- family disturbances

- unemployment, change in occupational or financial status

- rejection by a significant person, for example, a relationship break-up

- recent discharge from psychiatric hospital or prison.

Because of the stigma of suicide and the state of mind of those people who are feeling suicidal, people are often reluctant to talk about it. However, it is very important to talk to someone if you are feeling suicidal as they may be able to help you make and implement a plan to improve things in your life so that you can live well in the future.

It is not abnormal to think about suicide. It can be very hard for people with autism to explain how they are feeling, and it is understandably hard to tell someone you are thinking about suicide. However, you can approach family and/or friends, your GP, a crisis mental health team and/or a counsellor and/or a hotline/online support service. Talking to people can be very helpful.

Some early warning signs that someone may be at increased risk of suicide may include:

- threats to hurt oneself or suicide, including looking for the means of suicide (pills, weapons etc.)

- talking or writing about death or suicide

- acting recklessly or engaging in risky activities

- increased use of alcohol or other drugs

- withdrawing from friends, family or society to a greater extent than usual

- noticeably increased level of agitation

- dramatic changes in mood

- feeling that there is no reason for living, no sense of purpose in life.

If you are experiencing any of these things and are worried about suicide, seek help from a mental health professional.

If you know someone you think may be at risk, it is okay to talk to them about it. People used to think that talking to someone about suicide would encourage them to try to kill themselves but we now know this is not true. In fact, the only way to assess the real risks around suicide is to talk about it. The important questions to ask yourself are:

- Are you thinking about killing yourself?

- Do you know where you want to do this?

- Do you have a plan of how to do this?

- Do you have access to the things needed for your plan?

If you answer 'yes' to more than one question, your risk of suicide is much higher than if you say 'no'. People rarely change their method, if they have planned a method. If the person goes to act on their plan, but there is a barrier to the plan (e.g. the road is closed so they cannot get where they wanted to go to commit suicide), then they do not usually go through with their plan. This means that interrupting their suicide plan is very useful. However, with young people or people who are drunk or high on drugs, their inhibitions and impulse control are much lower, so it is more difficult to support them.

It is vital to refer someone who says 'yes' to all these questions to a mental health crisis intervention team immediately. If you answer 'yes' to these questions, seek help as soon as possible. If you do not know where to get help from, try phoning a mental health crisis line and explaining that you are a danger to yourself as you are struggling with severe suicidal ideation.

Approximately 90 per cent of those who commit suicide are experiencing mental illness at the time of their suicide. Undiagnosed and untreated mental illness is the most common risk factor for suicide. This is because being unwell mentally can change your thinking as well as the way you interpret and interact with the world as well as increase a sense of hopelessness and helplessness. People with autism already interpret and interact with the world differently from most people, so professionals and family members who do not understand the autism spectrum can sometimes miss or misdiagnose the autism and/or the mental illness.

It is perhaps because of the differences in perception that are experienced by people with autism, and the difficulty that many may have in finding a sense of belonging and purpose in the world, that can lead to increased risk of mental illness and increased suicidal ideation among this group. However, finding a sense of belonging and purpose can be much easier for people with autism when they meet online or in real life other people on the autism spectrum. Feelings of hopelessness and helplessness can be challenged and overcome when you find out how other people with autism manage some of the same challenges that you face. Having people who have similar experiences and shared ways of thinking can help you feel included and part of a group where you may not have in the past. This inclusion in a group of other people with autism, whether online or in real life, can help to provide a sense of hope that life will and can improve, and that hope is one of the most effective tools to prevent suicide. It also helps prevent social isolation and forge new support networks.

Some people with autism feel very alone, whether or not they live alone. This feeling is not 'just a part of autism'; it can change when people find others who are similar. For those with autism with or without a diagnosed mental illness, who live alone and who have little contact with others, the isolation can be both comforting and a source of pain at the same time. This isolation can make it harder to reach out for help if they have suicidal thoughts. However, it is important to seek support, as the sooner someone gets help, the sooner they can be on the recovery journey to live well.

The difference between thinking about and attempting suicide is often dependent on 'protective factors', which include:

- effective clinical care for mental illness, autism, physical illness and/or substance abuse disorders

- limited access to means of suicide (pills, weapons etc.)

- strong connections to family and community, which can include online autism or mental health communities

- acceptance by and involvement in a community (e.g. the autism community, social media, work colleagues, mental health community etc.)

- having a positive relationship with mental health clinician/s

- having meaningful activity to do and a sense of purpose (e.g. work, study, passionate interest)

- resilience

- having pets to care for

- belonging to a philosophy, culture or faith that discourages suicide and promotes positive views of life.

Try to ensure that you have some of these protective factors in your life, as they may mean the difference between thinking about suicide and acting on those thoughts.

One of the best preventers for attempting suicide is to be future-focused. This means having goals and plans for the future. It can be difficult for some people with autism to set a distant goal because of the difficultly of planning to do something that so many things could interfere with or impact on. If you are one of those people, make plans for next week or even tomorrow rather than next month or year. Goals can be very small, such as reading one library book next week, or very big, such as becoming an accountant. The key is to have a plan as to how you are going to achieve a goal and what you are going to do if problems arise.

Some people have tick charts as their goal and plan combined, and the plan consists of just doing the next thing on the tick chart. However, many people with autism have executive functioning difficulties (they find it hard to think how to organise and sequence events), so this would probably not work for them. If this applies to you, take your goals to a friend/family or professional and ask them to help write up a realistic plan as to how you can achieve your goals.

Many people who suffer from suicidal ideation have talked about the importance and helpfulness of both contact with other people or pets and things to look forward to, such as having a treat at a cafe or buying a new graphics card for their computer. You might like to save a small amount of money every day in a jar for a special treat, and as the jar fills, you can decide what treat you would like.

For some people with autism, suicide can appear to be the logical answer to their difficulties. Using the idea that 'if I do not exist, I will not suffer anymore', they may come to the conclusion that suicide is a legitimate answer for them. The problem with this logic is that suicide has a huge impact on other people. For example, family, friends, neighbours and even acquaintances can be hugely negatively impacted by suicide. Children or other close family members become more at risk of suicide if a parent or other family member ends their own life.

One way of understanding this is to see that suicide is extremely selfish. The person who you buy your milk or bread from may be devastated if you kill yourself, wondering if there was anything they could have done to prevent it. And if someone with a passing knowledge of you feels this way, imagine how people closer to you, like family members, your mental health or autism workers or friends, will feel. Your perception of how others see you can be skewed by loneliness, isolation and depression or anxiety. While you might think that nobody cares about whether you live or die and that others must all dislike you, the opposite is often true. Many people are willing to help, but do not know that a suicidal person needs help. This is why it is important to say that you are feeling suicidal.

When people have suicidal thoughts, they can often catastrophise events, which is something that many people with autism also have difficulties with. The expression 'don't make a mountain out of a molehill' tries to give a visual example of catastrophising things that are small to make them into huge problems. Often people with autism don't realise that they are doing this, and are convinced that the problems really are huge, if not insurmountable. For example, a person with autism who does not get the first job they apply for is more likely to think that they are never going to get a job than other people. Other people may well be upset, angry or frustrated, but they will say things about how hard it is to find work at the moment and they have heard that you need to apply for 60 or even 100 jobs before you get offered a job.

Peer mentoring advice

- Very few problems in life are truly insurmountable. With nearly everything there is hope and people willing to help, if only you ask.

- Often, the 'danger period' for suicide is quite short, even as little as 20 minutes – if you are having strong urges or wishes to act on suicidal thoughts, those urges generally don't last for more than a short while at the same degree of intensity. If you can get through that period of intense distress, the suicidal thoughts will probably become less severe. This doesn't mean that the suicidal urges won't return at a later time, but if they do, try to view that crisis period as being short-lived, and understand that if you can get through it, you will be stronger. That period of extreme crisis is the time to focus on crisis measures – calling the mental health crisis response team or a suicide counselling line, asking someone to come to your house and stay with you, or practising distraction techniques.

- Having another person with you during crisis periods is a good strategy as the other person can help focus your attention away from the suicidal thoughts and urges. Most people also find it a lot harder to go through with the act of suicide when another person is around. If you don't have anyone you feel comfortable enough to ask to spend time with, you can use your pet (if you have one) as another person. Imagine your cat or dog being in your house all by themselves with no human companion to feed them and to love them and how sad and scared they would be. Alternatively, if you are capable of this during a crisis, go into a place where there are other people, such as a park or cafe. Most people find it very hard to commit suicide in a public place.

- Restrict your access to the means of suicide (pills, weapons, etc.). If you need to have such things in the house (such as your medication), put them in a place where you need to make a conscious decision to be able to access them, such as a cupboard or drawer in a room you rarely use or in your car. If you are really troubled and frightened that you may act on the thoughts, ask a friend or family member to look after your medication while you are experiencing the crisis. If you do not have anyone who can do this for you, many mental health crisis services will look after your medication for you and dispense it as you need it.

- Sometimes people save up medications with the intent of using them for the purpose of suicide. If you do this, throw out the additional medications you have saved. It takes a lot of courage, but it is the best possible action you can take. If you are concerned about having too much medication in your house, when you fill in the prescriptions form, consider asking the pharmacist to pack your medications in a Webster pack or dosette. These systems mean that you only collect one or two weeks' worth of medication at one time. This is a good strategy for people who have issues with stockpiling medication.

- Always take somebody's statement that they are thinking about suicide seriously. Don't offer to keep their 'secret' from others. Encourage them to get help. If there is an immediate threat, call the ambulance or the police.

- If you are feeling suicidal, think what you would say to someone you care about if they said they were having suicidal thoughts. This exercise can help put your thoughts into perspective and realise that you, too, are a valuable and worthwhile person.

- Try to think about what legacy you will leave for your family, workplace or people you know if you commit suicide. This legacy will be entirely negative and tragic. Your life may be remembered by those who know you as marked with tragedy. Any positive memories of good things you accomplished will probably be eclipsed by the manner of your death.

- It is often said that suicide is a long-term solution to a short-term problem. Remind yourself that the feelings you are experiencing now will change and move on. You do not know what tomorrow may hold.

6

PSYCHOSIS

Psychosis is the name given to the experience of a set of symptoms when they appear together. These symptoms do not all have to happen at the same time for the person to be said to be experiencing psychosis. To gain a diagnosis of psychosis, the person must be observably unable to distinguish the effects of their psychosis from reality. In addition, a person can be wrongly diagnosed with psychosis, when the treating clinician is unable to gain an accurate understanding of what the person is experiencing. 'I am not what happened to me, I am what I choose to become' (Jung, nd). Someone who is experiencing psychosis is sometimes described as 'psychotic'.

In general, when trying to find out if someone is experiencing psychosis, their clinician will be looking for:

- Disordered thinking – the everyday thoughts that let us live our daily lives become confused and don't join up properly.

- Delusions – false beliefs held by a person that are not held by others of the same cultural background, in other words, believing something that is not possible in reality, or a culturally accepted belief.

- Hallucinations – where the person sees, hears, feels, smells or tastes something that is not actually there. The hallucination is often of disembodied voices that no one else can hear.

It can be difficult for clinicians to distinguish between hallucinations and extreme sensory sensitivities, or there can be miscommunication that leads the mental health professional to believe that the person is hallucinating when they are not. Many people with autism can hear, feel and smell more acutely than other people, and so may report hearing things that others around them cannot. People with autism can also notice details in the environment that go unnoticed by others, and this may be misinterpreted unless the person with autism is very clear in their description of what they are seeing.

For some people with autism, the way that they present when in the midst of a meltdown can superficially be mistaken for psychosis. All these possible misunderstandings can be compounded where there is not yet a formal autism spectrum diagnosis. This is not to say that people with autism cannot experience psychosis; they can. Sometimes, once a clinician knows that someone is on the autism spectrum, they may discount other mental illness and put everything down to autism. This can be highly counterproductive where someone is actually experiencing mental illness symptoms such as psychosis, and needs an intervention for that in addition to any interventions around their autism.

Psychosis can be a single brief episode, or it can recur a few times, or it can accompany a long-term mental health condition such as schizophrenia or bipolar disorder. The causes of psychosis are still being investigated, but it seems that some people have a genetic vulnerability, and if they then experience things that might not cause psychosis in someone else, they can have a psychotic episode. The rate at which psychosis occurs is about 3 per cent, which means that approximately three out of every hundred people will experience a psychotic episode in their lifetime. For most people, this occurs when they are young adults, from their late teens to early twenties.

There is some evidence around certain substances triggering an episode of psychosis. These include high THC (tetrahydrocannabinol) cannabis and hallucinogenic drugs such as LSD and psilocybin ('magic mushrooms'). Evidence on how this process works is not conclusive, but it would appear there is a link between these substances and the onset of psychosis.

Psychosis is a very frightening state for the person experiencing it, particularly for the first time. Psychotic symptoms can be very convincing, so somebody having a psychotic episode may be completely convinced that their experiences are real, despite others challenging them. Even very intelligent people can believe that what they are experiencing is real. Wisdom and insight are important factors in addressing psychotic symptoms.

There are often differences between people on the autism spectrum who experience psychosis and neurotypical people. Autistic traits such as sensory sensitivity may combine with hallucinations and delusions to make them more convincing. For example, somebody may have the delusion that they are being poisoned as part of a process of psychosis. Their senses may be heightened due to autism, and they may taste some of the additives in tap water that will confirm their belief that the water is poisonous.

In a clinical setting, autistic people who are suffering from psychosis may present differently to their neurotypical peers. This can lead to issues with gaining an accurate diagnosis and effective treatment. As is often the case with autistic people with a mental illness, there may be a lack of understanding of autism among mental health clinical professionals. If someone does not have access to the right medication, it may result in them begin significantly unwell for a long period of time – bearing in mind that even in a hospital setting, the right medication may be a case of trial and error, and a few drugs may need to be tried before the most effective one is found.

Accessing help – medication

If you experience a psychotic episode, chances are you will need medical intervention such as medication and maybe a stay in hospital (usually no longer than a few weeks, but it can vary depending on the severity of your symptoms and how well you respond to medication). In the past, there was no pharmaceutical treatment for psychosis and people were kept in institutions. Now there is a large range of anti-psychotic medications that can help reduce or eradicate people's psychotic symptoms. These are very strong and can have a number of side effects. Sometimes people will only need to take medication for a short while, but others are on medication for a long period of time, even for the rest of their life. It is important to have a professional (i.e. psychiatrist) prescribe these drugs. Your GP may be able to continue writing the prescriptions for you, but the decision to put you on what dose of which drug should be made by a psychiatrist. Knowing about psychiatric medication is one of the main roles of a psychiatrist, and they are the experts.

When you are taking anti-psychotic medication, you will need to make sure this is monitored and you have regular check-ups to ensure it is effective and any side effects aren't too troubling. Anti-psychotic medications may become less effective over time, so it important to report any psychotic symptoms or concerns to your doctor. Despite the potential for side effects and the inconvenience of having to take medication, if you have an psychotic illness, taking anti-psychotic medication can enable you to live a more productive and happy life free from severe illness symptoms that would probably be impossible if you were experiencing significant psychotic symptoms.

One important thing to note about anti-psychotic medication is that you must never stop taking it without consulting your psychiatrist. This could result in an acute psychotic episode or physical health issues. Ideally, your relationship with your psychiatrist should be one of dialogue and respect, so if you wish to stop taking the medication, you will hopefully be able to have a rational and equal discussion with your psychiatrist about the pros and cons of ceasing medication. Consider, however, that sometimes a mental illness process – and particularly psychosis – may trick you into thinking something is right when in fact it isn't. Bearing this in mind, take notice of what your psychiatrist says around medication, although you can seek out a second opinion if you wish.

Living well

There is nothing to say that people with a psychotic illness cannot live full and rewarding lives. Psychosis is quite misunderstood, and there is often a lot of stigma and prejudice. In fact, many people with a psychotic illness such as schizophrenia feel they need to hide it from work colleagues and friends, as do some people with autism spectrum conditions. For people with both autism and a psychotic illness, they can feel very vulnerable and afraid to disclose, given the stigma for both diagnoses. Sadly the less people there are who disclose, the less people are likely to, so it becomes a bit of a vicious cycle.

Just as there is no shame in being autistic, so, too, there is no shame in having a psychotic illness. Because people do not disclose their illness, people with a psychotic illness who are in responsible roles at work or who are in the public eye are often almost invisible, leading to a belief that there are no people with schizophrenia or bipolar or other illnesses in the workplace or the public eye. People like the actor and comedian Stephen Fry, who has a diagnosis of bipolar disorder, are doing a great job. And as an Indigenous Australian business consultant once told me, "If you can't see it, you can't be it." In other words, if there are no role models with psychotic illness or autism (or whatever) in a particular role or position, it is very hard for others with a psychotic illness or autism to aim for that role.

JENNY'S STORY: A sort of accidental role model

I have been at my current job for quite a long time – nine years. I started as an intern after university. About six months after I started, I was doing a training course, and a woman I had spoken to twice before said in the break "I have schizophrenia. Please don't tell anyone." I told her that I did too, and I wasn't about to disclose her confidence. A year later a woman in my team who I had just met got talking to me in the corridor and said, "I have bipolar disorder. Please don't tell anyone." I reiterated my advice to the other woman that I wouldn't betray a confidence, but I didn't think bipolar disorder was a shameful thing. I am very visible at work, particularly around autism, but I also talk about my illness. I don't see either of them as anything to be ashamed of, and if anyone is prejudiced, well, I'd rather know it and deal with it than assume that everyone will hate me when probably only a couple of people will be discriminatory. I am happy to discuss autism, mental illness and anything related with my colleagues, and most of them seem to be really appreciative of that. I also don't get annoyed if someone says something wrong or rude through ignorance rather than hatred or prejudice. I mean, we all say silly or uninformed things. So I just use it as a teaching opportunity. I love my job and I love being 'out' – both as an autistic and also as a person with schizophrenia – at work.

Peer mentoring thoughts on psychosis

There are many myths around psychosis.

- People with psychotic illnesses have jobs, houses, children and partners. They study and participate in all the activities of life that others do. It is true that many people with ongoing psychotic illnesses struggle to live independently and to hold a job, but this is far from the whole picture. Stereotypes such as people being unable to work or study or have a family can perpetuate poor outcomes and poor self-image for those with psychotic illness.

- People with psychotic illness do not necessarily need to be hospitalised for long periods of time. In the past, people with serious mental illness were housed in institutions for many months or years, but with the advent of anti-psychotic medications and other more effective treatments, many people with a psychotic illness are able to live independently and do all the things other people do.

- Find a good psychiatrist if you can. This can make all the difference while you manage your illness. A good psychiatrist is usually one who listens to you and discusses treatment options with you rather than simply imposing them. You can ask for recommendations for a psychiatrist from other people you know who have used the services of a psychiatrist or those with family members who have.

- Ideally, your relationship with your psychiatrist should be one of dialogue and respect, so if you wish to stop taking the medication you will hopefully be able to have a rational and equal discussion with your psychiatrist about the pros and cons of ceasing medication. Consider though that sometimes a mental illness process – and particularly psychosis – may trick you into thinking something is right when in fact it isn't. Bearing that in mind, take notice of what your psychiatrist says around medication. You can seek out a second opinion if you wish.

- Psychosis is not an intellectual disability.

- Some people on the autism spectrum are misdiagnosed with a psychotic illness such as schizophrenia. However, it is not always a misdiagnosis – it is possible for you to be autistic and also to have a psychotic illness.

- You do not have to use drugs like cannabis to get a psychotic illness. People who do not drink alcohol or use illicit drugs can also develop psychosis.

- If you have a family history of mental illness, particularly things like bipolar disorder or schizophrenia, be very careful around using illegal drugs, especially things like marijuana, stimulants (like methamphetamine) or hallucinogenic drugs (like LSD or 'magic mushrooms'). These substances can exacerbate mental illness symptoms or bring on an episode of psychosis. The best option might be not to use such substances at all or if you do use them, to only use them very infrequently.

- Psychosis does not necessarily occur throughout a person's lifetime. Some people have just one psychotic episode, while for others it will be an ongoing, chronic condition which interferes with their ability to enjoy life and participate in society. Psychosis is different for everyone who experiences it.

- People who experience psychosis are not necessarily violent. In fact, people with a psychotic illness who are currently under treatment are considerably more likely to be the victims of violence than the perpetrators. In people with untreated psychosis there is a slightly increased risk of aggression, but you are more likely to be assaulted outside a nightclub waiting for a taxi than by most people with a psychotic illness. SANE Australia has this to say about psychosis and violence:

  > Violence is not a symptom of psychotic illnesses such as bipolar disorder and schizophrenia.
  >
  > There is a slightly increased possibility someone with a psychotic illness may be violent if they are not receiving treatment, have a previous history of violence, and are abusing alcohol or drugs.

Symptoms of psychotic illnesses may include frightening hallucinations and delusions as well as paranoia. This means there is a small chance someone who is experiencing them may become violent when they are scared and misinterpret what is happening around them. If a person is being effectively treated for psychotic illness and is not abusing alcohol or drugs, there is no more risk they will be violent than anyone else.

(SANE Australia no date)

JENNY'S STORY: Psychotic illness

When I was 20, I was diagnosed with Asperger's syndrome. A year later, I was diagnosed with schizophrenia. I didn't understand what either of them meant at the time. I have had a few psychotic episodes since then, the most recent in 2011. I didn't realise I was getting unwell. It came on over a period of about a year so it crept up on me. I left it up to the point where I thought I had died and was in purgatory and God was punishing me and I couldn't use the appliances at home or have a shower before I accessed help, and only then because someone told me to. Over the next three years I was in hospital a lot and residential services. I was very vulnerable and scared the whole time. I nearly lost my job and my home, but I learned a lot from the experience. I have a lot more insight about my illness and how it works now. And I don't get so freaked out by the odd psychotic symptom or other. In the past, I think my anxiety about things being 'weird' contributed hugely to the illness and made me feel much worse. Now I just think 'oh, there's a ghost in the lounge-room. Hello ghost' and leave it at that. I'm much stronger now, and if I start getting unwell again, I think I'll notice before it's been going on for a year.

7

COMMUNICATION PROBLEMS

Autistic people generally communicate in a somewhat different manner from non-autistic people, and difficulties in typical social communication lie at the heart of an autism spectrum diagnosis. This can lead to misunderstanding, exacerbate mental health issues and lead to incorrect assumptions around diagnosis and treatment of mental health conditions. Autistic people often have difficulties understanding communication methods that non-autistic people understand easily, such as the use of body language or non-verbal communication – 'The single biggest problem in communication is the illusion that it has taken place' (Shaw, nd). Even when it comes to speech, the neurotypical person communicates in a different way from the autistic person. There may be different inflections or tones of voice that are lost on autistic people. There are often also many levels of meaning and subtle nuances within the words. Neurotypical people frequently use such communication devices as sarcasm, idioms, manipulation and hidden meanings that can be viewed as misleading or dishonest. To most autistic people, communicating with the neurotypical world and its inhabitants can be like navigating a minefield. This is at the heart of one of the difficulties of being on the spectrum and being articulate – people struggle to conceive that autistic people might miss common understandings and that they struggle to explain meaningfully why they missed the subtext, which seems to be so obvious to everyone else.

Autistic communication styles tend to be less socially driven and based more around exchanging thoughts, events and ideas, discussing areas of interest or passion. Autistic people often gain the majority of the meaning from the exact words that are said rather than non-verbal cues or hidden meanings within the words. This is often described as the literal interpretation of language, or the logical use of language to communicate.

Things such as body language and multiple levels of meaning within a conversation are often confusing or inaccessible to people on the autism spectrum. Eye contact (a cornerstone of conveying meaning for many neurotypical people) is often viewed as invasive or overwhelming by those on the autism spectrum. This means that all that meaning which non-autistic people are passing on to one another doesn't get interpreted in the way it is meant. Non-autistic people are often unaware of this and think that the autistic person is either rude or stupid for not 'getting it' when neither of these is the case. Autistic people are generally direct, honest and respectful. Any 'errors', misunderstandings or rudeness are usually the result of an oversight or mistake or a lack of awareness of the social implications of a comment rather than any actual malice. Autistic people often prefer to be friends, partners and colleagues with other autistic people, and this can be as a result of the stress of trying to understand what is essentially another language and to make themselves understood.

GRETCHEN'S STORY: 'It's like you speak another language'

I am 23 and have a diagnosis of Asperger's syndrome. I got my diagnosis when I was 11. My mum and sisters always sort of treated me like I was stupid, when I didn't get all of what they were saying. It used to really upset me. I wasn't trying to annoy them, I just don't see things the way they do. I tried to explain this, but they didn't seem to get it.

Our family is German. Every few years we go back to Germany to visit family. My sisters and mum and me all speak fluent German. Last year, my older sister Sami went to France for a holiday. She ended up getting lost and nobody spoke English. She called us up at 4 in the morning, freaking out. I could hear her on the other end of the phone speaking in German to the French people, because she was so anxious. She sounded really stressed, and she was saying 'surely you understand me?' I got mum, and they sorted Sami's issue. But it got me thinking. Later that day I told my mum 'That's what it's like. It's like you're speaking in French expecting me to understand you, but I'm speaking German. And you get mad at me, because

I'm speaking German.' 'Mum' I said, 'It's like we're speaking different languages, and you expect me to understand, and I can't.' She understood much more after that. It's much better. (And Sami was okay too.)

People with autism may appear different or odd to neurotypical people due, in part, to their communication styles and preferences. While sometimes this offers an opportunity for 'cross-cultural communication' and an appreciation of difference, sadly it can also result in discrimination or bullying. Autistic people can become bewildered, frustrated and distressed at the reactions from others in situations where they are unaware of miscommunication taking place.

LYNNE'S STORY: Communication is complicated

I was on holiday, and when talking to a local, I said that I could never live there as the weather was way too humid for me. It was awful. My partner (not-autistic) suddenly started talking about how wonderful the place was and how much we liked the city (which we didn't). Later she told me that the local person was really upset by my comments, and she could tell because of the facial expression on the local person's face. It is all so complicated. I have no understanding of why someone would be offended that I don't like or want to live in their home town because of the weather, and I had no idea that the person was offended. I find it emotionally exhausting trying to successfully navigate all the social consequences of everything I say. When I am just around other people on the spectrum, it is so much easier. For example, I could say that I was tired and wanted to go home, and no one would mind. If I say that to typical people, they try to pressurise me to stay, because I could have so much fun!

A lot of people make assumptions about a person's communication and think that the level of verbal fluency (how much a person talks) indicates their general intelligence and their level of understanding of others. This may be one reason why people, including professionals, assume that non-verbal autistic people have an intellectual disability. Autistic people can be completely non-verbal or partially verbal or usually verbal. When stressed, distressed or overwhelmed, many autistic people are less able to communicate verbally, and some are not able to speak at all in these circumstances, although they can at other times. Many people – including mental health professionals – lack a thorough understanding of how autistic people communicate.

The mental health 'system' – which includes psychiatrists, psychologists, hospitals and residential services – is often not geared towards awareness, acceptance and respect of people on the autism spectrum. In some instances, mental health workers are quite inexperienced in working with people with autism. People can gain misdiagnoses of psychotic illness, personality disorders and other conditions based on their communication style. Things such as literal interpretation of questions asked by doctors and misinterpretations of behaviours like meltdowns or self-injury can result in some diagnostic errors or inappropriate treatment.

In the documentary 'Alone in a Crowded Room', autism advocate, academic and author Dr Wenn Lawson describes a visit to the psychiatrist as a teenager:

> 'Wendy, do you see things?' asked the psychiatrist. I answered, 'yes, I see things', 'Wendy, do you hear voices?' asked the psychiatrist. Silly man! I thought. Voices are meant to be heard. 'It depends which one it is,' I said 'You hear more than one?' asked the psychiatrist. So his understanding that I had visual and auditory hallucinations, based on my literal understanding of seeing and hearing, meant that I got a diagnosis of schizophrenia and spent a lot of time in places like these. So when I was in my forties and got a diagnosis that says I have Asperger syndrome, it meant a lot of things made sense.

While this is a rather extreme example, people with autism spectrum conditions often struggle to be understood and heard by the health professions due to communication differences, and the expectations and assumptions around what is 'normal' or expected communication. When a person is acutely unwell, difficulties understanding others and being understood can be exacerbated. It can be very hard for somebody who has an autism spectrum condition and who is unwell with mental illness to make themselves understood. This frustration can contribute to a worsening of mental illness symptoms and can be extremely distressing. For people who do not speak ('non-verbal'), it can be a struggle to be understood anyway. When that person is in a mental health clinical setting, is unwell and may not have access to the usual supports (such as communication aids or support people), the communication difficulty can impact severely on their mental illness.

At the more extreme end, this frustration, mixed with emotional distress, can result in meltdowns, self-injury or even physical violence. In these situations, people can engage in behaviour that is vastly out of character due to a combination of illness symptoms, being overwhelmed and frustrated and not being heard. Meltdowns can be an area of particular concern when somebody is in a clinical setting such as a hospital. Some mental health professionals – like many people in the wider community – do not understand meltdowns and see them as poor behaviour or attention-seeking outbursts. This can result in a spiral of inappropriate treatment and apparent 'poor behaviour' from which people struggle to escape.

TOM'S STORY: Meltdowns and aggression

I have Asperger's syndrome and major depression. When I was 22, I got really depressed and went to psychiatric hospital. I didn't have the skills I do now in communicating. I was so depressed that I didn't care what happened. I was also really angry about life. I had been bullied at school and was still dealing with that, I couldn't find a job anywhere, and I felt like everyone in the world hated me and was laughing at me.

When I first got to the hospital, I wanted to get my razor and shaving cream, which they had in the nurses station. It's really important for me to be shaved, as I hate the feeling of stubble on my face – it causes a severe sensory reaction. The nurses were busy talking about something else and wouldn't help me out. They were all behind the glass in the nurses station. I asked them through the glass but they ignored me. One of them said something to me which I didn't hear, and then they all laughed. I was furious! In my mind they were all laughing at me. When the nurse came out with my shaving cream and razor, I yelled at him. I was screaming and crying. I got right up in his

face and threatened him. Then five or six of the nurses came
and put me in the high dependency unit. I was there for ages.
I've heard about other autistic people who end up in prison and
in trouble with the law because of that sort of thing. I'm glad that
didn't happen to me but the whole hospital thing was like that
the entire time. I didn't know how to get the staff to meet my
needs and they always thought I was being difficult when really I
just wanted them to understand me, and it just made me angry.
They should have a book or something that tells autistic people
what to do in hospital and also that tells the staff how to treat us.

There can be assumptions around people's preferred communication
methods and settings, for example, group therapy versus one-on-one
counselling. Many mental health treatment programmes assume
that the most effective way to assist people with certain conditions
is through group interaction. While some people on the autism
spectrum are comfortable in a group environment, many others
find it overwhelming, and it actually has the opposite effect to its
stated purpose. Some programmes that might be tried and tested
for non-autistic people, such as '12-step'-type programmes, can be
extremely challenging for people on the autism spectrum. This can be
problematic where a person is referred to such a treatment programme
through the court or mental health tribunal orders.

The information in this chapter deals with general observations
around communication styles that typify autistic people. However, as
always, it is crucial to remember that all autistic people are different.
The way one person communicates will be more typically 'autistic'
than the way another does, and what works for one person in terms of
communicating clearly may not work for another. Communication
styles are distinctly personal. While there are a few general autistic
characteristics and shared experiences, each person is different and
has different preferences for communication.

Literal understandings of language

Autistic people tend to be very literal in their interpretation of
spoken and sometimes written language. This is not to say that they
cannot and do not learn to understand idioms and other non-literal

language. However, it is much more difficult for autistic people to generalise than for other people, so they often learn one saying at a time rather than realising that a person cannot possibly mean exactly what they are saying. In communicating with professionals this can pose a number of unintended problems for both the person with autism and the professional.

Professionals tend not to be explicit in their questioning or information sharing unless they perceive the patient/client to have an intellectual disability. People with autism tend to prefer to give definitive answers that are completely true and can struggle to do this for mental health and medical professionals. For example, when a health professional asks: 'Do you drink?', a person with autism will say 'yes', because they do. However, in response to the follow-up question of 'How much do you drink?', or 'How many units a week?', the person with autism who has not realised the question relates solely to the consumption of alcohol will provide a misleading answer. Answering at least a litre, and up to three litres a day (meaning water or milk) would give the impression of alcohol addiction or dependency.

The example provided by Wenn Lawson earlier in this chapter is another example of the literal understanding of people on the autistic spectrum accidentally misleading clinicians. However, clinicians can also mislead their autistic clients/patients when they do not take into account this literal use of language, as shown in the next story.

EDWARD'S STORY: A misunderstanding

The doctor told me that the reason I got a blood clot was because of plaque. I thought he meant plaque from my teeth migrated into my blood vessels and then stuck together forming a clot. For years and years I worried when cleaning my teeth that I wouldn't manage to spit out all the plaque I had cleaned off, and then I would get another blood clot. I only found out that it didn't relate to plaque on my teeth when I was watching a TV documentary about eight years later!

Logical language use

For many people, language is the tool that conveys emotions, creates social relations and sustains social norms. For people on the autism spectrum, language is more typically seen as the vehicle through which to convey needs and wants factually, and to share information. The social aspect of communication can be extremely bewildering and indeed missed completely by autistic people, even those with apparently fluent spoken language.

This logical use of language is most easily apparent in the honest responses of autistic individuals to questions that start with 'Do you' or 'Would you'. However, when asked, 'Would you like to come through to the interview room?' in a mental health setting, a response of 'no' can be interpreted as defiant or combative, when really it was just an honest and logical response. To prevent these sorts of misunderstandings, it is vital that professionals use clear language that says exactly what they mean, and that they mean exactly what they say. So instead of asking, 'Would you like to come through to the interview room?', the mental health professional could say, 'Come on through into the interview room now, thanks.'

This difficulty with social language can be successfully mediated by good friends/family who can give honest and clear feedback that helps logically explain a situation or question. When there is a gap in this feedback, as happens for many people on the spectrum who are studying or in employment or alone in a supermarket, for example, there can be a fractured moment. In these fractured moments calm can be shattered and shredded, cast apart like an exploding fractal. This can feel like there is a disconnect felt in every pore and every fibre of autistic being, which may seem like being suspended in outer space where space consists of nothing but desolation. Social support from friends or family can help to prevent isolation and desolation by ensuring social connections can be maintained.

Communication changes when distressed, stressed or overwhelmed

Most autistic people are less able to communicate when distressed, stressed or overwhelmed. However, this can also lead to them being unable to speak (they can find the words but are unable to actually say them), or becoming unable to adequately communicate. Where the other party does not understand or misinterprets the communication attempts, this can lead to meltdowns, shutdowns or exacerbations of mental health difficulties.

Autistic people who are usually quite calm can become very distressed if their attempts to communicate are clearly not working. For some people, this distress will manifest in tears or attempts to self-sooth through stimming, whereas for others this distress can turn into frustration and/or anger and/or aggression. Where a person is also psychiatrically unwell, this can lead to outbursts of violence.

Having in place a clear communication strategy or plan for times of immense stress of periods of illness can prevent some of the negative consequences of miscommunication. For example, even if someone cannot speak due to their emotional state, they may still be able to type or draw or write. Having information presented in writing or cartoons may be easier for autistic adults who are in sensory overload and may even prevent a meltdown. Additional strategies for professionals are to provide autistic people with time to calm or engage in self-regulatory strategies before engaging in conversations or trying to elicit information.

Peer mentoring advice

- It can be incredibly frustrating and irritating – not to mention invalidating – to have the majority of the population not understanding your communication style and not recognising it is an acceptable alternative to their style. Even people you are close to can dismiss or invalidate your unique way of communicating and denigrate it as somehow less 'real'. This is unhelpful.

- Your autistic communication style is just as valid as any other communication style. Just because you are not like the majority, this does not make the way you express yourself 'wrong'.

- Talking to friends who are also on the autism spectrum can be a great release valve for communication stresses. Autistic friends and peers can also help you to decipher messages from the non-autistic people in your life – you can share notes. You might even find yourself laughing at certain situations that had caused you stress or anxiety when you were just thinking about them alone.

- Telling people you have an autism spectrum condition is often the first step to them understanding or paying attention to what you have to say. A lot of difficulty arises where non-autistic people see an autistic person through a neurotypical 'lens'. Instead of thinking that you are an accomplished, acceptable and respectable autistic person, they think you are a 'weird', neurotypical person. It can take a bit of practice, but if you can identify any differences between your communication style and the 'norm', you can explain any needs you have around communication. It rarely works just to tell someone 'I have Asperger's' or 'I have autism' and offer no further explanation. This is because many non-autistic people only have a vague idea of what it means for someone to be autistic. And even if they have met another person on the spectrum, they may not understand that you and their other autistic friend or colleague are probably quite different. It is better to say 'I have autism/Asperger's' and then explain what that means in terms of your communication style and needs. You could even make a small 'business card' to give to people that explains your personal communication style/ strengths/difficulties. An example is given at the end of this chapter.

- If you can, advocate for yourself. If people don't seem to understand what you're trying to say, explain it to them. This may not only assist you in communicating with the person, but can also assist other autistic people they may meet later on. Write down/type out or draw key important messages to share with other people. If you do this before you meet with people, this can help you to get across all the information that you want to convey.

- When talking to mental health professionals, ask them to clarify questions if you are not sure what they are asking. In addition, try to explain what you mean clearly. As in the example with Dr Wenn Lawson earlier in this chapter, a professional's misunderstanding of what people can say around mental health problems and symptoms can lead to some harmful and inappropriate treatments. Don't be scared to speak up and tell your doctor, psychiatrist or psychologist:

  » if they have misunderstood you or misinterpreted things you have told them

  » to clarify what they have told you about any treatments, including medications

  » to clarify something they may have said that you don't understand

  » to explain your perception of what they have said to you or asked you to do

  » to answer any concerns you have or parts of the treatment or consultation that are making you anxious.

- It can be very difficult for people on the autism spectrum who are undiagnosed or self-diagnosed to access appropriate treatment. It is hard enough for people who have the diagnostic 'piece of paper' to use to improve their chances of being understood by the non-autistic world. Obviously the choice is up to you, but if you feel you need an 'official' diagnosis, get one. It can be expensive, but it could save you any number of indignities in the future in the mental health 'world' – from misdiagnosis, to treatments that are inappropriate and misunderstanding of your autistic communication style. Being self-diagnosed is viewed with incredulity by many psychologists and psychiatrists, although not all. They may disregard your self-diagnosis even if you know it to be accurate.

- It is always okay to ask questions of mental health professionals – ask them to explain what they mean, or write down what they are trying to explain. This is particularly helpful if you struggle to make sense of long complex chunks of spoken information.

- Sometimes when you in a clinical setting, such as a hospital, you may be so distressed you are unable to make yourself understood at all. You could make an 'advance list' of your needs in case this happens. Make the list with your mental health or autism worker (if you have one). Ask them to keep a copy on file, in case you need to go to hospital or a residential service with instructions to provide it to your treating team if you go into a clinical or residential setting. In the list, include information on:

  » anything that will make you uncomfortable, angry or distressed, such as negative sensory stimuli, certain individuals or situations. If something has triggered you in the past, include this in the list.

  » things that will make you feel better if you are distressed – such as positive sensory stimuli, music, certain people.

  » your key contacts – such as parents, partner, mental health or autism case manager, close friends – and their contact details and advice on what you will allow professionals to disclose to each of them.

  » any medications you are currently taking.

  » any negative drug interactions or side effects you have had from medications you have taken in the past. Including this in the plan should mean that you will not be given medications that you have had a bad reaction to in the past.

  » details of any commitments you have – employment, voluntary work, study, loans, mortgages, etc. This will mean that the hospital staff can contact your employer, bank, university etc. and let them know where you are, so that they don't worry about you or penalise you for non-attendance at work or university.

- Sadly, communication difficulties are sometimes inevitable, so trying to alleviate them in every circumstance may not be entirely realistic. Practise some strategies for dealing with frustration and anger around communication. Things such as mindfulness, deep breathing, distraction and 'self-soothing' techniques can help.

- If you haven't done it already, learn to value yourself as an autistic person. Make a list of your achievements, your positive attributes and remind yourself of them frequently. Try to surround yourself with people who value you – for example, make some autistic friends. You can also use CBT techniques to reframe how you view yourself. There is more information on these techniques in Chapter 13. Being a strong and proud autistic person who advocates for yourself and other autistic people can have a pleasant unintended consequence that you improve communication with neurotypical people. You will find it much easier to 'own' your communication style and explain it to others. Being proud of your autism is beneficial for a number of reasons.

  » It is good for self-esteem

  » It challenges negative stereotypes of autism

  » It helps you to feel confident

  » It helps you to understand yourself and the way you think better, leading to greater self-acceptance.

My name is……..
I am on the autism spectrum.
I am non-verbal/I have limited speech.
I can understand speech but it is easier if you write things down/draw things for me.
If needed please contact my partner/parent/friend……….
Tel……..

My name is…….. ·
I am on the autism spectrum.
I have large body movements when I am distressed. Please do not touch me as this is painful for me and makes me more distressed.
I can understand speech but I may not respond if I am stressed. My partner/parent/friend………. may be able to assist if needed.
Tel……..

My name is……..
I am on the autism spectrum.
I have a very literal understanding of speech and may need a minute after each thing you say to process and understand it. Please write down any medical information and results for me to take home and go through to ensure I understand fully. Thanks.

Examples of personal communication 'business cards'

8

STIGMA AND DISCRIMINATION

Many people experience feelings of stigma and discrimination in their lives, and this can be based on real experiences or as a result of miscommunication/misunderstandings. While in many countries it is illegal to discriminate against people with disabilities or mental health conditions, this does not seem to have eradicated it. Traditionally, stigma meant a mark of disgrace or infamy that existed to stain or reproach one's reputation; it is now more commonly understood to be an association of public disapproval or community disgrace.

> The unkind word, the glance aside, the social exclusions, higher insurance premiums or some denial of a human right. Stigma against those of us with a mental illness takes so many forms. It is insidious and it is all too common. Daily it accumulates and may erode our self esteem. Stigma robs us of opportunities others take for granted in society.
>
> (Champ 2002)

Both autism and mental illness are stigmatised by mainstream culture, although this has been changing over the last few years, with, for example, large public health campaigns seeking to end the stigma and discrimination around depression. These public health campaigns are often led by a high profile sports star, for example, which helps the general public to understand that *anyone* can experience depression. The campaigns are in direct contrast to the way that mental illness has been described and portrayed in popular culture over the years.

Neurodiversity and autism self-advocacy

Unfortunately, autism has not been so well represented in mainstream culture, with misunderstanding of what autism is and how it affects people remaining the norm in most countries. However, there are now very large self-advocacy groups and communities of adults with autism who offer a counterbalance to the negative perceptions of many. Within these communities and groups, adults with autism are able to meet others who are similar to themselves and some who express autistic pride and/or actively celebrate their neurodiversity. In addition, there have been a number of people with autism who have very high profile public lives, such as Carly Fleischmann, Temple Grandin and Stephen Shore. These people are able to explain what it is be non-verbal and exhibit challenging behaviour or attitudes and still go on to live well.

The blogosphere and Facebook have large numbers of people with autism sharing information and tips on living well, including living well with both autism and mental health challenges. These resources accept autism as another variant on 'normal', and can help people to build self-esteem and self-acceptance. However, there are some autism resources that remain less accepting of mental health difficulties. In part, this is due to the issues of misdiagnosis over the years, a belief by some that a diagnosis of autism is more socially acceptable than one of a mental illness, and that some people are claiming to be autistic when they are not, and have a mental illness instead.

This position is similar to the idea in the gay rights movement that bisexuals were less acceptable, and so were claiming to be gay when they weren't and were not welcomed by some gay organisations. Both positions are relying on stigma and discriminating attitudes and are unacceptable. People are people, and some have more difficulties than others, and some need more support than others to live well. People who encounter bigotry, stigma or discrimination when seeking support should acknowledge that those attitudes are the other person's problem, not theirs, and accept that they are not going to be able to provide the support that is needed. This is true for all kinds of bigotry, whether it is due to ethnicity, religious beliefs, sexuality, gender, mental health status or autism diagnostic status.

Impact of stigma and discrimination

For some cultural/ethnic groups the shame and stigma associated with mental illness and/or autism is far greater than others. It is important for people to understand that they are not alone, that people with autism exist across all cultures, and within that there are a large number of people who additionally experience mental health difficulties. If people believe that it is their fate or karma to experience a difficult life, this does not mean that they cannot still live well.

Within the adult autistic/Asperger's community there seem to be two distinct attitudes towards the existence of stigma and discrimination. One of these is to be extremely upset and/or frustrated by stigma and discrimination, whether it is directed at the individual or someone else. The other attitude is to not care at all what other people say/think/do. Many people with autism can display both attitudes at different times in their life. However, along with bullying, which can be a manifestation of stigma and discrimination, some people with autism are not aware of the negative way they are being treated. Sadly, some people with autism have experienced so much negativity from others due to stigma and discrimination, whether or not they have a formal autism diagnosis, that they begin to feel that all people are unkind or dislike them. This is often a protective strategy to try and not be hurt by others. Thinking everyone is mean or doesn't like you is counterproductive, as it can decrease a person's self-esteem and damage their wellbeing.

Stigma and discrimination can lead to feelings of shame, hopelessness, distress and a reluctance to seek and/or accept necessary help. These feelings can be compounded by being mentally unwell and can, in turn, hinder recovery if these feelings are allowed to grow unchecked. Stigma has long been known to promote and reinforce isolation among people who are experiencing mental illness as well as act as a barrier to living well and participating equitably in society.

Family members and friends can also affected by stigma, which can lead to a lack of support or to them becoming strong advocates for a person with autism as they observe how that person is affected by discrimination. For mental health professionals, stigma around mental illness can lead to them being viewed as abnormal, crazy or weird, and psychiatric treatments are often stereotyped or misunderstood.

Psychiatric treatments and perception

There is a widely held view, accepted and portrayed in the media, that ECT is both dangerous and undignified, resulting in people becoming a drooling mess with no memory. In reality, ECT is a very useful tool that can be highly effective in helping people with chronic drug-resistant depression. Although the way it is administered has changed significantly over time, and it does not result in huge convulsions or permanent memory loss, there is still stigma and prejudice in society around ECT and people who have ECT (also known as shock treatment). It has been misused over the years, including as a form of punishment for patients within psychiatric wards, which has contributed to the negative view of this effective treatment.

ECT is most effective for melancholic depression, a depression that has both physical and psychological symptoms – every system in the body experiences depression and so slows down. For example, the digestive system slows, which slows the bowels, which can lead to constipation. In some cases, people may be unable to get out of bed, or they may even experience catatonia (a state of immobility).

The benefits of ECT for people who are severely depressed with significant physical symptoms of depression are that improvements are very quick in comparison to medications used to raise the levels of serotonin and/or noradrenaline in the brain. ECT uses low dosage and short duration bursts of electricity via electrodes on the person's scalp to stimulate and 'excite' the neurons in that person's brain. The mass excitation of neurons causes a generalised seizure of the brain, which is, in this case, desirable, to release large amounts of the neurotransmitters serotonin and noradrenaline into synapses within the brain. This immediate increase in central nervous system neurotransmitter activity is generally associated with a clinically significant improvement in symptoms within a few treatments, but if no discernable clinical improvement is observed, the diagnosis of depression should be reconsidered.

Modern ECT does not target both sides of the brain, which it did in years gone by. Nowadays, the electrodes for the ECT are usually placed on the right side of the scalp, because most people are left hemisphere-dominant for speech/language, even those who are left-hand dominant. Initiating seizure activity in the non-dominant right hemisphere reduces the potential neurocognitive side effects, including short-term memory deficits. Although the main documented side effects of ECT are short-term memory loss around the actual ECT, given that memory loss is also frequently associated with depression, it is unclear to what degree ECT contributes to memory impairment. Clinicians should therefore discuss with people the risks of short-term memory issues in relation to the long-term benefits of relief from depressive symptoms, so that they can determine whether or not the benefits outweigh the risks. Modern ECT also involves a much lower electrical current than in years gone by – the dosage of electricity is individualised to ensure minimum dose with maximum benefit, and the time duration is usually only about ten seconds.

People are also now given a short duration anaesthetic and a muscle relaxant prior to receiving ECT. This puts the person to sleep temporarily (usually for a maximum of ten minutes), and once this is effective, the muscle relaxant is administered, which reduces the side effect of muscle aches and pains that used to accompany ECT, and also prevents the huge muscle seizures during ECT depicted in some films.

For some people, ECT can completely resolve their depression; for others it still provides significant relief. Some require maintenance ECT to keep their depression at bay, for example, once every month or couple of months. People can have up to three ECT sessions a week initially, for example, on a Monday, Wednesday and a Friday, for a couple of weeks. By the second week, as long as the diagnosis is right, the person will show significant improvements in both their physical symptoms and their mental wellbeing. The patient may not notice the improvements, but they should be clear to the treating clinicians and family members – for example, they may be speaking more and finding it easier to get out of bed.

Discrimination and psychosis

Another popular misconception that has led to widespread stigma and discrimination is the idea that people with schizophrenia are likely to be violent. Schizophrenia is a major illness of the mind, where the person continually misinterprets the world around them through positive and negative symptoms, including, for some, paranoia and fear. It is the misinterpretation arising from paranoia and fear experienced by some with schizophrenia that increases their risk of harming themselves and/or others.

The brain is not dissimilar to but infinitesimally more complex than the electrical wiring in a house, but using this analogy, visual hallucinations (i.e. psychosis) could be likened to a light bulb that illuminates a darkened room without an external precipitant (i.e. no physical activation of the light switch). Misinterpretation of something that actually exists is called an illusion, whereas a hallucination is seeing, hearing etc. without an external precipitant. Illusions are relatively commonplace and are not always pathological, whereas experiencing hallucinations generally only occurs in disorders such as schizophrenia or in the presence of 'mind-altering' drugs such as PCP (Phencyclidine).

Another way of describing the misperception that underpins psychosis is that the brain, like a computer, should take data and process it in a way that consistently generates the 'correct answer', for example, $1 + 1 + 1 + 1 + 1 + 1$ should equate to 6, whereas in someone with schizophrenia, the brain, when attempting to calculate the same equation, may produce an incorrect answer, 42.

A primary function of the brain is to integrate and interpret complex sensory inputs from multiple afferent pathways, or put more simply, the brain takes sensory information (from multiple modalities), integrates it and then formulates a 'response'. The brain's integration and processing of sensory information is designed to improve our understanding of the world and to reduce miscommunications. This filtering, integrating and analysis of complex electrical and neurochemical communications is flawed in people with schizophrenia, which, put simply, results in the 'brain playing tricks', resulting in the individual's internal perception of reality significantly differing from the general population. Hence, incorrect neurosensory processing can result in people experiencing sound auto-generated within areas of the central nervous system devoted to 'hearing', which understandably leads to misperception, misinterpretation and, at times, significant confusion for the individual over what is and what is not. This is further complicated by the fact that 'reality' tends to be a social construct that is shared between individuals, so when a sensory mismatch occurs due to a disorder such as schizophrenia, significant interpersonal conflict and mistrust can arise.

Alterations in reality as a consequence of misperceptions are referred to as hallucinations. Although these can arise from any sensory modality including touch, taste and smell, the most common tend to be auditory and visual. When they occur, the brain attempts to make sense of them, which is in part how delusions arise. For example, if someone is in the garden and experiences a spontaneous activation of their auditory pathways, which sound to them like someone is calling their name, their brain will attempt to rationalise it. During attempts by the brain to integrate and interpret this misinformation, further mistakes can occur. For example, the person might decide that it was their neighbour calling their name, even though they can't see their neighbour. Because they can't see their neighbour, the person's brain will try to come up with an explanation for their neighbour to be calling their name without being seen. This explanation might be that the neighbour is trying to identify the person so that an unknown person can attack them, which can, in turn, provoke anxiety, fear and even paranoia.

Auditory and visual hallucinations do not have to be hugely complex, although they can be. In some people with schizophrenia, the visual hallucinations they experience are more misperceptions of an actual stimulus (i.e. an illusion rather than a true hallucination), or for others, their brain can attribute excessive value to generally innocuous external stimuli, for example, a glancing look by a stranger could be misperceived as 'staring', which in turn provokes, aggravates and/or drives the person's paranoia.

The human brain is very complex, and in schizophrenia, instead of taking in information that exists and interpreting it in ways that are common, it takes in information that is not there, creating a story to match the information. So the person described above may end up thinking their neighbour wants to kill them, whereas if they had not had the original auditory hallucination, they would have continued to garden contentedly.

Some of the stigma and discrimination around schizophrenia is related to the way that people with schizophrenia can act differently, for example, talking to themselves or not interacting in common ways. Media representations are usually very negative, although the film 'A Beautiful Mind' was far more positive and realistic. Most people with schizophrenia do not commit violent acts, but the media focuses on the negative or violent acts of a single person, suggesting that violence equates to schizophrenia, which it does not.

Anti-psychotic treatments can be very useful for some people with schizophrenia. These are based on the dopamine hypothesis that suggests that too much dopamine in the mesolimbic region of the brain causes schizophrenia. This can explain the positive symptoms of schizophrenia such as delusions, hallucinations, thought insertion and labile affect. For people with mostly positive symptoms of schizophrenia, using drugs that block dopamine-2 receptors, the dominant receptor in the mesolimbic region can result in a resolution of symptoms. Some people can have one or two episodes of schizophrenia with positive symptoms, but if they stay on their medications for the rest of their life, they can then often live symptom free.

Early discontinuation of treatment results in relapses in symptoms that become progressively more difficult to treat. The longer delusions are in place, the harder they are to treat. Areas of personality, memory and intelligence can be affected with relapses of schizophrenia symptoms. The negative symptoms of schizophrenia are things such as social isolation, flat affect (lacking a normal range of feelings and behaviour), lack of motivation and inability to do basic everyday self-care tasks. These can be very frustrating for family members, who may not realise that these are symptoms of the person's illness and not laziness or the person being deliberately annoying.

The newer anti-psychotic medications, although still antagonising dopamine, tend to be dopamine-2 receptor sparing, and so are associated with less medication-induced movement disorders and medication-induced elevated plasma prolactin levels. Negative symptoms are thought to be in part due to a neurochemical imbalance between dopamine and serotonin in areas such as the prefrontal cortex of the brain. These newer medications also target serotonin receptors in the prefrontal cortex, and may help decrease negative symptoms.

People with schizophrenia that is resistant to traditional treatments can be offered atypical anti-psychotics, which theoretically have less movement disorder side effects. Typical treatments can result in stiffness or tremors within the body. The greatest therapeutic gain for drug-resistant schizophrenia is clozapine, which binds to multiple receptors in the body. Over time people who trial clozapine are deemed treatment-resistant, but often have a significant improvement in symptoms. For some people, clozapine enables them to work, live comfortably within their families and to live well. For other people, the gains are not as big, but still enable them to have a better quality of life than prior to the clozapine. Clozapine can have some significant medical side effects, however, and requires ongoing monitoring every three to six months, usually at a clozapine clinic through the mental health service or via the person's GP. Clinicians should explain the possible side effects as well as the benefits clearly.

Perception around independence

Discrimination can also come about in relation to money, especially the ability to be responsible for your own spending. Back in 1999, Pescosolido *et al.* reported that people with schizophrenia were regarded as unable to manage their own money in contrast to the acceptance of corporate fraud and large-scale fund mismanagement. Many people with autism are also wrongly described as unable to manage their own money. While this is true for some people who may also struggle with literacy, numeracy and/or difficulties that make shopping very difficult or impossible, most people can learn how to manage money successfully. For those subject to a guardianship order that grants someone else control of their finances, it is important to seek help to learn how to budget before trying to challenge the guardianship order.

For some people, managing money well is impossible when they are mentally unwell, especially if one of their behaviours when ill is to spend compulsively. For example, people experiencing mania or hypomania may spend excessively while acutely unwell. In you are struggling with managing money while unwell, either share control of your money or let someone you trust handle it for you. If you decide to do this, it is useful to have a written agreement detailing how much freedom you will have with your money and when this will be.

There can also be discrimination in the workplace. If you work and become unwell and are hospitalised under the Mental Health Act, you may be reluctant to let your employer know. However, it is important to do so as you may be in breach of your employment contract if you do not. In addition, it is good to tell your employer as they can then provide you with any extra support you may require, for example, a graduated return to work. If you are applying for a new job, the application form usually has a question that says something along the lines of: 'Do you have any physical or mental health conditions that will prevent you from carrying out the duties of this position?' Think carefully about how you answer this question. There is no denying that many employers discriminate against jobseekers with mental illness and/or autism, but if you do not declare them and become unable to carry out the work *because* of your mental health issues and/or autism, you could be in breach of contract. Some autistic self-advocates suggest that everyone with autism should declare it in response to the question on the job application, while others refuse to disclose their autism diagnosis as they say it has no bearing on their ability to do the job and/or it would result in them not being offered the job. While technically an employer is not legally allowed to discriminate on the basis of disability (which autism is classified as), there is no denying that anecdotal evidence suggests that this happens fairly frequently. And it can be almost impossible to prove whether an employer has discriminated against you in recruitment, as they will most likely say that you were 'not the best candidate for the position' rather than citing your health conditions or autism as a reason. If you do choose to declare your autism and/or mental health issues on the application and/or during a job interview and are given the job, this declaration enables you to seek out reasonable accommodations under equal opportunity or anti-discrimination laws in many countries.

Anti-discrimination legislation

Relevant laws to address discrimination on the basis of disability or mental illness in employment (and other areas) and government bodies that support them across the English-speaking world include the following:

- United Kingdom: the Disability Discrimination Act 2005 aims to protect people with disability and mental illness in the

UK from discrimination in employment, accommodation, commerce, transport and building accessibility. It is supported by the UK Office for Disability Issues.[1]

- Australia: the Disability Discrimination Act 1992 protects people with disability or mental illness and makes disability discrimination unlawful. It promotes equal rights, equal opportunity and equal access for people with disabilities. It is supported by the Australian Human Rights Commission (no date).

- United States of America: the Americans with Disabilities Act 1990 addresses discrimination against individuals with disabilities in employment, housing, public accommodations, education, transportation, communication, recreation, institutionalisation, health services, voting and access to public services.[2] The US Equal Employment Opportunity Commission is responsible for enforcing federal laws that make it illegal to discriminate against a job applicant or an employee because of a number of characteristics, including disability or mental illness.[3]

- Canada: the Canadian Human Rights Act 1985 is the instrument that aims to address discrimination on the basis of disability and mental illness in Canada. It covers discrimination in employment, equal pay and provision of goods and services. It is supported by the Canadian Human Rights Commission.[4]

- New Zealand: discrimination on the grounds of disability or mental illness is addressed in the Human Rights Act 1993. It is supported by the New Zealand Human Rights Commission.[5]

---

1   See www.gov.uk/government/organisations/office-for-disability-issues, accessed on 26 January 2015.
2   See www.ada.gov/archive/adastat91.htm, accessed on 26 January 2015.
3   See www.eeoc.gov/eeoc/index.cfm, accessed on 26 January 2015.
4   See http://laws-lois.justice.gc.ca/eng/acts/h-6/fulltext.html, accessed on 26 January 2015.
5   See www.hrc.co.nz/, accessed on 21 October 2015.

- Republic of Ireland: discrimination on the basis of disability or mental illness is addressed by the Disability Act 2005, which is supported by the National Disability Authority.[6]

Telling your boss and/or your colleagues about your autism and/or your mental health issues can bring about support and friendship, or it can cause difficulties when they are afraid of, or confused by the labels. If you do disclose, it can be helpful to provide a small amount of information, such as a leaflet, that explains what these labels mean when applied to you, and what supports you may need.

JOE'S STORY: Understanding, not discriminating

I have autism and depression. This means that I avoid social chit-chat, because it makes me uncomfortable. When I am depressed, this means I don't talk at all. It is okay to tell me you are worried I am depressed, and ask if I need some support. Also I can get quite upset by very loud noises, so if there is a fire drill, it would be helpful to let me know before it happens. If there is a real fire alarm, it would be helpful to have someone offer to walk with me to the evacuation point. If you do this, please only touch my shoulder and nowhere else on my body.

Tackling stigma and discrimination

Stigma and discrimination reduce when people are educated and understand what they previously did not. You will not be able to educate every person who reacts negatively to you, but you may be quite pleasantly surprised by how kind people can be once they understand you. For example, a teacher with autism was supported with her hand sensitivities by other adults who would get out and clear up the Play-Doh for her.

One of the things that people with autism find particularly difficult to understand about being a member of a group that is stigmatised is the stupidity of discriminating against people because

---

6   See http://nda.ie, accessed on 26 January 2015.

of their differences. In general, people with autism view people as all more or less equal and tend not to notice differences that are socially/culturally important, such as clothing style or skin colour. However, society tends to sort and hierarchically order people in a myriad of ways. These ways vary between and within cultural groups – old people are revered in some cultures, but not if they are homeless or have dementia. In other cultures, old people are often ignored, unless they have dementia, in which case they are looked after.

Discrimination usually occurs in relation to not having particular traits or characteristics that are most valued in that society or having attributes that are viewed as aberrant or strange. A person who moves around the world may well be highly valued in some countries and be discriminated against in others. This is irrational and can result in identity confusion and distress. In addition, traditional cultures can revere or despise things that modern culture places the opposite value on. Many people with autism felt discriminated against in school if they were less social than their peers and/or not good at sport or struggled to talk or write. The impact of these feelings can last a lifetime unless they are confronted as belonging solely in the past.

Being confident about who you are and your value in the world can really help to combat negative feelings associated with stigma and discrimination. In addition, it is very difficult for others to project their negativity and ideas that you are less than them if you are presenting with confidence and self-acceptance. This is the case even when legal discrimination remains in place, as it does in large parts of the world in relation to lesbian, gay men and transsexual/transgender people.

Becoming part of a community, whether in real life or online, can also help to diminish the effects of stigma. One of the huge benefits of belonging to any self-advocacy community is your ability to help create change, and so make the world a more accepting and caring place for others who do not yet have the courage or ability to demand acceptance and equality. Yes, it can be frightening to make contact with others and to get to know them and share your own knowledge and skills and difficulties, but in the long term it can be of great benefit to you, and help you to live well.

Peer mentoring advice

- Everyone's experience of stigma will be different. Stigma ranges from paternalism, hostility, denial of employment or other positions, hate speech, name-calling, denial of medical treatment and a host of other negative actions.

- Stigma about autism or mental illness is just as negative and destructive as racism, sexism or homophobia; it is never okay to discriminate against someone because of their autism or mental illness.

- Some people can become quite worn down by stigma and discrimination and lose their confidence and 'fight'. This means that they may feel that they cannot participate in activities such as employment, civic life or social activities, even if they are highly capable and would provide a great benefit to themselves and society through their participation.

- Stigma can severely impact on confidence and self-esteem. Some people internalise stigma and view themselves through a hate-filled lens as a result of experiencing discrimination from others. This self-stigma can completely destroy a person's confidence.

- Stigma can come from many quarters including work colleagues or managers, strangers, family or friends, health professionals, the media and even yourself. Recognise it is harmful and illogical, and challenge it if you can, or choose to ignore it.

- It is okay to be who you are. It is okay to be on the autism spectrum, to live with autism, to be autistic, to be an Autie or an Aspie. It is good to decide how you want to describe yourself and claim the right to do so. Include any/all aspects of yourself that you want to. It is okay to be on a mental health journey. Most people in the world are seeking happiness, or a way to live well. You are no different from anyone else in this aspect. Your journey may be harder than some people's, but it may well be easier than some other people's too.

- You deserve love, acceptance and respect, not stigma and discrimination. If people discriminate against you, this usually says more about their own shortcomings than it does about yours.

- To counter the effects of stigma, try to do things that will build your confidence as a person with a mental illness and autism. This may include befriending others with similar issues and comparing stories and supporting each other, or it could mean challenging yourself to do something that the stereotypes around your illness claim that you shouldn't be able to do, such as a particular job, physical activity or social event. You could read some accounts of people dealing with similar difficulties to you, or get involved in autism and/or mental illness conversations in social media. You could start writing an article, book or blog about your experiences. Do whatever works, but make sure your goal is increasing your confidence and feeling good about yourself.

JENNY'S STORY: Stigma from health professionals

Most people might expect to find stigma in the workplace or social situations, but in my experience the most stigma I have suffered has been from certain health professionals who do not understand how my autism and mental illness impact on me. In one instance, I was severely discriminated against by a nurse on a surgical ward in hospital. She seemed ignorant of the issues around mental illness and treated me like I was a whinging, spoilt teenager. This admission occurred when I was quite unwell with psychosis as well as having a physical complaint in need of surgery. I was very weak – emotionally and physically – and felt powerless and unable to protect or defend myself.

I would like to see a world in which there is no stigma about mental illness or autism. To make this world happen, we need to educate others about mental illness and promote neurodiversity and love and accept ourselves. While this may not bring about a perfect world, it will go a long way towards doing so.

9

FAMILY INCIDENCE OF AUTISM AND MENTAL ILLNESS

For most people, the relationships they have with family members are the closest relationships they will have with anyone. Children usually grow up within a family unit, and this shapes their futures, their identity and their beliefs. 'In every conceivable manner, the family is the link to our past, the bridge to our future.' (Haley, nd). People with autism spectrum conditions often come from a family where many members have either a diagnosis of autism or some autistic traits. In some instances, family members will have autism as well as mental health conditions or will have undiagnosed autism and/or mental health conditions.

The US Centers for Disease Control and Prevention (CDC) provides the following statistic around the prevalence of autism spectrum conditions and co-morbid conditions in families:

> Studies have shown that among identical twins, if one child has ASD, then the other will be affected about 36–95% of the time. In non-identical twins, if one child has ASD, then the other is affected about 0–31% of the time.
>
> Parents who have a child with ASD have a 2%–18% chance of having a second child who is also (on the autism spectrum).
>
> ASD commonly co-occurs with other developmental, psychiatric, neurologic, chromosomal, and genetic diagnoses. The co-occurrence of one or more non-ASD developmental diagnoses is 83%. The co-occurrence of one or more psychiatric diagnoses is 10%.
>
> (CDC no date, b)

This means that about eight out of ten people on the autism spectrum have another developmental condition, such as dyslexia, dyspraxia, and/or an intellectual disability. About one in every ten on the autism spectrum will have an additional mental health condition. It should be noted that this does not include anxiety. Nearly all people on the autism spectrum experience anxiety, although most of these people will not get diagnosed with an anxiety disorder – they will either be viewed as not anxious enough, or that the anxiety is inherent in the autism diagnosis.

The UK National Autistic Society provides the following advice on heritability and autism:

> Recent studies...have highlighted an important difference in the types of families that have members with ASD. There are some families where only one member has a diagnosis of ASD, and no one in the extended family has a diagnosis. Such 'one-off' incidences of autism are referred to as 'simplex' autism. Recent research suggests that some of these might be due to 'de novo' changes in DNA sequence (e.g. a rare sequence variant or a copy number variation), i.e. a one-off change that happens during the formation of gametes. It is believed that these rare variants can account for nearly 10% of all people diagnosed with ASD (Sebat *et al.*, 2007). On the other hand, there is a multitude of families, where more than one member of the extended family has a diagnosis, or several members have very high levels of autistic traits – even though they might have never received a formal clinical diagnosis. Such families are referred to as 'multiplex' families. It is believed that there are specific genetic variations, passed down through generations, that might underlie the increased incidence of ASD in these families.

> (The National Autistic Society no date, a)

What this means is that about one in ten people on the autism spectrum will be the first in their family history to be on the autism spectrum, while the rest of the people on the autism spectrum will have relatives that are also on the autistic spectrum, whether or not they have been officially diagnosed.

A 2013 study also looked at the incidence of autism within families:

This study looked at parental incidence of the Broad Autism Phenotype (BAP) and its impact on the incidence of Autism in their children

Although parental pairs of a child with autism were more likely than comparison parental pairs to have both parents characterised by the presence of the BAP, they more commonly consisted of a single parent with BAP features. The presence of the BAP in parents was associated with the severity of autism behaviours in probands, with the lowest severity occurring for children of parental pairs in which neither parent exhibited a BAP feature. Severity did not differ between children of two affected parents and those of just one.

Collectively, the findings indicate that parental pairs of children with autism frequently consist of a single parent with BAP characteristics... The evidence of intergenerational transmission reported here also provides further confirmation of the high heritability of autism that is unaccounted for by the contribution of de novo mutations currently emphasised in the field of autism genetics.

(Sasson *et al.* 2013)

What this means is that most children on the autism spectrum have one or both biological parents who have traits of autism or who are on the autism spectrum, whether diagnosed or not. This accords with the previously discussed study that suggests that nine out of ten people on the autism spectrum have inherited genes that are implicated in the autism spectrum. How these genes are expressed (in other words, how the functions of the genes are affected) is dependent on a number of factors, including epigenetic factors. Research into epigenetics and autism as well as epigenetics and mental illness is growing, and may help people to manage their lives in the future.

Prevalence of mental illness and autism in families

As demonstrated earlier in this book, there is a high prevalence of mental health conditions among people who are also on the autism spectrum. People with autism are more susceptible to the range of mental illness diagnoses, particularly anxiety and depression. Given that there has only recently begun to be a focus on parents who are also on the autism spectrum, it is difficult to know what that relationship may be between parents who have an autism spectrum condition and a co-morbid mental illness, and whether their children develop a mental illness and/or autism.

Of course, the statistics have a human element. Families with many members on the autism spectrum, with or without mental illness, can experience difficulties, both from within the family and in their relationships with people outside of the family unit. There is a growing movement around raising awareness of parenting on the autism spectrum, particularly for mothers who are on the autism spectrum. Organisations such as the Autism Women's Network are focusing on some strategies to assist mothers of children on the spectrum who are also on the spectrum themselves. This could certainly be an area for further research in the future.

Some of the issues faced by members of 'multiplex' families where some or many members, and particularly one or more parents, have either diagnosed autism spectrum condition or have autistic traits include:

- difficulties between family members knowing when others are upset or having difficult experiences. Alternatively, autistic family members may be extremely sensitive to others' emotions and may find siblings', children's or parents' distress triggering and overwhelming.

- judgement about parenting styles from other parents, health professionals or friends.

- self-doubt around their parenting style or skills.

- family members – including parent/s – being overwhelmed or depressed and feeling unable to support other members.

- meltdowns in one family member triggering meltdowns in other family members

- lack of support services aimed at autistic parents.

- autistic parents having difficulty in setting and enforcing boundaries with children (especially teenagers), or having boundaries that are too strict and do not allow for teenagers to grow into independent adults.

- extreme parental anxiety. Autistic parents can be very worried about their children, considerably more so than many neurotypical parents. This can impact on the parent–child relationship, particularly for teenagers.

- disagreements and problems relating to non-autistic extended family members, including judgement and pressure on autistic parents to change their parenting styles.

- mental health issues and crises being triggering for other family members and in turn sparking off mental health crises in them.

Despite these potential issues, there are a large number of positive elements of being a member of a family with many autistic members, including parents. Children of autistic parents often report that they have a stronger relationship with their parents, because they share a lot of traits and a common understanding. Autistic parents may be less judgemental about things that concern neurotypical parents, such as gender identity or sexual preference. Many autistic children of autistic parents report that they have their closest relationship with their autistic parent because they understand where the child is 'coming from', and that they can tell their parent anything. Autistic parents can provide support for their children based on a genuine connection and understanding. If the child is experiencing bullying at school, having a parent who has a lived experience of what the child is going through, and has had a lifetime of learning how to advocate for themselves, can only be a positive thing.

In families where one parent is autistic and the other is not, these parents can find that their parenting styles suit autistic and non-autistic children really well. Autistic parents often share their autistic children's understanding of and responses to the world, and can prioritise the teaching and learning of skills that are particularly needed by autistic children, such as an understanding of how the social world works. This can be harder for non-autistic parents to teach their autistic children as they have an innate rather than a learned understanding, making it more difficult to scaffold and explain that knowledge.

While there are not many services specifically aimed at autistic parents, knowledge around their needs and experiences is growing. There are a number of advocacy groups supporting parents who are on the spectrum.

Siblings

There is a lot of material available about the challenges faced by neurotypical siblings of autistic children. Parents focusing on meeting the needs of their autistic child or children may have less time to spend with the non-autistic child or children. Some stressors non-autistic siblings can experience include:

- embarrassment around their peers

- jealousy regarding the amount of time parents spend with their brother/sister

- frustration over not being able to engage or get a response from their brother/sister

- being the target of aggressive behaviours

- concern regarding their parents' stress and grief

- concern over their role in future caregiving (Autism Society no date).

There are a number of strategies parents can use to build a meaningful relationship between autistic and non-autistic siblings. The nature of these relationships will differ across families, as families comprise individuals requiring different sorts of communication and interaction. However, some general points to improve sibling relationships and family dynamics include the following:

- Parents should explain autism to the non-autistic child(ren). There are a number of resources available for doing this, including books and films. The Resources section later in this book includes a selection.

- The conversation around explaining autism to non-autistic children should be had as early as possible, and the description made relevant to the particular family.

- Autistic and non-autistic children should be encouraged to play together. This can require give and take from both the autistic and non-autistic children. Learning how to play together will almost certainly improve both children's communication and empathy skills.

- There are sibling groups in many cities and regional centres as well as online and through social media. These can be especially helpful for teens and young adults.

- The concept of potential should be explored with all the children in a family, so that everyone understands that what each child is like today is not what they will be like in 5, 10, 15 or 20 years time.

- Children should get to celebrate all their achievements – not just school-based, but also those based on compassion, kindness, sharing and humour.

- Parents should make time to spend with each child one on one, even if this is only for five minutes a day. For large families, this will be more difficult, and the time may need to be scheduled weekly or even monthly.

- Autistic children should be involved in chore rosters alongside their typical siblings. This helps everyone to learn skills needed for later in life, and helps foster a sense of equity and equality in the family.

- Siblings who are both/all on the autism spectrum may be similar or very different. It is important not to compare children with value judgements, but to see all children as having the potential to grow and develop new skills and knowledge, whatever that might be.

JENNY'S STORY: 'My mum is my best friend'

When I was a kid and a teenager, my mum was my best friend. I could tell her anything. I'd stand behind her for hours, brushing her hair and talking to her about all the goings on in my life.

I was diagnosed with Asperger's syndrome when I was 20. The psychologist who diagnosed me said that Asperger's was often present in many different members of the same family. She said that one of my parents might be on the spectrum too. I didn't think about it much at the time but as the years went on, I thought that maybe my mum was an Aspie too.

I ended up getting a bit of exposure in the autism world. I was asked to speak at various things, I wrote a book and some magazine articles. One question I was asked at pretty much every talk was whether any of my family members were on the spectrum. I was never quite sure how to respond. I thought that all my immediate family could be somewhere under the umbrella of autism, even if none of them had a diagnosis.

A couple of years ago at Christmas, my mum came up to me and shoved a little card she had made in my hand. It had a photo of a butterfly on it. 'This is a little un-Christmas present,' she said. Intrigued, I opened it and saw she had written 'I am going to get an autism assessment'. Knowing my mum, I was pretty certain this was being done to support me and make me feel more included in the family. My mum got her diagnosis a few weeks later (I have a friend who is a diagnostician). And now my mum and I are our own little club of two. It's wonderful. I feel so much closer to my mum.

Family dynamics

So how do all these diagnostic considerations and clusters of people with autism and/or a mental illness in one family play out in terms of family dynamics? Most people would agree that families and family relationships can be difficult – communication issues can arise for both autistic and neurotypical family members. However, families comprising some members on the autism spectrum and some who are not can be strengthened by the different perspectives and the capacity for neurotypical members' ability to 'interpret' for autistic members (and vice versa). Conversely, a 'mixed' family can have tensions between members with different neurological presentations. Like more 'typical' families, the strength and cohesion of an autistic family depends on the individual family and its members. Different factors will be at play in each family. Whatever the situation, family relationships are very important and impact on our sense of identity and self-worth.

If one family member uses an alternative or augmentative communication system such as sign, PECS and/or iPad/tablet-based systems, it is important that everyone in the family learns to use this system too, so that the individual is able to participate in family discussions and decisions. Non-verbal family members must be supported to learn to use a communication system that works for them, and this support includes the family learning alongside the individual.

Peer mentoring advice

- A good family dynamic can help improve your health and wellbeing and that of your partner, parents, kids and/or siblings. Attributes of functional families include:

  » clear communication between members

  » friendships between members irrespective of the fact that they are related

  » mutual respect

  » people who listen to each other

  » people who love one another and express this love

  » relationships that are resilient and 'bounce back' after something goes wrong

  » family members who support each other and back each other up

  » the relationships are not characterised mostly by bickering and complaints about other family members.

- Communication is essential for good family relationships. Try to keep an open discourse within your family about your autism and/or mental illness and how it affects you. Nurture and encourage communication. Keep in regular contact with family members you do not live with if you can.

- Try not to make assumptions about why a family member is behaving in a certain way. If in doubt, ask them why.

- If you are the only family member with a diagnosis, try to imagine how your family members might feel about your autism or mental illness. This does not mean minimising your own experiences, but should involve you trying to imagine the world from their perspective. Ask family members how they perceive you (but be prepared to feel uncomfortable as they might say something frank or honest which upsets you).

- Remember that your family members may have autism, a mental illness or autistic traits themselves, even if they do not have a formal diagnosis. They may not be aware that they are autistic or they may have some idea about it but be in denial. Knowing this may result in better communication between and foster greater understanding and connectedness.

- Some families can be quite toxic and you may be better off spending time without them. This includes families where there is ongoing abuse – physical, sexual or emotional – where members take pleasure in belittling you, deliberately invalidate your experiences and views, and play cruel emotional games at your expense. If this is your family, you might want to avoid them and try to make a new 'family' with friends who value and respect you (or even with your pets). Caring people do not use hostile language or actions to others. You do not have to spend time with people who are unkind or uncaring towards you. It will negatively impact on your mental health to be around people who are constantly criticising you.

- Consider how you and your behaviour affect your family dynamic. If you are not sure, ask others to let you know when you are doing something that concerns them. Make changes if you feel you need to.

- If family members are doing things that upset you, call them out on it. Politely mention to them that when they do X you feel Y. Do not blame or insult them; just tell them how their behaviour impacts on you. Hopefully, this will spark a conversation and start you on the road to improved family relationships.

- Some of the things people might do when they are unwell with mental health issues or as a result of autism – self-harm, manic behaviour, suicide attempts or meltdowns – can have a negative impact on relationships within families that may continue into the future. Even if you think that they should forgive you and move on, try to be mindful of how these actions might impact on your family members, people you are close to. This doesn't mean that you should 'beat yourself up' over them and feel guilty, but rather try to think about how these actions would impact on you if one of your family members did them. Try asking them how it made them feel when you do X, and explain to them that you were unwell when you were doing this, and what steps you are taking to try and ensure that this does not happen again.

- Families can bring out our rawest, most difficult emotions. We tend to care more what our family and partner think than what anyone else does. Remember this when having issues with your family members, and try to consider that they probably care about you and your opinions similarly to how you care about their views.

- Your relationships with your family will be ongoing throughout your life. If you want to improve the dynamic between yourself and family members, try to see it as an ongoing 'project'. Even if relationships are strained at present, they may not be in the future.

- Try to focus on the good in each person in your family. You could even make a list with each person's name and the things that they are good at and ways in which they are nice people. Then if you are feeling sad or angry, look at the list to see which family member would be the one to understand that particular feeling the best, and then reach out to them for support.

- If your family support you financially, practically and/or emotionally, it is a nice idea to do something for them from time to time. This could be something free, such as helping out with the cooking or housework, or something that costs money, such as a present or a meal at a restaurant. When you do something for your family, it helps them to understand that you appreciate them and are not taking them for granted. This can maintain and improve family dynamics as well as be very meaningful to individual family members.

10

STRATEGIES TO AID SLEEP

Benefits of sleep

Sleep is an essential element for staying physically and mentally healthy. It is vital to get enough rest. Sleep disturbances can impact negatively on our health and wellbeing, and on our energy levels and ability to focus and go about our lives. 'It is a common experience that a problem difficult at night is resolved in the morning after the committee of sleep has worked on it.' (Steinbeck, nd).

However, autism and mental illness can play havoc with the amount, length and quality of sleep. People with autism frequently report insomnia and some mental illnesses, or their treatments can cause insomnia or increased fatigue. People's needs regarding sleep vary with each individual, but people usually know when they are not getting adequate sleep or are oversleeping. Issues with sleep can include not being able to get to sleep at night, waking frequently and having trouble getting back to sleep, waking too early, waking up feeling exhausted or oversleeping.

People with autism and/or mental illness may have issues getting a suitable amount of quality sleep for a number of reasons, including:

- anxiety interfering with the ability to get to sleep

- nightmares, night terrors or intense dreams

- thinking about or remembering traumatic experiences

- biological factors (brain chemistry during episodes of illness)

- disorders such as sleep apnoea or restless legs syndrome

- issues with the physical environment (e.g. too light, too warm/cold, too loud)

- sensory issues (e.g. itchy or uncomfortable bedding or pyjamas, distracting sounds or visuals)

- depression

- some medications (e.g. some anti-depressants, thyroid hormone, cold and flu medications)

- being woken by children or pets

- poor understanding or practice of sleep hygiene.

A common recommendation from health professionals is to improve sleep hygiene, which does not mean ensuring that you are clean before you go to bed! 'Sleep hygiene' is simply the clinical term for having enough sleep every night. Poor sleep can contribute to both physical and mental illnesses, and without enough quality sleep, our sympathetic and parasympathetic nervous systems are unable to function properly. In addition, the body releases growth hormones during deep sleep that are vital for children and young adults. Sleep is thought to be involved in a range of processes that enable the body to recover from stress and to maintain optimal health.

As many people with autism are aware, it is not always as simple as going to bed and going to sleep, especially if you have fixated thoughts and ruminate about events in the evening. If you have difficulty sleeping, you can choose to make some changes to your environment and yourself and/or ask for a referral for medication to assist with either falling asleep and/or staying asleep through the night.

If you work shifts, sleep can be particularly difficult to achieve, and can cause long-term problems for some people. Constant shifts, however, are easier on the body than shifts that change regularly.

What is sleep?

Sleep consists of light and deep sleep as well as a stage called rapid eye movement, or REM sleep. Each phase of sleep is useful in maintaining physical and mental wellbeing.

Sleep can be described by stage, type and function, as explained in the following table:

Stage	Type	Function/what happens
1	Light	Interim stage of sleep between sleep and being awake
2	Light	Heart rate slows down, brain becomes less active
3	Deep	Body makes repairs
4	Deep	Body temperature and blood pressure decreases
5	REM	Increase in body temperature, blood pressure, heart rate and REM – when dreams occur

A person cycles through the five stages of sleep a number of times during the night, and it is after REM sleep that people often wake up, as they have moved from deep back into light sleep. The decrease and increase in body temperature can help to explain why people may wake up hot or cold when they had previously been comfortable.

Insomnia

Insomnia is a sleep disorder characterised by a lack of sleep or extreme difficulty getting to sleep, and can cause a number of issues during the daytime, such as increased irritability and stress, fatigue and memory difficulties. Primary insomnia is environmentally influenced, whereas secondary insomnia is caused by (is a side effect of) some other thing, such as alcohol consumption, some medications, some health conditions and some mental health issues such as anxiety. An acute period of insomnia may last only a few weeks, whereas chronic insomnia is where the person has been unable to sleep for at least three nights a week for over a month. Acute insomnia is usually caused by something significant happening, such as the death of someone close, losing a job or home, divorce or even getting married. In addition, being physically unwell can cause difficulties sleeping for the duration of the illness. Some women are unable to sleep well during menstruation due to the pain and/or hormonal changes.

Some cold or allergy or depression medications are stimulants and can therefore disrupt sleep. There are often alternative non-stimulant medications, so if sleep is an issue, you may wish to discuss this with your doctor.

Light, noise, smells and bedroom temperature can all cause sleep difficulties, as can shift work. Chronic pain and stress, as well as depression, anxiety and the menopause, can all cause chronic insomnia. In these cases, the underlying condition needs to be treated which will often solve the sleeping difficulties.

Medication and sleep

Medication is sometimes prescribed for insomnia, and these medications are commonly referred to as sleeping tablets. Treatment for other sleeping disorders such as sleep apnoea and periodic limb movement disorder are different, and these conditions require specialist diagnosis, often through a sleep clinic. You should never take someone else's sleeping tablets, especially if you are taking any other medications.

Just like medications to treat mental health conditions, there is no 'one size fits all' sleeping tablet. What will work for one person will not work for another. In addition, the dosages required for adults on the autism spectrum may be much lower or higher than for neurotypical people. To further complicate things, some medications are not authorised for use in some countries as sleeping aides, but are authorised in other countries. In countries where medications are subsidised by the government, which sleeping tablets are subsidised and for which types of sleep issues varies.

This section provides a brief overview of the medications both prescribed and 'natural' that are commonly taken by a range of adults on the autism spectrum. It is important to note that you should never drive or operate heavy machinery after taking sleeping tablets, as your ability to do these tasks will be impaired.

Melatonin

Many people on the autism spectrum have tried using melatonin in one form or another as an aide to sleep. The availability of melatonin has been restricted over the last decade, however, and a prescription is often required. The liquid form (drops) can be hard to source, and it is usually prescribed as a tablet.

Melatonin is also known as N-acetyl-5-methoxytryptamine, and is a naturally occurring human hormone made by the pineal gland in the brain, although bought versions are synthetically produced. It was previously used to combat jet lag, as it seems to be the key regulator of a person's body clock in terms of when to sleep and when to wake. This is also called the circadian rhythm, the pattern of waking and sleeping over time. Darkness falling triggers an elevation of melatonin levels, and this appears to prepare the body for sleep. Once the day dawns, the light seems to trigger a decrease in melatonin, and the body prepares to wake up. This is why it is recommended that the area you sleep in is dark when you go to bed, as this will naturally increase levels of melatonin. It is advisable to have a bedtime routine as it is thought that a person's circadian rhythm can be adjusted through regular times for going to and getting up from bed.

For some people, taking melatonin approximately 1–2 hours before attempting to sleep may help them to fall asleep. Dosages will differ for different people, and should be worked out with a GP. For those who struggle to get to sleep (delayed sleep phase syndrome), melatonin may be helpful, but if you struggle to sleep because you are reviewing your day or analysing issues/events from the day or having fixated thoughts, melatonin may not help.

Research has indicated that melatonin use is safe for up to two years, although within one year of stopping it, people for whom it was effective can lose the benefits and return to poor sleeping patterns. Side effects can include daytime sleepiness, headaches, short-term feelings of depression, dizziness, stomach cramps or irritability.

Tart cherry juice is said to contain a high level of melatonin, and some people choose to trial this instead. Pigeon *et al.* (2010) found that the tart cherry juice blend they investigated was beneficial for some older adults with insomnia, and that this benefit was either larger than or the same as the benefits demonstrated in studies of valerian (see below). Benefits when compared to melatonin tablets were inconclusive as some studies showed greater and some lesser effectiveness at aiding sleep.

Valerian

Valerian medications/therapies are made from the root of the valerian plant. It is thought that valerian increases the amount of gamma aminobutyric acid (GABA) in the brain. GABA is a chemical that helps regulate nerve cells and is thought to have a calming effect on anxiety. Valerian is sometimes chosen to try and help with sleep because it is a natural product, although the evidence for its effectiveness is contradictory and variable.

Valerian may help some people fall asleep faster and help some to have a better quality of sleep than they would otherwise, but it may not work at all, or take up to a month to be effective, for others. The quality of valerian products is variable as it is not a regulated prescription medication, and this may affect its usefulness to aide sleep.

In many cases, valerian is sold in a mixture with other herbs such as lemon balm and hops, and used in hot water as a herbal tea, to be drunk an hour or so before bedtime.

For some, valerian can increase anxiety and restlessness. In this case, it should be stopped immediately. As with all medications, natural and synthetic, there are a number of potential side effects and possible interactions with other medications. Always discuss whether or not to take any additional non-prescription medications with your family GP. Possible side effects from valerian include headaches, restlessness and anxiety. The University of Maryland Medical Center suggests that valerian can alter the effectiveness of many medications used to treat mental health issues such as benzodiazepines, tricyclic anti-depressants as well as interacting with anti-convulsant medications, antihistamines, statins and even some anti-fungal medications.

Valium and temazepam

Valium and temazepam are common sleeping tablets that are also sometimes used to treat parasomnias, which have been assessed by sleep specialists. Parasomnias are disruptive sleep disorders that usually occur during arousals from REM sleep or partial arousals from non-REM sleep, and include things such as night terrors or sleepwalking. Night terrors can result in a person suddenly waking up from their sleep feeling terrified. They are often confused and unable to communicate for a period of time during which they usually do not respond to voices and may be difficult to wake up completely. After a while, the person settles and seems to go back to sleep. People who have night terrors often don't recall what they were experiencing when they wake up in the morning. Night terrors are more extreme than nightmares, and occur most often during a person's deep sleep. Sleepwalking happens when a person is moving around and may look as if they are awake, but they are actually asleep. The person may even talk or interact with others while they are sleepwalking, but will have no recollection of this in the morning. It usually occurs during deep non-REM sleep early in the night, although it can also happen during REM sleep in the early morning.

LAURA'S STORY: Sleepwalking and nightmares

I used to sleepwalk and talk as a child, apparently even coming out to sit with my parents and play cards with them. I never recalled this in the morning, but when I went to boarding school, I remember being really worried in case I went sleepwalking because the school rule was that we were not allowed out of bed after lights out until lights on in the morning. I don't know if I did sleepwalk at all at school, but I know that I always had big problems getting to sleep after that and I would have these recurrent nightmares that I was in a tiny cardboard box and the box was put on the road in between the wheels of a truck. I always woke up just as the truck was rolling and about to squish me. Some mean kid told me if I didn't wake up before I got run over I would die in my sleep, and this made sleeping even more difficult for me. Now I take sleeping tablets about once a month to help me have a really good night's sleep, and then I am okay for another month or so.

Valium and temazepam are benzodiazepines that act on GABA receptors in the brain, causing the release of the chemical GABA. GABA is a neurotransmitter that is thought to assist in keeping the chemicals in the brain in balance, and is involved in inducing sleepiness, reducing anxiety and relaxing muscles. Benzodiazepines can be used for short-term treatment of severe anxiety associated with insomnia. They can decrease the time taken to fall asleep and minimise the number of times a person wakes up during the night as well as decrease the time spent awake then. When combined, this increases the total amount of time spent sleeping. However, they are only suitable for short-term treatment of insomnia and anxiety, as they have a high potential for dependence and addiction, and can cause drowsiness the following day for some people, even at quite low doses.

Side effects of benzodiazepines include feeling restless, agitated, irritable or aggressive, experiencing delusions, rages, nightmares or hallucinations. They can also interact with a number of other medications, so it is important to make sure that your prescribing doctor is aware of all your medications, and that you do not take anyone else's medications.

Evening routines to aid sleep

- Don't drink caffeine or alcohol in the evening. For some people who are caffeine-sensitive, drinking caffeine after lunch may be enough to prevent them from sleeping.

- Drink enough water during the day, but not just before bed, as this can make some people wake up needing to go to the toilet in the night.

- Try to eat your meal several hours before bedtime, as it is harder for your body to digest during sleep.

- Cut down on nicotine or, ideally, quit smoking altogether. Nicotine is a stimulant and can prevent good sleep for some people.

- Exercise regularly.

- Do something relaxing just before bed. This may be listening to music, having a bath or meditating or something else. Try *not* to think about things that may have gone wrong in your day or worry about things that are coming up.

- Establish a regular bedtime and wake-time. It is thought that going to bed at the same time and getting up at the same time every day is helpful to develop good sleep hygiene. However, for some people with sleeping difficulties it may be that on days when they are not working it is beneficial just to have extra sleep.

Simple changes to help with sleep

The place that you sleep needs to be conducive to sleeping comfortably, if at all possible. This means you should think about what you need to feel relaxed about going to sleep. Both your bed/what you sleep on and the blankets/covers are as important as the space in which you are sleeping. If you can, have a separate room to sleep in; however, if you live in a studio/one-room apartment, this may not be possible. In this case, it is even more important to ensure that what you sleep on and under are suitable for sleeping well.

Beds, sofas, blankets, covers and duvets

A bed may be equally comfortable to a sofa or less comfortable, depending on the mattress. Some people like sleeping on a sofa, sofa-bed or futon, while others can only sleep in a bed. What you prefer is what you should choose. If you can afford to, get a new mattress or sofa cushions every five to ten years as they become less supportive with age. Lie down on the mattress/cushions before committing to buy them.

Once you have your furniture to sleep on, pick out your sheets and blankets/duvet etc. to sleep under as well as think about what you want to sleep in. Just because you wore pyjamas to go to bed when you were growing up does not mean that they are useful or helpful in having a good night's sleep. For some people, any clothes in bed are seriously uncomfortable and can stop them from feeling relaxed and drifting off to sleep easily. For others, having the air touching their bare shoulders or feet can be annoying. There are no right or wrong things to wear or not to wear to bed. And there are no correct or incorrect sheets and covers.

If you can afford to, choose a fabric that you like the feel of. Rub the fabric between your fingers when you are browsing in the shops. It will feel a bit harder than once you have washed it, but washing it will not make it super-soft if it is a naturally stiff fabric. Whether you have old or new sheets and covers, you can make them smell fresh by washing them every one to two weeks and hanging them outside to dry if possible. Or try adding a few drops of lavender or another essential oil to the washing machine when you wash them, as lavender can help some people to sleep better if they can smell it when they go to bed.

Once you have your sheets to sleep on top of, you may want to have a cover to sleep under. For some people with autism a weighted blanket is very effective as a sleep aid, but for others the cover needs to be as light as possible. Only you can find out what works for you. You could borrow a weighted blanket to see if this helps. If it does, you either buy one or make one yourself. For people who would like a duvet (or 'doona' as it is called in Australia), the most important choice is between a feather or synthetic filling. Feathers can irritate or itch some people even though they are not actually touching the skin. If you are not sure, go to a shop and touch the display duvets to see what you like. Buying online can save you a lot of money, but if you plan to do this, ensure that you know exactly what you are buying and that you are happy with your choice.

Position your bed/sofa wherever you like in the room. Some people like to sleep jammed between the mattress edge and the wall, or in the corner of a sofa. This may not be possible if you share a bed with someone, so if this is the case, it may be that a weighted blanket would be helpful.

Bedroom/room issues

Where you sleep needs to be relaxing. If your room is full of things or has things in it that you associate with stress, change the way the room is organised. It is generally thought that the bedroom should be set up for sleeping and nothing else, although if you are in a relationship, it may be where most of your sexual intimacy takes place too. If you are going to rearrange your room, the following are some ideas to help:

- Make sure you can get to and from the bed easily – try and make sure there are not things all over the floor.

- Make sure that the room has had some fresh air during the day – open the window in the day.

- Have the room at a comfortable temperature for you to sleep; this is different for every person, however, and if you are in a relationship with someone, it will need to be negotiated. You may need to have a small heater or fan.

- The room should either smell neutral or of something that you perceive of as relaxing.

- Darkness helps people to go to sleep, and light helps people to wake up, so ideally you want your room to be as dark as possible at bedtime and be able to let light in when you wake up in the morning – black-out blinds or thermal-lined curtains can help.

- There should be nothing in the room that provokes stress or anxiety. If possible, remove anything that may do this and replace with a photo or picture that you find relaxing or positive.

- If you have your clothes in the same room, try to have these stored either in a wardrobe, drawers or in boxes. If you need to have your clothes for the next day laid out ready for the morning, put these on a chair, not on the end of the bed or floor. If they are on a chair, you can have them so that the first things you will put on are on top and the last on the bottom.

- Have a drink of water by the bed, so that if you wake up in the night, you can have a drink and go back to sleep, without having to get out of bed and walk around, which may wake you up.

- If you get hungry in the night, put a snack by the bed too.

- If you have a pet that you like to sleep in your room or even on your bed, make sure they are settled before you get into bed.

- If listening to music or audio books helps you to relax, you may like to have a CD player or radio in your bedroom. You can also use online radio stations that you can preset to turn off after 15, 30, 45, 60 or 90 minutes.

- If you need an alarm clock, try to have one (or use your phone alarm) that does not tick or glow in the dark, as these can make it difficult to go back to sleep, if you wake up 30–45 minutes before you wanted to.

Peer mentoring advice

- Try some relaxation techniques before you go to bed. These could include taking a bath before bed, drinking a hot drink (which doesn't contain caffeine), or listening to your favourite (and preferably relaxing) music.

- Try not to do any activity other than sleeping or sexual intercourse in bed. This will ensure that you view bed in a particular context. When you use your bed as an extension of your lounge room – say, for watching TV or reading – you can blur your mind's understanding of what it is for. This means that when you go to bed, you may not be in 'relax and go to sleep' mode; you might be in 'watch the news' mode. This is generally not conducive to good sleep.

- Limit screen use before bed and during the night, especially backlit devices (such as tablets, e-readers or mobile phones).

- Make your bedroom a comfortable, safe, pleasant environment that you want to spend time in. You don't need to spend a lot of money to do this. For example, you could put up artwork – make them yourself, if you are creatively minded – or display photos of places, people or pets that you have positive associations with.

- Each person has a different requirement for light levels in the bedroom, but make sure you have a level of light that helps you get to sleep.

- Even if you don't have much money, investing in a comfortable bed is well worth it. You will be rewarded by years of good sleep.

- If possible, avoid napping during the day.

- Keep a similar bedtime and a similar getting-up time each day, if possible. (Although people working shifts or those with small children may not be able to do this.)

- If you take medication that interferes with your sleep, talk to your doctor about whether it is possible to change either the medications or what time you take them.

- Alcohol and illicit drugs can interfere with your sleep. Drink in moderation and avoid illicit drugs, especially 'uppers' such as amphetamines or cocaine.

- Medications – whether 'natural' and/or prescribed – can be useful tools to aid sleep, but may have significant side effects and/or the potential for addiction, so should only be used under the direction of a medical doctor or specialist. You should never drive or operate heavy machinery after taking sleeping medications. In some countries doing so is illegal, and you could be prosecuted.

LYNNE'S STORY: Restless legs syndrome

I have very bad restless legs syndrome, which means that when I sleep or try to sleep, my legs keep moving – it looks like I am running in my sleep. I suppose it is good exercise, but it also means I am always exhausted and my knees can hurt in the mornings. I went to see a sleep specialist and was prescribed some medication that really helped for about a year. Then it stopped working. The specialist got me to take another medication too, to enhance the first one, but it didn't really help so I stopped taking it. After a few months I got so tired I could only just manage going to work. I am really sensitive to sleeping tablets and they knock me out and leave me really groggy the next day so I can only take them at weekends. I find that if I take one sleeping tablet once every 3–4 weeks on a Friday night and sleep until lunch on Saturday and then just relax for the rest of the weekend, I am okay to work normally. I usually sleep for a few hours, wake up for a few hours and then go back to sleep for a few hours. It is like I am catching up on my missed sleep once a month!

11

THE VALUE OF PETS

Most people respond positively to pets. A dog with a wagging tail or a purring cat can make us feel instantly happy and relaxed. 'There is no psychiatrist in the world like a puppy licking your face' (Williams, nd). There is a great deal of research showing how and why living with pets is good for our mental health. It has been found, for example, that animal-assisted activity is as effective as commonly used mental health service stress management programmes, decreasing depression and anxiety, as well as decreasing the negative effects of pain (Nepps, Stewart and Bruckno 2014).

Many people have a pet – most commonly a cat or dog – but there are many other animals that people like to share their home with. If you are allergic to or afraid of dogs, this doesn't mean that you cannot benefit from having a pet. Researchers have found positive effects for people who care for a variety of other animals, even birds and fish. Studies have found that:

- pet owners are less likely to suffer from depression than those without pets

- people with pets have lower blood pressure in stressful situations than those without pets

- playing with a pet can elevate levels of serotonin and dopamine, which calm and relax people

- pet owners have lower triglyceride and cholesterol levels (indicators of heart disease) than those without pets

- pet owners experience a notable improvement in their ability to communicate and interact with others (see Rossetti and King 2010)

- pet owners over 65 years old make fewer visits to their doctors than those without pets.[1]

Research has demonstrated that dog owners exhibit greater benefits than non-owners across a range of areas including self-esteem, physical fitness, sociability, happiness and general health (McConnell *et al.* 2011). Some studies have shown that dog ownership has also been implicated in helping to alleviate symptoms of depression among terminally ill patients, older people and people suffering from post-traumatic stress disorder (PTSD). But you don't need to own a dog to reap the benefits of pet ownership; people gain mental health benefits from other pets too. It is important to choose a pet that you are able to afford and can physically care for, however, or the pet may cause you more stress!

Some people enjoy having non-traditional pets such as stick insects, which require very little physical interaction and minimal costs, or reptiles that vary considerably in cost and care needs. You may need to check with your local council and/or landlord what kind of pet you are allowed to keep. Even places with a no-pet policy will usually allow animals such as fish or stick insects.

People on the autism spectrum may feel that their pets are more important to them than almost anything else. Children with autism can feel closer to their pets than to the human inhabitants in their life. Likewise, adults with autism may feel closer to their pets than they do with people. Many people with autism have a bond with animals and the natural world. They may have skills at understanding and communicating with animals that others lack. People with autism often seek out the company of animals and feel a strong connection with them. For these people, having a pet or keeping chickens or working with animals can be very positive life choices.

Pets can mean the difference between a person on the autism spectrum and/or a mental illness being lonely and isolated or feeling supported and connected.

---

1   See www.helpguide.org, accessed on 24 January 2015.

LUCY'S STORY: Comet, the pet cat

I have a diagnosis of Asperger's syndrome and depression. For years I struggled with feeling isolated and alone. One day someone at my workplace suggested that I get a pet. I have always loved cats, so I got myself a little white kitten that I called Comet. Comet is the most important thing in my world, and I feel more attachment to him than anyone else. Comet has helped in my recovery from severe depression. When I cuddle him, all my sadness and anxiety seems to drain away. Before I got Comet, I dreaded going home at the end of the working day, but now I can't wait to unlock the door and give him a big cuddle. I think having Comet is as important in my recovery as taking medication or seeing a psychologist. I think everyone with depression should get a cat.

Some organisations provide assistance dogs and cats specifically for people with autism or those with a mental illness. These are working animals – much like the assistance dogs used by people who are blind – and their job is to be a good friend to a person with autism and/or a mental illness and to comfort them when they're having a hard time. For people who may be isolated and lonely, these assistance animals perform an invaluable role, bringing connectedness, love and attachment. Initial research has provided preliminary support for the concept of therapy/assistance dogs for some individuals with autism, through increased social interaction and communication as well as reduced behaviours of concern, anxiety and stress (O'Haire 2013). It is, however, quite difficult to get a therapy/assistance dog as they are expensive to train and there is usually a waiting list. If you feel that you would prefer a trained therapy/assistance dog to a pet dog, approach your local guide dog association to discuss this with them.

Interaction with pets has been shown to provide people with autism and mental illness with a wide range of benefits, including emotional, psychological, physical and physiological benefits (Morrison 2007). Healthcare professionals are increasingly recognising the potential for using animals in therapeutic settings and interactions for treating a range of issues, including providing support for people with autism (Mallon 1992; O'Haire 2013).

Pets have a large number of benefits to improve mental health and wellbeing. They have been shown in numerous studies to reduce stress levels. Owning a dog helps people to be active and to get outside – both things that improve mood – and they are a great distraction from difficult emotions, anxiety and depression, and give people a sense of purpose and meaning in their life.

In recent years there has been considerable research into the benefits of assistance animals and pets for people – and particularly for children:

It has been noted by many authors that assistance animals provide… wider therapeutic benefits to both the child and family, in particular acting as a transitional object, facilitating more positive social interactions with others in a variety of ways (Davis *et al.* 2004). For example, assisting with activities of daily living (ADL); making daily routines and outings possible and more pleasurable for the entire family (Davis *et al.* 2004; Burrows *et al.* 2008); and decreasing anxiety and behavioural outbursts (Martin and Farnum 2002).

(Reynolds 2012)

Owning pets can be a highly effective intervention to address mental health issues and suffering. A cat or dog often loves their human 'parent' unconditionally. Walking a dog can help people to address social anxiety as their canine best friend is right there with them, supporting them while they are out in the world. People can talk to their pets and share any issues they may be experiencing. Most cats and dogs are affectionate and will want strokes and cuddles from their human owner. Some sleep on the bed with their owner. Many pets demonstrate their love and appreciation for their owner that will almost certainly alleviate stress or depression.

Pets can give people a sense of responsibility. That sense of responsibility can also encourage people to do everyday self-care things like cleaning the house or eating regular meals. Having the responsibility of looking after a pet for people with autism can also translate into a sense of responsibility in other areas of life such as employment or study. It can be less frightening to look after a pet than to interact with other people, as pets do not judge, and they tend to instantly forgive any mistakes someone might make. Pets can be a protective factor against becoming unwell or going to hospital, due to owners wanting to stay well and stay home to look after their pet as well as the more obvious attribute that they are loving companions and help the owner to feel loved and needed.

Owning a pet can be a point of commonality between a person with autism and other people. There are clubs and societies for most companion animals – dogs, cats, guinea pigs, rabbits, mice, rats, lizards, birds etc. Some dog clubs have activities for dogs and owners to do together. Other people with autism have pets too, so it might be possible to make friends with them through a shared interest in pets. Having a peer group of autistic people can be a strong protective factor to help address isolation and mental health concerns. Being friends with others on the spectrum can help people to feel included and have a sense of belonging where they may not have done in the past. Social media is also a good way to meet others on the autism spectrum, as there are many groups and pages for people with autism. This is also true of mental illness, so people can connect with other people with autism or mental illness and discuss their pets. This helps in connecting with other like-minded people.

Pet owners should be aware, however, that most animals live considerably shorter lives than humans. Dogs live on average for around 12–15 years, cats around 15–18, small mammals like rats and mice usually only live between 1–3 years, although some birds and reptiles can live for a long time – cockatoos for around 100 years and tortoises for a similar length of time. As most people will own a cat or a dog, preparing for the terrible day that they will lose their furry friend can be very difficult, so it is good to develop some strategies for managing the loss of a pet. One of the most important strategies is to accept that the animal is going to die within the next X amount of years, although it could be sooner due to ill health or accidents, or it may be longer. There is information available online and in books about grief – and mourning the death of a pet can be just as difficult, or more difficult, for people on the autism spectrum as mourning the passing of a human family member. If approached in a positive and accepting frame of mind, however, dealing with the grief around losing a pet can prepare someone for other difficult losses that may occur in their life and can help them build resilience (see also Chapter 17 for more on resilience). There is no 'right' or 'wrong' way to grieve a loss – everyone approaches it differently. It may or may not be helpful to keep photos of the pet or their favourite toys as reminders of them after they are gone. When dealing with grief, people should simply do what works best for them, and it is okay to ask for support if needed. It is also okay to get a new pet straight away or to wait a while.

Practical considerations around pet ownership

It is important to understand what the responsibility of looking after a pet entails, and to assess whether you will be able to take it on at this point in your life. Some pets require a lot of work and financial input, such as dogs, which need to be walked at least once a day, fed twice a day and require ongoing medical attention such as worming, flea and tick treatments and booster vaccinations at the vet. Owning a dog – especially a large one – can be quite expensive. And with dogs, you need to be the 'boss', so to speak, as they are pack animals and their behaviour can become problematic if they perceive that their 'position' is above yours in the pack hierarchy. Cats require a little less attention, but still need twice-daily feeding, worming and flea treatment, booster vaccinations from the vet and attention. Some lower-maintenance pets include reptiles, insects or birds. It is important to know what you will need to provide as an owner for the pet you choose before going out and buying it. Talk to people you know who own pets, and find out what's entailed in looking after them, or do some research online prior to making the decision to get one.

- One way of determining whether you will be responsible enough to look after a pet is to offer to look after a pet for a friend or family member when they are away. Observing things such as how confident you felt looking after it, whether you remembered to feed it or walk it, and how happy you felt with it is a good way to work out whether you are about to, and indeed enjoy, looking after a pet.

- Most people respond better emotionally to mammals – furry creatures that are capable of affection. This is why animals such as cats, dogs, horses, guinea pigs and rabbits tend to be more popular than insects and reptiles. However, if you have a lifelong love of snakes, spiders or lizards, get one of those instead.

- Pets cost money. You'll need to budget to see if you can afford it. Expenses include food, worming medication, flea and tick treatments, vet bills (these can be unexpected and very expensive), de-sexing, microchipping, vaccinations, toys and pet insurance, if you choose to buy it.

- It is a good idea to get your cat or dog microchipped. If they run away or get lost, whoever finds them can take them to a vet or animal centre to check the registration and owner details from the microchip. Vets can insert the microchip, which is inexpensive and painless for the pet. Some organisations will de-sex and microchip your pet for free, if you cannot afford it.

- It is also a good idea to get your dog or cat de-sexed or spayed – the world already has a lot of feral cats and stray dogs, and you don't want to add to their number! De-sexing also tends to make male animals less aggressive and more affectionate.

- Find someone – a friend or family member – who can look after your pet if you go away. Confirm this person's agreement and capacity to look after your furry companion prior to bringing it home. It is very important to have somewhere for your pet to go when you are away, as most animals need feeding daily. If something comes up suddenly, make sure you tell the person looking after your pet about the situation as soon as possible. If you can, ask a few people if they can care for your pet when you are away. Then, if one of them cannot take care of your pet, you have a back-up plan. Make sure you pick someone who is trustworthy and reliable (someone you do not mind having access to your house, who likes your pet, and is usually reliable at keeping appointments).

- If you get a dog, consider taking it to obedience training. This is often run by animal welfare organisations such as the RSPCA. As dogs are pack animals, it is important to let them know that you are the pack leader. Failing to do this can result in poorly behaved or aggressive dogs. Autism and mental health assistance dogs will probably have had a high level of training before you get them, however, so you will not need to take them to obedience training.

• Consider getting your pet from an animal shelter or pound. While some people want a particular breed, the reality is that huge numbers of animals are euthanised each year because they cannot find a home. Giving a pet a second chance at life is wonderful. However, if you get an animal – particularly an adult animal – from a shelter, make sure you enquire about their health and any problems with their behaviour prior to deciding to keep them. Ask to visit the animal a number of times before committing to owning it, so that you can check that you like their temperament and feel comfortable around them.

LYNNE'S STORY: Getting the wrong pet

I love furry cuddly things; touching soft fur really helps me calm down. I saw this gorgeous puppy, soft curly black fur. It was so cute and so soft, I decided to get it. I knew I could afford to keep a dog as I already had one, and I knew how much they cost. What I didn't know, however, was that the dog I already had was very sensitive to my Asperger's and my distress when I was overwhelmed. The new puppy just wanted to sit on me and lick me whenever I was stressed or upset. I hate being touched when I am stressed, so it was awful. I knew the puppy was just loving me, but it made my life worse. It took ages for me to find a new home for the puppy, as no one would believe me that he was a lovely dog. Both the puppy and his new family are really happy. His new owner loved his affection and kisses, so they were perfect for each other. I need a dog that comes up for a quick pat and then just lies down near me, not one that wants to sit on me all the time.

- You are responsible for your pet when it is healthy and when it is sick. While vet bills can be expensive, your pet deserves the best care you can give them. Tragically, many people abandon their pets to die, because they cannot afford the bill for treating them. If money is an issue, consider taking out pet insurance. This usually involves paying a small fee monthly or annually and is well worth doing. You also need to plan for the end of your pet's life. If they are very unwell and there is no cure, what will you do? Vets will offer to euthanise animals that are suffering so that they do not continue to suffer. You will need to think about what is best for the animal, and how you will manage this emotionally.

Despite all the expenses and responsibilities, owning a pet can be incredibly valuable and worthwhile. Pets can give you unconditional love and companionship that is hard to find anywhere else.

Therapy and assistance pets – how to access these services

There are different organisations offering therapy or assistance animals (mostly dogs) for people with autism and/or mental illness. There is a list of some of these organisations in the main English-speaking countries in the resources section of this book. It is not an exhaustive list, however, and you may benefit from doing some additional research on what is available in your local area.

12

MINDFULNESS

Although many people may associate mindfulness with Buddhism, it is essentially a way of interpreting and reacting to experiences, and can be accessed by anyone. Mindfulness is literally about being mindful – being aware of and paying attention to the here and now. It can be non-religious or faith-based, and can be practised as part of meditation and/or in everyday life and during everyday activities. If you already practice meditation, this means that mindfulness can be carried out during meditation and during your meditation break. If you do not want to meditate or you do not like meditating, you can still use mindfulness.

A part of some cultures for thousands of years, the concept of mindfulness became accepted in psychology during the 1980s following the development of mindfulness-based stress reduction (MBSR) (Kabat-Zinn 1980). Dr Kabat-Zinn defined mindfulness as 'the awareness that emerges through paying attention on purpose, in the present moment, and non-judgmentally to the unfolding of experience moment by moment' (Kabat-Zinn 2003, p. 145). These experiences include thoughts and feelings. As you pay attention to what is happing and how you are thinking and/or feeling about it, when practising mindfulness you just accept everything as temporary mental phenomena that do not need to be analysed. 'When we are inattentive, the mind is most vulnerable to slipping into the habitual mode of rumination and worry. This mindset is central to depression and anxiety' (Hassed 2011). It is a proven way of avoiding dwelling on the past or worrying about the future, but staying focused on dealing with what is happening in the here and now. You are not aiming to change your thoughts and feelings as you would if you were engaged in CBT. This concept of mindfulness uses the concept of acceptance, which is fundamental in ACT (Hayes 2004).

Mindfulness approaches have also been found to:

- help remediate suicidal depression (see, e.g. Hargus *et al.* 2010)

- help people to live well with mood disorders (see, e.g. Raes *et al.* 2009)

- be an effective way to a self-manage and significantly reduce aggressive behaviours in people with and without schizophrenia and/or people with autism (Singh *et al.* 2011)

- reduce anxiety, depression and rumination, intrusive thoughts in people with autism and/or mental health issues (Hassed 2011; Spek, van Ham and Nyklicek 2013; Segal, Williams and Teasdale 2002)

- increase compassion, empathy and sleep quality (Hassed 2011).

Engaging in mindfulness is about being actively engaged in your life, being aware of what is happening and how you are responding to it. When you are not focused on what is happing or what you are thinking and/or how you are feeling, you can easily become preoccupied with intrusive or ruminating thoughts.

LYNNE'S STORY: How mindfulness helps

Like most Aspies, I don't sleep well, and I can respond over-emotionally to events. For the last few years, I have been practising mindfulness, although I don't do this all the time, I try to do it whenever something really stressful happens, like when a car nearly crashed into my car in the car park. Usually, I would get really angry and overwhelmed, which often leads to a meltdown. This time, I did my breathing in and out to remind me to be mindful, to focus on what was happening and what I was thinking. When I did this, I realised I had been frightened that they would crash into me when I heard the brakes and angry that I hadn't seen them. I thought I was angry with them, but when I focused on my thoughts I could see I was just cross with myself. I accepted that I was angry and scared and that feeling like this would end, that bad things sometimes happen and it's okay. After a minute I was able to drive home reasonably calm. I didn't obsess about what had happened, which I used to do all the time, it would go round and round my head like a broken record. I managed to go to sleep without any more problems than usual too. I wasn't awake till 3 in the morning thinking about what could have been.

Lynne mentioned her breathing in and out, which is central to many versions of mindfulness, although not all. Essentially, to be mindful you have to first manage to distract yourself from your own inattentiveness in order to focus. Here are some exercises to try:

- Breathe in through your nose, focusing on how the breath feels on the nostrils as it enters your body. Breathe out through your nose, again focusing on the breath. Do not analyse; just do.

- Breathe in through your nose, focusing on your lungs and feeling them expand as they fill with air. Breathe out through your mouth, feeling your lungs deflate. Again, do not analyse; just do.

- Stay where you are and do a body check – think about how each part of your body is: is it hot, cold, warm, tingly, tired, are the muscles taut or relaxed, are body parts tense, etc.? Check what sounds you can hear, focusing only on what you can hear. This can be hard for people with autism as they usually hear, see, feel, etc. all at the same time. This exercise trains you to focus on one sensory aspect at a time. Do this until you have checked in with all body parts and all of your senses.

- Standing up with bare feet, feel how your feet are connected to the ground. Feel the sensations of temperature, texture and the sense of touch. Just feel; don't respond.

Once you have tried one or more of these exercises for a short period of time, pick one that you find calming or that helps you connect with yourself more. Then use this technique to interrupt yourself so that you can practise mindfulness. Because mindfulness is about accepting and being non-judgemental, don't worry about doing it wrong. When you start using mindfulness, it is important to just keep trying every now and then until you feel comfortable with it and it feels useful to you. Useful mindfulness will help you to reduce anxiety, stress, anger, frustration, meltdowns etc.

There are a wide variety of mindfulness techniques and rationales, and you can try one or lots of them. You may choose to practise one type exclusively, or to use a number of them over a period of time. For some people, different types of mindfulness work in different circumstances. Essentially, there are mindfulness practices that are inwardly focused and those that are outwardly focused, and then there are those that are a combination of the two. However, for all types, the central premise is the same – being present and aware without judging yourself or others/things.

> Mindfulness is simply the knack of noticing without comment whatever is happening in your present experience. It involves just seeing from moment to moment what the mind is up to; the endless succession of ideas and feelings and perceptions and body sensations and memories and fantasies and moods and judgments arising and passing away.
>
> (Claxton 1990, p. 111)

Mindfulness is very helpful for living well and decreasing stress, anxiety, ruminating thoughts, anger and aggression because it enables people to safely observe their world and themselves. It is safe because of the commitment to acceptance without judgement that is made when practising it. This creates time and space in which to process and to be, until the events and/or emotions have changed. This can be a powerfully positive and self-caring strategy that both centres a person to reality but also grounds someone to a less volatile or stressful way of being at the same time. In this act of observing with acceptance and without judging, it is possible to see what causes distress without having to stay distressed for long periods of time. Over time this technique can help people to understand who they are.

TYSON'S STORY: Mindfulness to help anxiety

I was always so anxious, though I didn't actually realise I was anxious. Even when my psychologist told me I had so much anxiety it was like a disorder, I didn't believe her. With mindfulness I have learned to actually feel my heart start beating really fast and to accept that I am anxious. Often I am just laying down reading when this happens, so it is not an event that is making me anxious, just the cumulation of the day catching up with me. I can just be aware of this now, and observe my heart beat until it slows down again. I don't beat myself up about it any more. It just is. Now that I think like this, I am not having this everyday anymore. Probably once or twice a week and it doesn't last so long. I now accept I am quite an anxious person, and I am more aware of all the things in my day that cause me lots of anxiety, so I can plan for these things, which really helps. One of the things I do that helps is keep change in my car for parking meters, as I realised worrying about parking was one of the things causing me lots of anxiety.

As this story demonstrates, mindfulness can help someone to acknowledge and accept, and thus slow down or stop automatic or habitual reactions to events, people, places or things. This, in turn, enables people to see things more clearly and to plan and implement more effective and positive strategies for use in daily like. Mindfulness also helps in developing a better emotional balance in life and build resilience. It is not about emptying your mind or getting cross with yourself when you are trying to be present and thoughts start rushing into your head. Instead it is about being aware of those thoughts and just letting them go.

Imagine, for example, that your mind is the sky, and when you are practising mindfulness you are looking at the sky and your thoughts are the clouds. Sometimes the sky will be cloudless, deep and expansive. At other times there will be fast moving clouds or huge black thunderclouds, passing through. If you are not being mindful, you might get caught up in the exact shape, size and texture of each of the clouds, and begin to worry about why they are there and what effect they are going to have. At these times, just watch the clouds as they go, acknowledging and accepting their presence.

Here are some examples of mindfulness techniques:

- *Breathing:* take notice of and focus on your breathing. When you are aware of thoughts drifting into your focus, return to focusing on your breathing and let go of the thought. You can do this anywhere – it is very useful on public transport or in public places if you can find somewhere to stand or sit for a few minutes.

- *Body focus:* take notice of and focus on an aspect of your body. This can be in relation to an activity or emotion. If in relation to an activity, for example, filling in a form, try to become aware of every detail of your body in relation to that task. Are you gripping the pen tightly? Are you pressing hard on the paper? Is your back tense? Is your breathing shallow? As you become aware of each detail, just accept that is how it is and move on to notice the next detail. You may choose to incorporate or only focus on emotions or feelings, and this could be in regards to the same activity or at an entirely different time. You might ask yourself, am I stressing? How do I know I am stressing? What signals am I getting from my body? How am I externalising this with my body?

- *Daily living:* if you are doing the washing up while being mindful, pay attention to and be aware of every detail within the task. You might notice that the water is slightly too hot for comfort on your hands, the washing up liquid is a greeny-yellow with a light scent of chemical and lemon, the drops of the washing up liquid fall into the water and move a particular way through the water, and so on. This sort of mindfulness in daily life will help you to really be in the present moment and to experience deeply and slowly.

When trying out these mindfulness techniques, start off with one of the breathing or body focus activities first. If, after a few seconds or so, your mind starts to wander and you think about other things, instead of saying or thinking *I need to focus*, take a few breaths in and out until you are focused on your breath, and then return to the mindfulness activity you had started. You could do this for a minute or two when you start out, and then maybe for longer as time goes by.

Some people with autism and/or mental health difficulties can spend five or so minutes several times a day, some several hours a day, being mindful, while some find it such a useful technique that they try to be mindful all the time.

For some people with autism, it can be very difficult to focus on their body, however. If you find it frustrating, just try a different form of mindfulness, such as noting down all the things that you can see, hear, feel, smell, etc.

Below is an example of a mindfulness cycle for a person who is using breathing as their mindfulness technique.

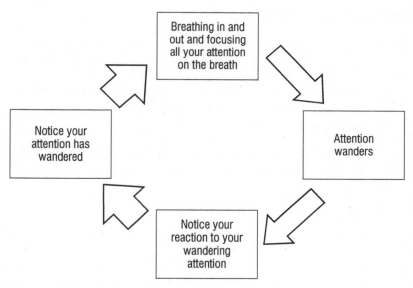

The mindfulness cycle

If you have experienced trauma in your life, mindfulness can help you to stay focused in the present, and to understand how you are reacting to things. This can help you to work out how you can experience less anger and more happiness as you identify things in your present that provoke these feelings. For some people who have experienced trauma, there may also be residual feelings of shame and/or self-hatred. Mindfulness can help end these feelings, enabling people to focus on and accept what is happening without judgement. Once it becomes habitual to accept and not judge things in the present, it is harder to judge yourself and not accept yourself for who you are. During mindfulness activities you may become aware that you are being critical towards yourself, which you may not have actively been aware of before. Once you have awareness, through acceptance of yourself, you can then learn to be kinder to yourself, and show yourself compassion.

Juliet Adams, founder of Mindfulnet.org and director of *A Head for Work*, has written an ABC of mindfulness that summarises what you should do when being mindful:

The ABC of mindfulness

- *A is for awareness:* becoming more aware of what you are thinking and doing, what's going on in your mind and body.

- *B is for 'just being' with your experience:* avoiding the tendency to respond on autopilot and feed problems by creating your own story.

- *C is for seeing things and responding more wisely:* by creating a gap between the experience and our reaction to it, we can make wiser choices.

13

PSYCHOLOGY AND PSYCHOTHERAPY

The goal of psychological treatment is primarily to address the issues related to a person's thinking (including reliving or being affected by past trauma), attitudes and approach to life. 'Thinking' or psychological elements impacting on mental illness include things such as emotional, physical or sexual abuse, bullying, isolation, social anxiety, obsessive thoughts, a negative or pessimistic focus or difficulties relating to others. A primary concern of psychotherapy is the way people cope with situations and solve problems. These 'thinking'-type issues can combine with chemical and environmental issues to form part of a mental illness process, or they may exist in isolation. 'Psychotherapy is a sanctuary; it is a battleground; it is a place I have been psychotic, neurotic, elated, confused, and despairing beyond belief' (Redfield Jamison, nd). The different elements of mental health issues often interact dynamically, so that psychotherapy, addressing environmental issues or medication alone, may be less effective than a combination of strategies. Which combination is very much an individual thing, and finding the most effective treatment is a bit like buying the perfect pair of shoes – you need to get not only the right size, but also the correct level of comfort for walking in the heat and the cold, with the shoes made out of a material that does not bother you in any way.

Treatment from a psychologist or psychotherapist usually involves 'talk therapy' where clients discuss psychological issues and aim to lessen their negative influence as well as improve their coping strategies. For people with a diagnosed mental illness, psychology is often combined with medication therapy to address a number of elements of the illness. Psychology or psychotherapy can help people with a variety of mental illness and personal issues. Some people who do not have a diagnosed mental illness also make use of psychotherapy to improve their thinking and approach to problems, and to build a more positive and fulfilled life. Some therapists specialise in helping people with autism with issues they may have while some have a very limited knowledge and understanding of autism. While a lack of knowledge in itself is not a barrier to being a good therapist, a lack of acceptance of and understanding the experiences of an individual with autism as they present during therapy should be an indicator that the therapist may not be the right person to help.

A number of types of clinician can practice psychotherapy, including psychologists, psychiatrists, counsellors and social workers. It is important to ensure that the therapist is reputable and legitimate. If in doubt, research the therapist and the field of psychotherapy in which they are practising. Be wary of anything that promises miraculous results or a cure or that seems a bit 'wrong'. If in doubt, most countries have a board or registrations agency for therapists administered through the relevant government body, and if you have doubts about the therapist, you can check to see if they are registered.

It is important to be on your guard when searching for a psychotherapist as there are some unethical people who may pretend that they are qualified or who may see clients as a money-making opportunity and are therefore not aiming to help as this would end the client–therapist relationship (and their source of money). If you are concerned by your therapist's behaviour, either simply cease the therapy or discuss your concerns with a trusted friend or family member, and see what course of action they suggest.

In many countries it is possible to receive a number of free or government-subsidised sessions with a psychologist. For example, in Australia, if you have a mental health plan written with your GP, you can access six free or subsidised psychologist sessions each year.

LYNNE'S STORY: Therapy, not for everyone

I was diagnosed with Asperger's in middle age, but when I was younger I had an eating disorder, and my GP recommended therapy. I didn't have much money and being gay wanted to find a therapist who was non-judgemental and didn't go on about how being gay must have caused my eating disorder, so I randomly chose a therapist in a gay directory. The first one told me I needed to stop eating chocolate, because it was making me store fat. As chocolate was pretty much all I ate other than bread and milk, I figured this was stupid at the least, and indicated a complete lack of counselling skills. I then made sure the next person I picked was actually registered and qualified. They did this therapy where you sit in a chair and talk to your imaginary self or imaginary whoever is causing the issue while looking at an empty chair opposite. Then you swap seats and reply as that person. In my logical way of thinking it was simply idiotic! The therapist said that she could see the style of therapy wasn't helping and that it was important not to intellectualise everything in therapy.

I gave up at that point and just decided to meditate and practice mindfulness, which have really helped me.

Psychotherapy models

Clinicians use a variety of psychological therapy 'models' to assist their clients. It is important to note that all of the main psychotherapy models are valid, although some work better for some people than others, and some are more effective at treating certain problems.

One of the most important elements of psychotherapy is to have a good therapeutic relationship or alliance. A therapeutic alliance refers to the relationship between a professional (e.g. psychologist, counsellor, social worker or psychiatrist) and their client. There is evidence that a strong therapeutic alliance results in better outcomes in therapy. This is demonstrated by the client feeling comfortable with their therapist, having a perception of a common purpose with the therapist, and feeling a sense of trust in the therapist and the therapy process.

There are three basic elements to a good therapeutic alliance:

- the relationship or bond between the therapist and client

- consensus between the therapist and client regarding the techniques/methods employed in the therapy

- consensus between the therapist and client regarding the goals of the therapy.

There should also be the following in a positive and productive therapeutic alliance:

- flexible relationship that allows the client to discuss issues that are important to them

- respectful relationship

- warm, friendly and affirming relationship

- open and honest relationship

- trustworthy relationship (see Ackerman and Hilsenroth 2001).

The nature of the therapeutic alliance may be even more important than the psychotherapy model being used. An unproductive, negative or inflexible therapeutic relationship, even one that uses a therapy model that is best suited to the client's needs, may be considerably less useful than a positive, trusting and productive therapeutic relationship using a therapy model that might seem to be ill suited to the client. It is vital to find a good, trustworthy, respectable therapist.

The therapeutic alliance is particularly important for people with autism. They may have issues trusting others and have more difficulty than neurotypical people in knowing who is and isn't trustworthy. They may also share either considerably more information about themselves than most non-autistic people, or considerably less. Having a therapist who understands the particular needs of not only autistic people generally, but also the autistic individual they are working with, can be seen as essential to a good therapeutic alliance for autistic people.

For those who struggle to communicate using spoken language, this does not mean that they cannot access psychotherapy. A good therapist will be willing to work effectively, and this may include the use of 'homework', where the client writes down all the things they think of after an appointment that they did not discuss in the session, and this written information will then form the basis of the next session.

Cognitive behaviour therapy (CBT)

CBT is based on the idea that how we think, how we feel, and how we act affect each other. CBT uses a variety of techniques to help people become more aware of how they think, so that they can change their thinking patterns and style, and from that, their behaviour. Some forms include keeping a diary in order to record feelings and behaviours, or making a 'happy box' filled with items that have pleasant associations. It is used to address a variety of psychological issues, and is considered particularly helpful in helping people with depression or anxiety. CBT essentially involves reframing negative thoughts and changing thinking patterns to be more positive.

The underlying concept behind CBT is that our thoughts and feelings play a fundamental role in our behaviour. For example, someone who spends a lot of time thinking about health issues and disease will probably worry about their own health. The goal of CBT is to enable people to take control of how they interpret and deal with things in their environment.

It is often a short-term treatment option. There is a form of CBT called mindfulness-integrated CBT that integrates mindfulness principles into CBT practice. People who find mindfulness beneficial may gain some value for mindfulness-integrated CBT. Robertson (2015) suggests that mindfulness-integrated CBT is useful to change a number of negative thinking patterns common in the autism spectrum, such as:

- magnification and minimisation – see all the negatives, overlook the positive

- catastrophising – straight to the worst possible scenario

- emotional reasoning – 'I'm so overwhelmed that there is nothing I can do' –> more problems

- 'should' statements – rigid rules set by yourself or others

- labelling and mislabelling – defining people by overgeneralisations

- self-blame – for situations over which you have no control or blaming others for your feelings.

For further information on mindfulness, refer to Chapter 12 earlier in this book.

CBT can be helpful for individuals on the autism spectrum. Some find it very helpful in alleviating their anxiety or depression symptoms. According to the UK-based Research Autism website, describing the value of CBT interventions for those on the spectrum:

> There are several multi-component CBT programmes which use a variety of techniques and which have been adapted specifically for use with people on the autism spectrum. There are also numerous other autism interventions which are based on, or which incorporate, the principles of CBT (such as social skills groups and social stories).
>
> (Research Autism no date)

It should be noted that some autistic people report that CBT is unhelpful for them, and so it is not a 'one size fits all' approach to therapy, although others find its practical and action-based nature helpful.

Dialectical behaviour therapy (DBT)

DBT was initially developed for the treatment of borderline personality disorder, particularly for people who engage in self-harm and/or suicidal actions, and who have ongoing issues with suicidal thoughts. DBT is now applied to a range of other psychological disorders and problems, including eating disorders and major depression. It combines approaches from CBT with techniques such as mindfulness and acceptance. It usually involves therapists teaching a range of 'skills' – often in groups in a classroom-type setting – and starts from the premise that people are coping as well as they can with the set of skills they already possess. It aims to equip people with skills they may be lacking in. DBT techniques may assist in crisis situations such as meltdowns or when someone is experiencing suicidal ideation.

DBT is divided into four sets of skills:

- *Mindfulness skills:* these have to do with self-awareness, and are seen as the most important skill set in DBT. Mindfulness forms the foundation for all the other skill modules.

- *Interpersonal effectiveness skills:* these assist people to become more skilful during interactions with others, particularly in interactions that may result in conflict. The skills in this module can be valuable for people on the autism spectrum.

- *Emotional regulation skills:* these enable people to better understand and manage intense emotions. Topics in this module include:

  » function of emotions

  » relationship between an interpretation of an event and the subsequent emotion

  » bodily responses to emotional states.

- *Distress tolerance skills:* these simply refer to the ability to manage a crisis. They are based on the concepts of mindfulness and acceptance (Hoermann, Zupanick and Dombeck 2013).

DBT is based on the same general principles as CBT, but is applied differently. While in CBT the focus is on trying to manage responses to the external environment, in DBT the focus is on the individual and how they can learn to accept and understand themselves. While it was designed for people with borderline personality disorder, some people on the autism spectrum may find DBT helpful, particularly the mindfulness and acceptance elements of the therapy, and the interpersonal effectiveness skills. And some people on the spectrum find the way the therapy is delivered – as skills in a classroom-type setting – is more accessible than one-on-one talk therapy with a therapist (Linehan 1993). Further information on DBT and the skills are available in the Resources section at the end of this book.

Acceptance and commitment therapy (ACT)

ACT (pronounced as the word 'act') works from the premise of 'accept what is out of your personal control, and commit to action that improves and enriches your life.' ACT differs from CBT through not working to reframe negative thoughts but by accepting that difficult issues exist in life and learning skills to deal with painful and negative thoughts effectively and so they have less impact. Similarly to DBT, ACT focuses on mindfulness and acceptance.[1]

Author of *The Happiness Trap* and proponent of ACT, Russ Harris, provides information on the aim of ACT:

> The goal of ACT is to create a rich and meaningful life, while accepting the pain that inevitably goes with it. 'ACT' is a good abbreviation, because this therapy is about taking effective action guided by our deepest values and in which we are fully present and engaged. It is only through mindful action that we can create a meaningful life. Of course, as we attempt to create such a life, we will encounter all sorts of barriers, in the form of unpleasant and unwanted 'private experiences' (thoughts, images, feelings, sensations, urges, and memories). ACT teaches mindfulness skills as an effective way to handle these private experiences.
>
> (Harris 2006, p.2)

Some people on the autism spectrum find ACT helpful. It can help address anxiety and promote a more positive view of the world and self-acceptance. The emphasis of mindfulness, and putting mindfulness into practice in the client's life, can be beneficial to people on the spectrum.

Solution-focused therapy

Solution focused therapy focuses on what a client wants to achieve through therapy, rather than on the problem that made them seek help. It is focused on the present and future rather than the past, and works on building solutions rather than solving problems. It aims to promote positive change rather than dwelling on past problems.

---

1   Acceptance in the context of psychotherapy does not mean thinking that negative events are okay or not being angry about people wronging you. Many people find it hard to be comfortable with acceptance in psychotherapy, because that is what they think it means. However, acceptance in the context of psychotherapy actually means understanding that an event has happened and that you cannot go back in time and change it. Practising acceptance is a way to avoid regrets and anger at things you can't change. The concept of acceptance is inexorably linked to mindfulness practice.

In solution-focused therapy, people focus on what they do well, and then set goals and work out how to achieve them. The therapist's role is to assist the client in producing a narrative of coping and success rather than one of failure or regrets.

Solution-focused therapy revolves around three questions:

1. What are your best hopes from this therapy?

2. What would your day-to-day life look like if these hopes were realised?

3. What are you already doing, and what have you done in the past, that may contribute to these goals being realised?

It starts from the premise that people are already equipped with the skills to create change in their lives, although they may need help in identifying and applying those skills. Similarly, solution-focused therapy recognises that people already have some understanding of what change is needed in their lives. The therapist will help the client to identify a time in their life when the current problem was either less harmful or more manageable, and determine what was different then, or what solutions may have been available. Solution-focused therapy is considered a 'brief' form of therapy where the therapist and client can effect a change relatively quickly (ICP no date). People on the autism spectrum who do not want to spend hours agonising over issues may prefer this. Its positive nature may be beneficial to those on the spectrum as they tend to focus on the negative, making more traditional therapies that delve into past experiences quite unhelpful.

However, for some people on the autism spectrum, solution-focused therapy can seem pointless, as the idea that they already have the skills but can't identify them can be quite challenging. They may find this type of therapy difficult to engage in.

Solution-focused therapy is based on the work of twentieth-century psychiatrist Milton Erickson, who also pioneered work on hypnotherapy and family therapy. Erickson believed that a therapist's duty was to first ease or remove the psychological distress. He said that if you could 'lift the handle a lot could be done with the pot' – in other words, he thought that a small change could influence effects that impact on other areas – for example, addressing a phobia can lead to increased confidence in other areas.

Each person is a unique individual. Hence, psychotherapy should be formulated to meet the uniqueness of the individual's needs, rather than tailoring the person to fit...a hypothetical theory of human behaviour.[2]

Creative expressive therapies

Creative expressive therapies involve the use of art, music, dance/movement, drama or poetry/creative writing in the context of psychotherapy. They differ from more traditional psychotherapy and counselling as they have several specific characteristics not always found in 'talk' therapies, including self-expression, active participation, imagination and mind–body connections (Malchiodi 2005). Proponents of these therapies suggest that they can help people to resolve issues and manage their behaviours and feelings, reduce stress and improve self-awareness and self-esteem. Their aim is not to produce a beautiful painting or a moving poem, however; rather, the creativity is a means to tap into the underlying message contained within the creative output to foster healing and understanding.

Creative arts (including visual art, writing, music, drama and dance) are often a major element of the lives of autistic children and adults. Indeed, many people on the spectrum find their career in creative endeavour. So many people on the autism spectrum find creative expressive therapies beneficial and accessible.

It should be noted, however, that creative expressive therapies may be seen as being more vague in their focus and less rigorous in terms of the evidence base for their effectiveness, but despite these considerations, they can be helpful for some.

There are a number of other therapies that people on the autism spectrum may find helpful. These include psychoanalysis, hypnotherapy and family therapy. It is important to understand that different people are individuals, and that a therapy that works for one person may not be helpful to another.

---

2   See http://erickson-foundation.org/biography/, accessed on 24 February 2015.

Peer mentoring advice

- You may need to do some research and shop around to find the right therapy model and therapist for you. For some people, talk therapy, psychotherapy and counselling are not helpful at all, while for others, they are life-changing. It is important to find the option that works for you. Even if a close friend or family member has a positive experience using a particular therapy or therapist, the same type of therapy or counsellor may be completely wrong for you.

- The therapeutic alliance or relationship is one of the most important elements of psychotherapy. Having a psychologist or therapist you do not feel respect for or who does not respect you, or who you find unhelpful, can be detrimental to your mental health. It may be a good idea to talk to friends or relatives who have seen a therapist and get recommendations from them (or advice of who not to see).

- A good place to start might be to see a therapist who specialises in helping people with autism. Some therapists who mainly see people with personal problems and mental illness may not be skilled in helping people with autism spectrum conditions.

- You do not need to keep seeing a therapist who you find unhelpful, even if they insist that you should. They are essentially being employed by you, so you have the right to stop seeing them if you choose.

- You may find it hard to talk about your feelings or experiences to someone you hardly know. Try to remind yourself that the therapist's job is to help people with their thinking problems and that they have heard many people talk about difficult things. Their profession is based on confidentiality and respect for people's privacy, so you shouldn't have to worry about them divulging your private thoughts to other people. If you are concerned about discussing your thoughts and feelings with a therapist, it might be a good first step to discuss your concerns with the therapist. The best results can be gained from psychotherapy when you are open and honest.

- You will probably need to pay to see a psychologist or therapist, depending on what the arrangements are in the country or district where you live. Some psychological treatment may be paid for through your health insurance, and in some places it is covered through the government's healthcare provisions. If you have difficulty paying, many therapists will come to an arrangement whereby you do not need to pay the full price, although do not assume that this will be the case the first time you visit the therapist, and make sure you ask about options if payment is an issue for you.

- A good therapist can mean the difference between experiencing severely troubling thinking and being able to get on with your life. If you choose to go down the psychotherapy path, take the effort to find a good therapist and engage in any activities they give you. If you put effort into changing your thinking patterns, and undertake the activities set by your psychologist, you may see improvement in your thinking sooner.

- There is quite a lot of emphasis on the need for psychotherapy in the mental health world. If you see a psychiatrist or mental health clinic they will probably recommend therapy. They may even have a specific therapy model or even a particular therapist in mind for you. It is important to have agency in any decision around therapy. You are allowed to decline a recommendation for a therapist from your doctor. You are the person who will be undertaking – and paying for – the therapy, so you should have the final say in who you see.

- Some people do not find any kind of psychotherapy helpful – therapy is not for everyone. If therapy makes your life – and mental health – worse rather than better, it is okay to discontinue it. There is not a one-size-fits-all therapy option. It is down to individual preference, so make sure you do what works for you. It can be a bit of a journey to work out which model and therapist – if any – is best for you, but when you find them, you can gain a lot of benefit.

JENNY'S STORY: Finding what works

I have Asperger's syndrome, and I've also had mental health issues for a very long time – including depression and post-traumatic stress-type problems. From as early on as I can remember I have been seeing therapists. My parents were advised that psychotherapy would help me be less quirky and troubled at school. Unfortunately, I went to school in the 1970s and 1980s when Asperger's syndrome was not known of, so these sessions didn't do much other than waste my parents' hard-earned cash!

I got a misdiagnosis of borderline personality disorder when I was in my early twenties. I had to attend a group programme doing DBT. Oddly enough, I found DBT quite helpful. The mindfulness element helped with my anxiety and obsessive worrying thoughts and the school-type setting made me feel successful and motivated. I always did well academically at school so I sort of viewed the DBT skills training as academic work and tried to excel at that too. After doing the DBT course, my mental health issues died down for a few years but then in 2009, I got really sick. I tried all sorts of different therapy models, but nothing really worked. This went on for years. I thought I was wasting the therapists' and my time.

In the end I found a psychologist who did CBT. A friend recommended her, and I was fairly certain she wouldn't be any good for me. I didn't really like the CBT principles. I thought it was better to learn to live with my issues and make the most out of life rather than simply reframing my thinking. But I developed an amazing rapport with my therapist, and that was what helped get me through the rough patch. I stopped seeing the sessions as 'CBT' and instead viewed them as 'Cathy and me time'. I got so much out of my time with Cathy. She helped me to understand triggers for difficult emotions and how to manage anxiety. While she wasn't a friend as such, we had an amazing relationship. I stopped seeing her a few years ago, and I'm going really well. I imagine that I carry a little piece of Cathy with me wherever I go. That helps a lot.

14

MEDICATION

Medications are at times useful tools for treating some of the distressing maladaptive/disruptive behaviours and co-morbidities associated with autistic spectrum disorders. Medications used to treat psychiatric conditions in 'neurotypical' people can also be effective in treating similar conditions in autistic people. This chapter presents information that clinicians should consider when prescribing medications to autistic people, as well as some that people on the autism spectrum can take into consideration when undergoing treatment with medication for mental illness.

The different medications used to treat mental health conditions include anti-depressants, anti-psychotics, anti-anxiolytics (anti-anxiety), mood stabilisers and neurostimulants. Psychiatrists prescribe medications based on the diagnosis and their observations of a person – there is no one definitive treatment that 'cures' mental illness symptoms. Some medications will be highly effective for one person and ineffectual for another with the same condition or symptoms. Finding the medication that works is often something of a process of trial and error, and patients find themselves trying a variety of different drugs before they start to feel better. Many people gain a lot of benefit from psychiatric medications, but some people's condition is 'treatment-resistant' and they do not respond to medications, 'Drugs are not always necessary, but belief in recovery always is' (Cordero Jnr., nd).

There are a lot of psychiatric medications available now and more are being released all the time. They have changed the lives of literally millions of people worldwide. They are a relatively recent phenomenon – with the first anti-psychotic drugs coming out in the mid-twentieth century – and have enabled people to live productive and fulfilled lives, free of the worst manifestations of mental illness, who would otherwise have been unable to do so.

As with the commencement of any new medication, the prescriber should discuss the risks (including possible side-effects, interactions, potential for neuroadaption and subsequent potential for tolerance, etc.) versus the benefits – some people find it helpful to do some reading/research themselves into the pros and cons of medications (but just remember that drug companies tend to list many side-effects that are incredibly rare and even idiosyncratic, i.e. specific to individuals).

It is also advisable, and in my opinion essential, to review each and every medication at regular intervals to ensure the benefits continue to outweigh the risks, especially as people get older – a drug and dose may have been appropriate at age 65, but at 85 the dose (and even the actual drug) may no longer be effective.

People with autism may respond differently to medication from neurotypical people, in that sometimes they require higher than recommended doses, while others may 'respond' and/or develop intolerable side effects to apparently low 'sub-therapeutic' doses. Despite diagnostic labelling and medical interventions, it is essential to remember that like much of medicine, psychiatry is more of an art than a science. Therefore, a 'one size fits all' paradigm in diagnosing and treating psychopathologies is incomplete at best. Prior to the introduction of psychotrophic medications, some individuals were confined for extended periods (some even for their entire lives) to institutions.

Psychotropic medications can be viewed as useful 'tools', particularly when used in conjunction with other psychological treatment strategies such as 'talk therapies' (e.g. CBT). However, generally speaking, mental illnesses are considered incurable (but not untreatable), and therefore most management strategies target the 'illness-related symptoms' rather than the actual cause (which tends to be complex and multifactorial). Hence psychopathologies are not diseases that can be 'healed or cured' but complex illnesses that can be present with or without an underlying disease process. A mental illness is diagnosed according to a collection of identified symptoms that in some way are causing impairment for the individual, but unlike 'disease' that can potentially be healed, mental illness – due to its complexity – invariably requires more time in a process known as recovery. Treatment strategies (especially pharmacotherapies) for symptoms associated with mental illness generally only temporarily alleviate rather than permanently extinguish distressing emotions, such as anxiety associated with depression and/or psychosis.

Deciding to take medication – or not

Most of the time, people with mental illness, including those on the autism spectrum, have the right to decline treatment with medication and to opt for psychotherapy or other interventions instead. Clinicians should provide autistic people with information on non-medication therapies such as mindfulness or CBT as well as information about medication that may help to alleviate their mental illness symptoms. The choice as to whether to use medication should be made by the person using the therapy, and, should they require, be made in consultation with their family, carers, partner or children.

Some people choose to take medication at the same time as undertaking other therapies, which can be undertaken individually, in groups, or with a spouse or partner, if wanted.

Academic and clinician Dr Luke Tsai (2007) formulated a series of questions for clinicians and their autistic patients to consider when making a decision about whether or not to take psychiatric medication:

1. What medications are typically used to treat the disorder in question?

2. How do the medications work in the human body?

3. How should the medication be taken?

4. How can you tell if the medication is working?

5. What should the individuals do (or their carers do) if there are side effects?

6. How long will it take for the medication to work?

7. Can the medication be used with other medications?

8. How frequently should the clinician see the individual?

9.   How long will the individual need to take the medication?

A psychiatrist prescribing medication to a person with autism needs to have a clear and thorough understanding of that person's needs, and how their autism and their mental illness impact on them. This means that people with autism need to be open about their autism when seeking support for their mental illness. It is crucial that an open and respectful relationship between the psychiatrist and autistic client is developed and maintained in order to avoid either party making incorrect assumptions around things such as medication, symptoms or diagnostic 'labels'. A greater understanding among psychiatrists of autism and how it interacts and influences mental illness processes can only be a good thing, as misunderstandings or ignorance of autism-related issues may lead to counterproductive and damaging treatment plans, including around medication.

TERRI'S STORY: Decisions around medication

I have a diagnosis of autism spectrum condition and post-traumatic stress disorder. I've never been on medication for autism or any psychological symptoms from co-morbid conditions. A few years ago, I would have been very against this idea. I have problems with emotional regulation and don't always notice things like anxiety and depression symptoms until they are fairly advanced. I was scared that medication would mask my emotions and make them even harder to recognise before they were beyond my control. Nowadays I would probably be a bit more open to the idea, if there was good reason to justify it, but I would want to have a treating doctor who made sure I was well informed about it all and was willing to listen to and talk through my concerns.

Medication for psychiatric conditions is intended to address a specific mental health-related problem that the patient is experiencing. For example, a person with bipolar disorder might be prescribed a mood stabiliser. However, some of the medications also provide relief from other problems that people on the autism spectrum might experience, sort of an unintended consequence of treatment. For example, a drug commonly used to treat psychosis, Quetiapine, has an additional benefit for many people who take it in that it can significantly reduce their anxiety. People with autism also sometimes have a reaction where the medication causes a different effect to what it is intended to (e.g. they may take an anti-depressant, and it makes them manic).

People on the autistic spectrum have at times unpredictable reactions to psychotropic medications, which can mean that some on the spectrum require much lower doses compared to the general population. Conversely, some individuals on the autistic spectrum require larger than typical doses. It is incredibly difficult to predict the reaction someone will have to a medication. Therefore medications are generally introduced at a low dose and slowly titrated (gradually increased over time) according to therapeutic outcome and side effect profile. Risperidone is the antipsychotic medication with the most evidence for people on the autism spectrum seeking to manage anger and outbursts that have been resulting in behaviours of concern. People on the autism spectrum may need very low doses of one medication in combination with more of another, with individual reactions needing careful monitoring and adjusting to find the optimal dosages.

Role of medication in treatment

Medication can treat or help alleviate the symptoms of a mental illness (e.g. such as depression) but does not really 'cure' the illness. Just as things such as social skills training or interventions to assist with sensory issues assist with managing but do not 'cure' autism, so psychiatric medications work to help reduce the symptoms and their impact, but they don't actually 'fix' the illness. Some people with a mental illness will need to continue to take psychiatric medication or undergo psychotherapy for a very long time, possibly for the rest of their life. The progression of a mental illness is different for each person, and it is difficult for clinicians – or anyone else – to predict what course an illness will take. Some people will have ongoing, serious issues for their entire life, while others will have a number of periods of illness interspersed with period of good mental health, and other people will need minimal treatment. It is different for each person.

Keeping a symptom diary may help to identify patterns of mental health and signal mental illness for people who have recurring episodes of mental illness over a long period of time. Many people with mental illness find that it helps to develop a varied set of skills to help them cope with the illness and its impact on their life. Medication is one part of this coping strategy for a lot of people, and can be combined with other strategies such as those outlined elsewhere in this book.

Contra-indications and side effects

Medications can interact adversely with other medications (known as contra-indications). It is very important that people taking psychiatric medication understand how their medication might interact with any other drugs they may need to take – either prescription drugs or over-the-counter medications. Potential contra-indications can occur with a wide variety of other medications, including cold and flu medications, painkillers and antibiotics, as well as hormone treatments (such as thyroxine or the birth control pill) and other herbal or natural remedies. People taking psychiatric medications should check with their doctor or pharmacist if they need to take any other drugs or remedies.

Medications used to treat mental illness can have side effects. These can range from being quite mild to being dangerous. Some side effects from medications used to treat mental illness symptoms include drowsiness, weight gain, dry mouth, muscle tremors or stiffness. Not all people on the autism spectrum are capable of recognising or communicating that they are experiencing side effects, so clinicians should closely monitor patients/clients on the autism spectrum when a new medication is introduced. Asking patients/clients to keep symptom diaries may help to identify side effects where these are explicitly explained.

JENNY'S STORY: Side effects of medication

When I was in my twenties, I was prescribed high doses of an anti-psychotic medication, Largactyl (Chlorpromazine). It was not particularly effective in helping my psychosis or depression. I took it for about five years. One day, my mum told me that my tongue flicked in and out of my mouth like a lizard. This sounded worrying, and I didn't know what might be causing it. I asked a bunch of people whether I did this with my tongue, and they all told me that I did. My psychiatrist sent me to some doctors who were movement disorder specialists. I'd never heard of a movement disorder before. They examined me and asked me questions and then told me I had a movement disorder called tardive dyskinesia, caused by the anti-psychotic medication I had been taking. Tardive dyskinesia is unusual. The doctors told me I had to stop taking the Largactyl and go onto a different medication. It actually turned out really well. My tongue stopped making its presence felt in embarrassing ways, and the new medication – Risperidone – was so effective that it changed my life. I enrolled in university later that year and have not looked back since. Medication is a pretty amazing thing, but I'm always aware that it can cause unwanted issues.

Medications each have different half-lives, which is the time taken for half of the medication to be eliminated from your body. A medication with a long half-life will take longer to have an effect than a short half-life medication, which means results won't be seen for longer. Additionally, effects can be modified by other medications and supplements that a person is taking, so it is important to be completely open with a doctor about what is being taken, including alcohol and other drugs, such as marijuana.

Peer mentoring advice

- Medication is but one weapon in the arsenal of measures to combat mental illness. It can be effective and can be combined with other measures such as psychotherapy, psychosocial rehabilitation and/or peer support. Your attitude towards life can be a powerful a therapy too.

- As medication is such a powerful thing and can have potentially negative consequences, carefully consider the decision to go onto medication. Discuss the pros and cons with your doctor, and make sure that they listen to any concerns you have. You can take a carer, partner, family member or friend along to the appointment as they may provide moral support and can objectively explain to you what the doctor is saying and help you get your point across if necessary. Make sure that the final decision about medication is your decision. If your doctor is persistent or doesn't seem to be listening to you, consider changing to a different doctor. Don't forget that the potential side effects listed for medications will not necessarily occur, and if they do, the side effects may not last long. Ensure you and the people around you understand which side effects require urgent action, if any.

- It can be hard adjusting psychologically to a life in which you need to take medication in order to stay mentally healthy. It may help to realise that many people have to take medications to stay physically healthy, and mental illness is only another form of ill health. Some people feel a sense of loss or grief around the fact that the life they had without a mental illness has changed and that they now need to access additional support – including medication – in order to feel okay. It is perfectly understandable to go through this kind of grieving process. You may feel angry, resentful, resigned or depressed about a new life that will possibly involve seeing mental health professionals and taking medication for a very long time. However, the course of an illness is never set in stone, and you might come to a point in the future where you can decrease or even cease taking medication, but it is important to talk with your doctor or psychiatrist about this, as many psychiatric drugs cannot be stopped suddenly. As you learn new strategies to minimise the impact of your mental illness on your life, this can be a good time to discuss decreasing medications. Try to keep an open mind about these things, and deal with life in the present moment and not worry about what might happen in the future.

- Try to be patient when you are starting on a new medication regime. You might have to try a few different drugs before you find the one that works. It can be a frustrating process but it's very beneficial when you get the right one for you. You might benefit from writing notes (a medication journal) about your experiences with the medication. When you start taking the medication, note down things like your mood (or the level of mental illness symptoms, if you can identify them), your energy level/fatigue and things such as the amount of food or number of items you eat during the day. Note down any strange physical sensations or experiences (such as a dry mouth, muscle tremors or sensitivity to the sun). You can refer to these notes and show them to your doctor to demonstrate whether the medication is having the desired effect and/or if there are any side effects you should be concerned about. Your doctor will be able to tell you how long it will take before there will be any noticeable effects from the medications being trialled.

- If you have difficulties being aware of your physical or mental state, make sure that the doctor prescribing the medication knows this. If you start taking medication and you have trouble being aware of your physical or mental state (e.g. you can't identify when you are depressed or how your body feels), enlist someone close to you to assist. Ask your doctor to write down a number of things to look out for (e.g. likely side effects or the expected impacts of the new medication on your mood or motivation), and give that to a parent, carer, partner or trusted friend. Your doctor, autism worker or psychologist can use the doctor's advice to make a list of questions, and then regularly ask you the questions, to ascertain what your mood and mental state are like and any physical issues you might be having, based on their understanding of your individual needs and feelings. And if you are aware of anything that seems unusual or odd about your mental state or physical condition, make sure you tell someone straight away – either the doctor, if you can, or your carer, parent, partner or friend who can then help you access assistance. Never worry about whether you are making a fuss over nothing. A 'false alarm' is much better than you not talking about something that could be detrimental to your health.

- Sometimes your doctor will recommend that you start taking a new medication or change from one to another. These transition times can trigger a relapse in symptoms or the onset of new side effects. Make sure that you regularly review your medication with your doctor, especially if you have recently changed from one to another, started a new medication or changed the dosage. Changing from one medication to another, reducing medication or stopping a medication needs to be done only under the direction of your doctor. Even under medical orders, these transitions can be very stressful and can sometimes result in an episode of acute illness. If you are changing any element of your medication regime, pay close attention to such things as your mood, your level of motivation, any unusual side effects or physical symptoms or any worsening of your mental illness. You can keep a medication journal (as outlined above) during the period of changeover and show it to your doctor. Report any worrying changes to your doctor. Never stop taking your medication suddenly or attempt to reduce it, even if you are feeling better. The effects of suddenly stopping some medications can be very unpleasant or even dangerous. If you want to reduce or stop taking your medication, discuss it with the doctor who prescribed it.

- It is also a good idea to familiarise yourself with the medication you are taking – what it is used for, why you are taking it, effects of different dosages and what side effects it commonly causes. Other information which you may want to know about your medication is whether it can be taken by pregnant and/or breastfeeding mothers (if you are pregnant or planning to become so) and if you need to avoid drinking alcohol while taking the medication. The doctor who prescribed the medication or the pharmacist should be able to give you information. Most pharmaceutical companies provide factsheets on the medication that include detailed information about the drug and its effects, and your pharmacist should be able to give you a factsheet on the medication you are prescribed.

- Never give another person your medication, nor sell or swap it, even if they have similar symptoms to you. The doctors who prescribe psychiatric medication are experts who have studied for many years and have a far deeper understanding of the medications and how they affect someone than an everyday person does. Your medication regime was developed for you by your doctor in order to help alleviate the individual mental health problem you experience. Even if someone asks you to give you their medication, always say no. You do not know what effect the medication will have on another person, and it could be dangerous for them. Also, if you give your medication to someone else, you are depriving yourself of it, and that could lead to a relapse of your symptoms. People who ask for your medication may be trying to exploit you or take advantage of you, and you have no obligation to do what they want. They are doing the wrong thing, so it is okay for you to decline their request and not give up your medication. It is also illegal to sell on many medications.

- Some pharmacies pack up medication for you for a small fee. This is especially helpful if you take a lot of different medications at different times in the day. As people with autism often have executive functioning issues, taking medication at the correct time every day can be very difficult to achieve. Having the medication packed by the pharmacist enables you to know when to take your medication, and you can check against the pack to see if you have already taken it (i.e. it is no longer in the pack) or whether you still need to take it. With a medication pack, all you need to remember to do is to look at the pack every day and make sure you take the medication from the right day. This is helpful, as some medications should be taken in the mornings, some with food, and others in the evening.

- If you are travelling overseas, there are a few things to take note of regarding your medication:

  » Make sure you get a letter from your doctor explaining what medication you take and the dosage. Slip a copy in your travel documents. This will ensure you don't have any issues going through customs.

  » Keep your medication in its original boxes with the sticker from the pharmacy listing your name and address. If your medication is in a weekly pack (Webster or blister pack), the information on the pack about the medication and who it is for should be enough information to satisfy customs officials.

  » Do not keep medication loose in your bag. Customs officers may think you are bringing the drugs into their country to sell them or to give to friends for recreational use. If you have the original box or pack with your name and the dosage of the medication you take written on it or a blister pack prepared by your pharmacist, customs officers will understand that the medication is for you and you need it for a medical condition.

  » If you are asked about your medication by customs officers at the airport, simply explain that you need it for a medical condition and that it was prescribed to you by your doctor. Show them the letter from your doctor.

  » You can also tell customs officers that you have an autism spectrum condition. Some people wear an alert bracelet that tells others they have autism. Try to stay calm and remind yourself that you have done nothing wrong.

  » Make sure you take enough medication to last for your entire trip. The pharmacy will dispense extra medication, if you explain that you are going away.

  » Pack the medication in your carry-on luggage, just in case your checked bags get lost in transit.

15

CRISIS MEASURES

Sometimes people with autism and mental health conditions experience a crisis. This is an acute onset of severe distress where the person is overwhelmed with negative emotions. For people with autism, meltdowns can indicate the onset of crisis, or they can happen without being followed by a crisis. A crisis is often triggered by an event. For example, somebody might be feeling very depressed but just about managing to cope when a colleague is rude to them. This one event, combined with an underlying level of mental health symptoms, may result in a crisis. A crisis can be an event with a sudden onset, particularly in response to a traumatic of triggering event. It can also be a more prolonged period of intense distress, for example, when somebody is experiencing a psychotic episode and is having overwhelming and frightening experiences of feeling outside of reality.

Not all people with mental health issues or autism will experience crises. It is different for each person who experiences it, and it is important to note that what for one person would be a manageable amount of distress for another will result in a crisis. Each person is different in terms of their triggers, their level of resilience and their response to events. People experiencing a crisis may have suicidal ideation or actions, may self-harm, become very angry, do or say things that may seem irrational or become very emotional. Often, an intervention is required for a person experiencing a crisis, either from the mental health crisis team, a hospital or a counselling service. For those experiencing a crisis, probably the most important thing to remember is that it will pass.

One way of addressing crises before they happen – including meltdowns – is to learn what triggers a crisis response and to try to avoid or mitigate it. For example, if you have post-traumatic stress issues that are triggered by a certain topic (such as sexual violence), try to avoid being in contact with your triggers or reminders of them (such as a television programme about police investigating sexual crimes), particularly when you are feeling more vulnerable than usual. Of course, you cannot avoid every potentially triggering experience, but you can deliberately not place yourself in a situation where you know you will be triggered. If you find yourself being triggered and it is possible to do so, remove yourself from the situation and do some activities that usually make you feel calmer, such as positive sensory experiences, meditation or deep breathing, talking to someone you value, or whatever works for you.

For those who are really unwell or struggling, they may find it hard to head off a crisis as they may find all sorts of interactions and events triggering, even just speaking to a person they dislike or receiving disappointing news. Sometimes things that other people would not even notice can trigger a crisis in a person on the autism spectrum if they are already struggling to manage on a day-to-day basis. Things that would usually provoke a meltdown in that particular person with autism, such as a strong sensory experience or a perception of discrimination, real or imagined, from a friend or acquaintance, may be so compounded by the existing struggling that a crisis ensues. A crisis is more than a meltdown, and it has even more of an impact in the short, medium and long term.

This chapter explores strategies to address the immediate issues arising from a crisis to strategies around insight and maintenance that will help people have less crises or lessen the impact of the ones that do occur.

Some things to do during a crisis include:

- if you can, tell someone you trust that you are having a crisis

- seek help from a mental health professional or emergency department

- practise distraction

- practise deep breathing and/or mindfulness

- practise self-soothing or positive sensory experiences/ stimming.

- Reassure yourself that the crisis will pass.

Some things to *avoid* doing in a crisis include:

- acting on suicidal or self-harm urges

- arguing with health professionals. Despite how it may seem, almost all of them will be trying to help you. If you can, remind yourself of this, and instead of arguing, clearly state what you need from them

- keeping 'secrets' about things that are important to your care (such as a recent break-up of a relationship, drug use or a disagreement at work)

- posting information about your feelings on social media. It might seem a good way to express how you feel, but some people can be quite judgemental about mental health-related symptoms and you may need to explain after the fact why and how you were feeling during the crisis. And once information is online it can be difficult to remove completely, and you may post something you regret at a later date if you are in a crisis.

Some principles of crisis interventions – from the perspective of mental health service staff to assist individuals experiencing a crisis – as described by Dr Jeffrey Mitchell, from the National Center for Crisis Management and the University of Maryland in the US, are:

- Brevity – a crisis generally lasts from minutes up to one hour in most cases.

- Innovation – crisis support services must be creative to manage new situations.

- Pragmatism – suggestions to address a crisis must be practical if they are to work.

- Immediacy – a state of crisis demands rapid intervention.

- Expectancy – the crisis intervener works to set up expectations of a reasonable and positive outcome.

A crisis plan

If you experience mental health crises or meltdowns, you may find it helpful to develop a crisis plan. This should ideally be developed in consultation with significant people in your life such as your partner, family or close friends, as well as with any mental health clinicians who are looking after you.

You could make a 'crisis card' to give to relevant people when you have a crisis. This might include the following:

- important phone numbers – who to call in the event of a crisis or an emergency, including who to call first and who to call if your first choice is not available

- the mental health professional who is looking after you (e.g. psychiatrist, therapist or psychologist)

- your GP

- a list of any medications you currently take, the prescribed dosage for each, and the times of day or night that they are to be taken

- a list of any medications or foods to which you are allergic

- any communication styles that will make you feel worse (shouting, physical touch, patronising etc.)

- any communication styles that help you to calm down and feel validated

- self-soothing activities that help you feel better (e.g. fidget toy, music, talking to pets etc.).

There are some drawbacks with a crisis card, as you may not remember you have it when you are experiencing a crisis or the information might be misinterpreted, but some people find it helpful. It can ensure that first responders make things better rather than escalating the issue.

Other similar tactics include advance agreements with mental health service providers (e.g. crisis team or hospital) that include the kind of information listed above, but instead of being written on a card, it is contained within their database, so when you call them they can access this information and have a better idea about how they might help you.

Clinicians – insight and hope

When people are experiencing a mental health crisis they may feel as if there is no hope for them, that they may never be able to live well or be happy. It is important for clinicians to express their hope that the person will indeed live well again in the future, that other people have been in the same place and have had improvements in their lives. When working with people with autism, this needs to be expressed very clearly and may need to be repeated during each consultation/conversation. This is because it can be much harder for people with autism to take information in, which is exacerbated by a mental health crisis.

The use of specific examples/stories can be helpful in these situations and can even be presented in a written/cartoon format for the person to read over as often as they would like to. People on the autistic spectrum are usually concrete in their thought processes, which can be harnessed by clinicians in clear treatment and safety plans.

Safety considerations

When experiencing a mental health crisis or a meltdown, autistic people may be at risk of self-harm or suicide. The overload of emotions and stimuli associated with a crisis is often overwhelming and impulsive, negative thoughts that would normally be dismissed might make sense. People in crisis often act irrationally and impulsively, and do things they later regret. People may feel an urgent need to act on the impulsive and destructive thoughts. Try to delay and put off acting on these thoughts, and remind yourself that they will pass. This is something that will probably get easier with practice. The emotional overload combined with impulsivity that occurs during a crisis or meltdown can be very dangerous. If you experience self-destructive urges during crises or meltdowns, it is extremely important to develop and apply strategies to help you cope with these things so that you don't act on something you will later regret.

While you are not in crisis, develop skills and strategies to help deal with impulsive negative thoughts. These will then form a core of skills and strategies that may improve your ability to refrain from acting on destructive thoughts during a crisis. You can do this by using mindfulness, practising distraction and self-soothing techniques, using DBT skills, resilience strategies, learning to seek appropriate help or a combination of these.

Distraction technique

Distraction is seen by some as the 'gold standard' in dealing with many psychiatric issues, and especially mental health crises. It is incredibly simple in principle, and involves doing something engaging or interesting and enjoyable to take the mind off the negative thought process someone is going through related to a number of mental health issues.

Some types of distractions that might help include:

- reading a book
- watching television
- going to the cinema
- learning about or taking up a passionate interest
- writing (e.g. poems, non-fiction or in a journal)
- talking to your partner or a family member or friend
- cooking something
- going to work
- playing computer games
- browsing the internet/social media
- playing with a pet.

Different distractions work for different people, so it pays to try out a few and see which is the most effective. Distraction works best when it is something that involves focusing most or all of a person's attention. Otherwise the negative thoughts or emotions find it easier to reassert themselves in the mind. Distraction is often a short-term 'fix' to be undertaken during a difficult time, and as such, it is a highly effective crisis measure. Sometimes, a few different distractions may need to be employed to get through a rough patch, but persevere, and it will almost certainly be of assistance during a crisis. You may need to remind yourself to use distraction at first, and you can do this by putting a sign or list somewhere around your house and/or places you spend a lot of time (e.g. in your desk drawer at work). As you get more practiced at distracting yourself over time, it will come to you naturally, without the need for prompting.

JENNY'S STORY: Distraction

I have had a mental illness diagnosis for over 20 years. I have learned a lot of strategies to deal with crises over that time. I was first introduced to the concept of distraction by the mental health crisis team when I was about 26. Every time I called they would say 'watch some TV or go for a walk. That will make you feel better.' I thought this was the most stupid piece of advice in the world and was a cop-out. I never actually did it, preferring to focus on my distress and negative emotions. I thought that the crisis team had no idea what they were talking about. I could have thought up their advice myself, and they were supposed to be professionals!

I had a few years' reprieve from serious mental health issues. The next time I became unwell, I was 35 and probably a bit more sensible and willing to listen to others' opinions if I thought they could help me. When I rang the crisis team and they advised me to go for a walk or watch television I tried it. And I was amazed to find that it did actually work. I started devising my own customised distractions and found that by far the most effective was going to work. Despite seeming a bit counter-intuitive – I mean, work is about being social and living up to others' expectations, all things which could be triggering – but for me, work was the ultimate distraction. I have a very strong work ethic, so that I will not allow myself to be miserable and unproductive at work. If I am having a period of illness or a crisis, being in the workplace is so beneficial, because I will not let my illness get in the way of my work. I focus completely on the task at hand and so I feel better. I'm not sure if work would be a good distraction for others, but it works really well for me.

Seeking help

When experiencing a crisis, seek help from another person or service. Human beings need connectedness and relationships with others in order to survive. 'No man (or woman) is an island.' Even introverts who are on the autism spectrum need human contact and support. Many of us know this in theory, but we can often find ourselves quite detached from the rest of the human race. We also tend to think that we should be able to fix our problems ourselves. This is especially true of mental health problems. We may not tell anyone what we are going through for fear of stigma or judgement, or because we are too proud to accept help, or simply because it does not occur to us that we need, or can receive, help from others. Sometimes people on the autism spectrum experience alexithymia, which means that they cannot connect with or are unaware of their emotions. They may not recognise that they are having a tough time until they are in a state of extreme crisis. Autistic people may push others away when they are struggling as well. They may isolate themselves and be unaware that accessing help may well help them to feel better. However, for those who are unwell, and especially when they are in crisis, it is important to seek help from the appropriate place. Accessing help can be hard, but it is often the best course of action, and help is usually available when needed.

People you can talk to when unwell or in a crisis include:

- your GP, psychologist, psychiatrist or autism support worker

- family members (parents, partner etc.)

- a counselling service (such as Lifeline in Australia and the US or the Samaritans in the UK)

- emergency department doctors and nurses (if your issue becomes severe or life-threatening)

- local mental health crisis team.

Sometimes, when people are in a crisis, they may feel an urgent need to speak to somebody to help them feel better. However, crises often occur outside business hours, so they may not be able to access their usual supports. In this instance they may need to call the mental health crisis team or a counselling service such as Lifeline. They might have to wait on hold for a while with these services, depending on how busy they are – their level of busyness depends on things such as the time of day, time of year (Christmas time and winter are often busy times for mental health and counselling services), and even events in the news that may trigger the symptoms of some people's illness, resulting in a high volume of calls to the service. It is very challenging to have to wait on hold when experiencing a crisis, so if people are really concerned for their safety, they should go to the emergency department of their local hospital. However, they may have to wait there as well, and many find the hospital environment very frightening and triggering. In these instances, they should remind themselves that the crisis team or a telephone counsellor will talk to them shortly.

If people have someone in their life they trust and can talk to about mental health issues, that relationship can be a useful crisis measure. If they live alone, being in a crisis while at home can be very frightening – if they have a trusted person whom they can go and stay with when they are in crisis, this can help them to get through it. When not in crisis, they should ask their trusted friend whether they are happy to be their 'crisis buddy' and help them out when they are having a difficult time. Most people find it easier to talk to a friend who knows them rather than a mental health worker they don't know, although sometimes the situation will require them to deal with mental health workers, crisis team staff or emergency services.

If speaking to the mental health crisis team, a counsellor or emergency services staff for the first time, people should make sure they tell them their current diagnoses (including autism or Asperger's), any medications they are taking and who their psychiatrist is (if they are seeing one). They may ask the person what or how they are feeling. For many people on the spectrum, this is a difficult question as they may not be able to pinpoint their feelings. If possible, the person should explain this to the counsellor and describe to them what things they are aware of, such as things they are thinking ('I'm thinking about hurting myself'), physical feelings ('My chest is tight. I feel like I want to run away'), and things they may have done during the crisis which are out of the ordinary ('I put my cat in the laundry room, because I'm scared to have him around').

It is a sign of strength, not weakness, to seek help for mental illness symptoms. Sometimes, it becomes essential to access help. In these instances, it is better if people are willing and able to accept help than if they are resistant to the idea. When it comes to mental health crises, the earlier a person seeks help, the better.

Building coping skills and insight

Building resilience and coping strategies can be one of the best ways to ensure crises occur less often and people are better able to deal with them when they do. (See Chapter 17 for strategies to build resilience.) Successfully getting through a crisis gets easier the more coping skills a person has. As time goes on, people can learn what their triggers are and what helps. They may even be able to distance themselves from the crisis as it happens and understand that it will not last forever.

One of the key methods for getting through a crisis is insight. Insight refers to the ability to view what is happening in the mind with a deal of objectivity. Having insight is like having the ability to metaphorically step outside of yourself and to see yourself as others see you (to an extent). To have insight means that you understand the reasons for your behaviour and can challenge things such as depressive thoughts, paranoia and delusions. For example, having insight might be accepting that you have a mental illness and that certain things (which you know about) can trigger you and aggravate your mental illness. It also helps people to understand and accept the need for treatment even when they are feeling well, as they know that stopping the medications and living well strategies can lead to relapses in their mental illness.

Insight is also an invaluable tool in dealing with crises as it allows people to more easily determine what triggers a crisis and to avoid it. And if someone does experience a crisis, if they have insight, they will be better able to see past the irrational and impulsive thoughts attached to the crisis and find a way to feel better. Insight allows people to understand that what is happening is actually a process of illness and is not objective reality, and that it will pass. Diminished insight or lack of insight can lead to people making inappropriate choices and increased risk of relapse, crisis and a poorer quality of life.

Insight is a highly valuable commodity in the journey to living a positive life and being mentally healthy. It allows people to understand why they might be having issues and not to be caught up in the overwhelming overload of a crisis. The first act of being insightful is to understand that the only person who can change your life is you. People who lack insight often blame others for their difficulties and struggles. They may believe that they have no power over mental health crises and that there is nothing they can do to help themselves get through the crisis and become more resilient. People with insight are more likely to understand that, even though certain circumstances may be outside their control, they are responsible for how they respond to those circumstances and take control of their life.

Insight is not something that can be manufactured. It usually comes through years of experiencing life and reflecting on the reasons why things have happened. However, if someone lacks insight, they can try to stimulate it by questioning what is going on when they are experiencing a crisis or other mental health symptoms.

Logic is also a useful commodity that can feed into the process of developing insight – and in this regard, people with autism may be at an advantage over others given that they tend to be logical.

Maintenance

A good way of looking at mental health is to view it in terms of maintenance. Dealing with a crisis is not usually a one-off occurrence. Crises may happen periodically, so the goal of maintenance is to improve health over a person's lifetime. While urgent and immediate crisis measures need to be implemented during a crisis, if people maintain their health and wellbeing, there may well be less need to employ crisis measures in the first place, as the incidence of crises may decrease or disappear altogether. Here is a metaphor about maintenance:

> If you own a car, you need to do a number of things to maintain it and keep it working well. You need to put fuel in it to make it

go of course, but you also need to change the oil and top up the water, have it serviced and get it repaired if anything goes wrong. Your mental health is a little like your car in this respect. You need to maintain your health and wellbeing. It's not a case of simply recovering from a crisis or an episode of illness and then living life as if nothing ever happened. Good mental health is not a given and, if you have a vulnerability to mental health issues – as many people on the autism spectrum do – you will probably need to engage in maintenance-type behaviour for the rest of your life.

Maintenance of mental health and wellbeing includes things such as taking medication as prescribed, seeing a psychiatrist, having counselling or seeing a psychologist if needed, surrounding yourself with supportive and caring people, avoiding excess alcohol and illicit drugs, keeping an eye on stress levels, practising being kind to yourself and avoiding doing anything that makes you too stressed. Insight into the best ways for you to live well is important in enabling you to live well. Maintenance of our health and wellbeing can become part of our daily routine – it doesn't need to be onerous.

16

SELF-ESTEEM AND SELF-CONFIDENCE

One of the most significant factors in improving your life and becoming mentally healthy is liking and respecting yourself. This can be quite a challenge for people with a diagnosis of autism and who experience mental health issues. People may have experienced bullying or abuse or people and society telling them continually that they are weird or disabled or incapable of living an ordinary life. People on the autism spectrum may have had years of invalidating and traumatic experiences, and as a result they can dislike or hate themselves. Additionally, mental illness itself can trick people into negative thinking and self-hatred. It is no mean feat to overcome these invalidating experiences and the overwhelming view that one is inferior or deserving of blame.

Self-esteem and self-confidence are extremely important to our sense of self, our psychological outlook and our health and wellbeing. 'Optimism is the faith that leads to achievement. Nothing can be done without hope and confidence.' (Keller, nd). Self-esteem is both a risk and protective factor in many domains of life. Social cognition is the descriptor used for the ideas about how people think about themselves and other people. It focuses on the steps people take and the conclusions they reach as they strive to make sense of themselves and other people and their social environment. In other words, how you see yourself is influenced by how you think others see you, and how you experience and interpret your environment. Having a positive view of oneself can contribute to academic achievement, productivity and performance at work and social interaction and relationships.

Self-esteem starts to develop from an early age. For people on the autism spectrum, negative social experiences such as bullying or victimisation as children or adolescents and messages from broader society devaluing the experience and ability of those with autism can contribute to a negative or poor sense of self-esteem. In psychological terms, a person's sense of self or 'I' can be negatively influenced by negative societal messages about them or a group that they are part of. These early messages and experiences can influence a person's sense of self-identity well into adulthood.

Events and experiences that help to us to form and establish our beliefs about ourselves often (although not always) start early in life. A person's experiences in childhood – in their family, at school and in their community – often have a strong influence on the way they view themselves.

Some early experiences that can impact negatively on self-esteem include:

- neglect or abuse

- failing to meet the standards of parents

- failing to be accepted by peers

- belonging to a social group or demographic that other people are prejudiced against

- parental/adult role models' indifference, lack of warmth, love or affection

- being ostracised, bullied or discriminated against, at home or at school.

Children and young people on the autism spectrum are at a higher risk of experiencing some of these factors than non-autistic children. As such, it follows that autistic people may be more at risk of experiencing low self-esteem as children that may flow into adulthood. In addition, opportunities to succeed may not be offered to children and adults on the autism spectrum due to a lack of awareness that people with autism can succeed in a whole range of areas, regardless of their verbal skills or perceived intelligence. This can lead to autistic people themselves assuming that they would not be able to succeed in their endeavours.

Poor self-esteem can impact significantly on a person's life and contribute to issues with appreciating oneself, which may, in turn, lead to self-defeating attitudes and vulnerability to mental illness. This can also be associated with mixing with negative and damaging peer groups and/or engaging in risky activities such as drug or alcohol abuse or criminal behaviour. This process can be exacerbated for people on the autism spectrum due to the impact of elements of autism such as social communication difficulties and a limited sense of self-awareness.

Self-esteem is also linked to the development of a number of mental illness conditions. In a range of literature, a negative or unstable self-view is cited as a significant component in the diagnostic criteria of many mental illnesses, including major depressive disorder, eating disorders and some personality vulnerabilities (Mann *et al.* 2003). Self-esteem can also be a factor in suicidal behaviour and/or self-harm.

Being confident and liking and valuing yourself is a good place to start if you want to promote good mental health. However, it can be difficult to build self-esteem if starting from a position of low self-worth and negativity. It seems a touch unfair that the one thing you need to do to overcome your illness and take your rightful place in society can be so very hard. There are, however, ways in which you can challenge self-hatred and lack of confidence.

JACOB'S STORY: School and self-esteem

When I was 16, I found out that I have Asperger's syndrome. It came a bit late for me, because I had been in school for a fair while, and I had already had a really hard time. I found it very hard to make friends, and some of the other kids were stupid bullies and seemed to enjoy making me a target. I was also not very good academically. This was mostly because of sensory issues. I also have Irlen syndrome, so when I was looking at books the words just danced around on the page. I had actually been out of school for about two years, when they found out about the Irlen issue. Nobody – teachers, parents, no one – treated me like I would ever do anything with my life. I had it from all angles – people picking on me at school, feeling like nobody would ever like me, getting bad marks in all my subjects. When I got the Asperger's diagnosis and then the Irlen one a while later, it was easier for me – and my parents and teachers – to understand why I was having trouble. Things did improve, but I still struggle with self-esteem now, and I'm 34. I think it's really important for people to understand that autistic people are just different and that is okay. If a kid isn't doing well, try to look for the reasons behind it, not just make them feel small and alone and like nobody will ever be their friend. We've got good qualities. There's things we're good at. Kids need to know that. These days I'm doing some volunteer work at the local high school, talking to the kids with autism and Asperger's and ADHD, and helping them to see their good points. I love doing this work. I feel like I'm sort of helping myself by helping the kids. Self-esteem is very important.

Self esteem and self-confidence can be a significant challenge for people on the spectrum and can be compounded by both autism itself and the onset of mental illnesses. People on the autism spectrum – and particularly women – can have issues with self-identity and awareness of who they are which can compound self-esteem issues. They can have such low self-esteem that they try to 'fit in' at any cost and as a consequence, they struggle to know who they are. This may come about due to years of masking their true self and trying to be accepted by various peer groups. Some people on the spectrum feel that they have lost – or indeed never had – an identity of their own. For people who also have mental health issues such as personality disorder or complex PTSD, this disconnectedness from self and self-identity can be compounded. If you feel disconnected from your sense of who you are, there may be some work to do on reconnecting with who you are or discovering your identity.

You can also take some steps to try to understand yourself. Ask questions like 'What are my specific likes and dislikes?', 'How would I describe myself to others?' or 'What do people that know me say about me?'

For some people, connecting with others on the spectrum can be a great way to forge an identity that is true to them, as they are able to just be around other autistic people without constantly trying to interpret the situation, and many find a helpful part of their journey to self-discovery includes becoming involved with an autistic peer group, although it can be daunting to join an autistic social group in real life, and some prefer to start or stay online to interact with other autistics. A common misconception that may prevent people from searching out other autistics is the idea that they do not want or need friends, and this can lead to people assuming that autistic social groups are pointless and/or non-existent.

Most autistic social groups have social media or web pages through which initial contact can be made. Some groups will have an official convener or organiser who will often agree to meet up with someone who is thinking of joining the group first, so that they can talk about what a typical meeting or event is and what happens. Meeting other autistic people online or in real life can help because the worldwide autistic community is huge and there is such a range of people within it. Most people can find at least one person they enjoy interacting with, and often find a sense of belonging and begin to understand how to feel comfortable in themselves as well as around others. In addition, meeting other autistic people can lead to peer mentoring where strategies for living well are shared, which can be formal or informal.

Other people may benefit from some psychological support or counselling to help them develop a positive sense of self and increase their self-confidence and self-esteem. (See Chapter 13 on psychotherapy, which may be helpful when looking for this type of support.)

One factor that can strongly affect self-esteem for people on the autism spectrum is the expectations of others. If those around you – family, partner, friend, work colleagues, clinicians etc. – only or largely focus on your deficits and what you cannot do as a person with autism, the chances are that your self-esteem and self-confidence will take a hit. Conversely, if people around you give you positive feedback and praise and focus on your strengths, your self-esteem and self-confidence will likely increase. This is commonly known as the self-fulfilling prophecy, as you begin to believe the attitudes and expectations of others defines and accurately describes you. And this issue affects all kinds of people, not just those with autism.

Negative attitudes and a focus on what autistic people can't do and have deficits in are currently pervasive in society, although work is being done to address this. Autism self-advocates, parent advocates, some clinicians and educators are working to make a world in which autistic experience is valued, and the unique strengths that autistic people have is made the focal point of interactions, rather than the negatives and deficits. Rather than believing what others are saying about you that is negative, search out positive sources of information about living well with autism.

There are a number of examples of non-verbal adults with autism who are challenging the idea that they are unhappy or unfulfilled, pointing out that life can be joyous and fulfilling without spoken language. Additionally, there are a large number of blogs written by adults on the spectrum and these may help you to develop your self-awareness as well as indicate the range of things you may be good at or enjoy doing.

Some things you can do to help improve your feelings about yourself include the following:

- Gravitate towards people who view you positively as an autistic person and respect that you are 'different, not less'.

- Focus on what you do well rather than what you struggle with. You can make a list if you like.

- If you are not already, think about becoming involved in autism support, friendship and/or advocacy groups.

- Read personal accounts of notable and influential autistic people, movies or documentaries with positive autistic characters or actors in them, or listen to music by autistic musicians. Some notable diagnosed creative people include actor and comedian Dan Ackroyd, actor Darryl Hannah, singer Susan Boyle, professional surfer Clay Marzo, lead singer of The Vines Craig Nicholls, author John Elder Robison, and author and autism advocate Dr Temple Grandin. There are also a number of notable autistic people in the world of the sciences, mathematics, IT, medicine, psychology, academia as well as many other fields. Seeing these people who are at the pinnacle of success in life may well inspire you and help you to identify with the amazing gifts that often come with autism/Asperger's.

- Start to identify when you say negative things about yourself or put yourself down in conversations. You can also ask trusted people to tell you when you are doing this. You may be surprised about how often you say something negative about yourself. Identifying the problem is a good way to start addressing it. You can either look for evidence that the negative thing you are saying about yourself is true (as it almost certainly won't be), or just make a blanket ban on putting yourself down. Come up with some alternative, positive things to say to yourself.

- Talk to yourself as you would talk to a person you care about. Be supportive, kind and understanding. Forgive yourself if you make a mistake.

- If you are aware that you have negative feelings about yourself, try to challenge them whenever they crop up. You might even want to make a list of challenges and arguments against them and draw on the list as you need to.

- Try to surround yourself with people who like and respect you and who are doing positive things with their lives. A good place to find friends is among others on the autism spectrum and/or those with mental illness. There are a large number of groups and forums where you can meet people with a similar diagnosis to you, from social media to support groups hosted by autism or mental health organisations.

- Be kind to yourself. This may sound trite and possibly unattainable, but it is a very important step in learning to value yourself. A practical way of doing this is to reward yourself for achievements. This could include buying yourself a little present when you do something well.

- Make yourself a 'good things about me' kit. This can include things that evoke positive feelings about yourself, such as photos of people you are close to or photos of your pets, a painting or poem you have written that you like, any awards you have won, nice notes, letters or emails people have sent you praising your character, your work or other activities, a list of your achievements, positive school reports etc. Include anything that makes you feel good about yourself or that you are proud of. You can look at this kit when you are feeling negative about yourself to help boost your feelings of self-worth.

- Appreciate your unique and amazing qualities. Try regularly reminding yourself of some of your good points. Some people do this standing in front of the mirror, but you don't have to do this if it doesn't work for you. Make a list of your good points and refer to it frequently. List your achievements and reflect on them. These do not need to be huge – they can include small achievements that you know are significant.

- Don't compare yourself to others. This is important, because it is very easy to look at people you think are more successful, more intelligent etc. than you, but actually, as humans, we tend to compare ourselves to people we perceive as being in a better position than ourselves. We can never know what somebody else is experiencing, and it is almost always unhelpful to compare ourselves in this way.

- Acknowledge the positive parts of yourself. If somebody gives you a compliment, say 'thank you'. Don't dismiss the good things about yourself. Be aware of your strengths.

- Try not to dwell on the past. Use the mindfulness skills outlined in Chapter 12. In the same vein, try not to worry about the future.

- Learn to be assertive and to stand up for yourself. You deserve to have your reasonable needs met. Assertiveness is something you can practice if you are not very confident with doing it at first. Try being assertive and stating your needs with people you feel are very 'safe' before trying it with people you find it difficult to assert yourself with. You will get better at it the more you practice. There are also assertiveness courses you can take. If you have an autism or mental health worker and assertiveness is a challenge for you, ask them about improving your assertiveness and if there are any courses you can take to build your assertiveness and boundaries skills. Some courses are delivered via the internet, and others are in person.

- Do things you enjoy. Everyone deserves to have some fun, and it is also good for your sense of self-esteem. Try to schedule enjoyable activities into every week. Obviously these will vary for each person, but you can make a list of things you enjoy and work through them.

- Try to reframe your view of yourself. You can start to do this by asking trusted people what they think you are good at and why they think you are a good person. Listen to them and try to accept what they are saying.

- Practice mindfulness as this is an evidence-based strategy to improve wellbeing. See Chapter 12 for ideas on how to do this.

- If you have issues liking yourself because you are on the autism spectrum or have a mental illness and you feel inadequate or less than others because of this, you could join some autism and/or mental illness self-advocacy groups on social media or read inspiring stories by impressive people with your condition. Some positive accounts of living well with autism are listed in the Resources section at the end of this book. Instead of focusing on your negative qualities or deficits, remind yourself about all the challenges you have got through to be where you are.

17

RESILIENCE

Resilience is essentially what is needed when a person has to push up against a challenge or difficulty in order to get through it. It is a characteristic that is built up when people are successful in dealing with their challenges. Being resilient means that a person is better able to 'bounce back' after a hardship or setback. Someone who is resilient has faced a challenge or difficult situation, worked out how to get through it and come out the other side, so to speak. Having resilience helps in building confidence and mastery around facing challenges in the future, and resilient people tend to do better at managing their lives than those who are not resilient. Working through an issue often teaches skills and wisdom in areas related to the issues that have been overcome, allowing this experience to be generalised out into wider areas of a person's life, 'Persistence and resilience only come from having been given the chance to work through difficult problems.' (Tulley, nd).

In medical terms, resilience is the ability to maintain biological and psychological homeostasis under stress (Depp and Jeste 2006). In other words, when you are stressed, if you are resilient, your physical and mental wellbeing do not alter much from when you are not stressed. Research has not found a definitive answer to the question of whether the most effective reliance is innate (a quality you are born with) or learned, or a mixture of the two. We do know that people can learn to modify their reactions to stress and build resilience through a number of channels.

Medications do not increase resilience, but they can provide supports to diminish anxiety, for example, which can then lead to people being able to implement strategies and to build their resilience through the successful use of such strategies.

Factors involved in innate resilience include temperament, which is known to have some level of heritability. 'Protective temperamental factors include sociability, intelligence, social competence, internal locus of control, warmth and closeness of affectional ties, and active emotional support relationships, and purposeful engagement' (Lavretsky 2010, p.13). Other than intelligence, these characteristics are ones that people with autism, by definition, have difficulties with. So, according to Lavretsky, this would mean that people with autism are lacking some of the key protective factors that boost resilience, and this may be one of the reasons why there is such a high level of mental illness among people with autism.

However, resilience has other positive determining factors that can be more easily increased than sociability and social competence. Self-esteem, personal coping strategies and even faith/spirituality are factors that can help build resilience and that are more accessible to people with autism.

Things that promote resilience	Challenges to resilience
Self-acceptance	Perfectionism
Positive self-image	Low self-esteem
Assumption of competence	Assumption of incompetence
Positive attitude towards challenges	Physical or mental illness
Social/emotional support	Disability
Exercise, meditation, mindfulness	Social isolation
Positive self-talk	Negative self-talk

The journey to living well with mental illness can be positively impacted by high levels of resilience, so it is important to try and build up your resilience over time to increase your ability to live as well as possible. You can do this on your own using strategies such as meditation, mindfulness and exercise that all modulate the body's immune system response to stress and decrease negative emotions (Lavretsky 2010), or you can do this with support from others. Wellbeing therapy (Ruini and Fava 2009) – a type of structured mindfulness – has been shown to improve symptoms of anxiety and depression in younger adults by developing and increasing environmental mastery, personal growth, purpose in life, self-acceptance, positive relationships with others and autonomy.

An understanding of an appropriate (correct) diagnosis and the use of effective medications and other treatments can help a person to grow and develop their resilience as they learn to manage life and to live better over time.

Resilience, wisdom and independence are all linked. While resilience helps build wisdom and a deeper understanding of the world and of oneself, those who are not independent tend to be less resilient, as they have less experience of challenging issues and gaining mastery over them. Building resilience will help you to become more independent and better able to take on new challenges.

Independence

People with autism spectrum conditions and with mental illness often struggle to become independent or to maintain their independence. And people or organisations that aim to assist may often inadvertently promote dependence instead of independence. Some institutions are particularly prone to this, such as psychiatric hospitals and residential mental health or disability services. When people enter these institutions they may be vulnerable and in need of assistance, but their structure may actually disempower the person, leading to increased dependence. In this manner, a hospital – which has a pivotal role in providing care – can have the perverse effect of making people less able to cope with life's challenges when they are discharged. To counteract this, it is important to develop long-term care plans that set out independence goals and day-to-day levels of independence to be maintained wherever you are. For example, you might need assistance to dress yourself, but want to maintain the independence to choose the clothes that you are going to wear.

With mental illness there can be a fine line between providing vital assistance and denying independence as some mental illness processes do, in fact, require significant interventions from health professionals to protect the person from self-inflicted damage or vulnerability to abusive people. If, for example, a person is severely manic, leaving them in control of a credit card is probably a bad idea, given that they may run up a large debt buying things they don't need.

It can be hard for health services to get the balance right between denying independence and providing a therapeutic environment. Autism and mental health consumer advocates can assist in these situations by advocating on behalf of people who may be unable to do so themselves due to an acute episode of illness. Future planning can be very helpful in these situations as advocates can ensure that the long-term care plan that has been developed goes into the case file as an active part of the therapeutic support plan.

People with autism and mental illness may have difficulties around resilience and independence that are beyond their control. Children and young people diagnosed with autism may be shielded from difficulties and challenges by their parents. This is not because their parents don't love them or want them to suffer a life where they aren't independent. Instead, the opposite is often true – shielding young people on the autism spectrum from adversity can be a misplaced manifestation of parental love and care. For people with mental illness in addition to autism, this can be especially true, with families shielding them from having to make decisions or take on responsibility. People with mental illness may also be subject to treatment orders and hospital admissions where their independence is essentially removed for a period of time. The people who most need to build independence and resilience may have that possibility severely challenged by mental health services and families who in fact have their best interests at heart. Sadly, these good intentions can backfire and lead to people being unable to live independently, either for a period of time or permanently. Striking the balance between protecting vulnerable people with autism and mental illness and stripping them of their independence is a complex area. An effective approach may differ from person to person.

Family group conferences or team meetings can be useful tools to both prevent and remediate this stripping of independence. It is also helpful to keep in mind that all people learn from their mistakes, and indeed that resilience is built through managing in difficult circumstances and/or overcoming challenges.

It is important to give people with autism and/or mental illness support to move beyond dependence. It is more helpful for people working with those on the autism spectrum and those with mental illness to start from a position of what the person can do, rather than their apparent deficits. This can be difficult and counterintuitive, as most funding and support services are dependent on what an individual cannot do, or needs support to do. However, as in education, it is more beneficial in the long term to focus on an individual's potential, rather than on their problems.

If you find that people are too focused on negatives and your apparent deficits, try to point that out to them and ask them to reflect on what you can do. It is important to try and counteract the self-fulfilling prophecy, which is the phrase used to describe the way that predictions of achievement or behaviour come true because of the feedback loop between belief and behaviour. It has been shown that teachers who can't see the potential in students with autism do not provide them with the learning opportunities to achieve their potential, and then when those students do not achieve, the teachers feel that they were correct about their lack of potential (Goodall 2013). This effect explains why some people on the autism spectrum may be so influenced by the dependence-promoting attitudes of society and others around them that they may believe that they are, in fact, not capable of living independently. If this is you, you might like to read some accounts of people with similar issues to you (e.g. autism and/or mental illness) who have achieved independence and who live well. Living successfully means different things to different people – for some people there will always need to be support from others in order to live well, and for others living successfully may mean being able to take care of not only themselves, but others too.

You can build independence through undertaking a small project, such as starting a group for friends with autism and/or mental illness on social media or doing something that you haven't done in the past (e.g. taking public transport, supermarket shopping or working). Independence and confidence at life skills is something that can be practised. It is like a muscle, in that the more you do the thing that might be challenging, the stronger you will get. And the reverse is also true: the longer you are dependent, the harder it will be to build independence. Needing support to do things is not the same as being dependent, however – you can be independent with high support needs, for example, requiring someone to do tasks for you that you are unable to do because of an additional physical disability. Dependence is about other people making all your decisions and having all the control over you and your life.

JUDY'S STORY: Hospitalisation and independence

I am 46 and have a diagnosis of Asperger's syndrome and bipolar disorder. I got both diagnoses as an adult. I have always been very independent and done everything for myself. I got my driver's licence when I was 18 with no special assistance and I moved out of home when I was 22. I have been working as a manager at a hotel in the city for just over three years. About ten months ago I had a bad episode of my bipolar and went to hospital for three weeks. When I first got to the hospital, I hated it. I am used to getting my own way and giving instructions to others, and here I was, being told when to eat dinner and having my medication locked in a room and given out by nurses. At the start, I wasn't even allowed to leave the ward. I wanted to leave every moment of the day and hated the nurses for having so much control over my life.

After a while, though, I became more comfortable with being in the hospital and stopped worrying that others had control over my life. When I went home, I almost missed being in hospital! It made no sense. Transitioning back into my independent life as a manager was really hard. I was on a graduated return to work for three months. I kept wondering what was wrong with me. I'm now back working full-time, and I feel much better. It was really scary seeing how quickly I become comfortable with being in hospital. I guess that I was in a bad way when I went there and they did everything for me. I didn't have to worry about looking after myself or making decisions.

Adversity

Our society places a lot of importance on things like success and happiness. There is almost an unspoken assumption that anything that doesn't go the way we would like is unfair or wrong. People get upset when things don't go their way. Most consider the old chestnut, 'why do bad things happen to good people?', to be a reasonable question.

We seem to want, and even expect, a world free of challenges and hardship. For those with autism and a co-existing mental illness, this might seem laughable. Their lives are by their very nature challenging and difficult.

Issues that people with autism and mental illness may encounter include:

- discrimination
- bullying
- trauma – present or past
- isolation or loneliness
- depression
- unemployment and poverty
- sensory struggles
- meltdowns
- feelings of alienation and not belonging
- anxiety
- communication differences and difficulties
- paternalism and people being condescending
- prejudice, poor treatment or misdiagnosis from the psychiatric profession
- intimate relationship issues
- issues with family
- executive functioning problems, leading to issues with things such as managing time, money etc.

In addition, mental illness can sap a person's enjoyment in life and impact severely on their ability to carry on their everyday life.

This is actually quite a short list of issues people with autism and a co-morbid mental illness may face. It would follow that building resilience might be a very helpful course of action. One thing people can try to do to build resilience is to view the hardship and difficulty as a teacher. Instead of being angry or depressed when faced with adversity, it is possible to work through the difficulty and, when this has been done, to look back and see how much has been learned and how you have grown through the process. It is very satisfying to review challenges or difficulties in life and know that you managed to get through. If you can share how you did this with others, it can be both empowering and helpful.

There is a relationship between thinking about difficulties as learning opportunities and mindfulness practice, and you can find out more about mindfulness and how it can benefit you in Chapter 12.

Building resilience

Building resilience requires a change of attitude for many people. People with autism and mental illness can be very negatively focused and may find it hard to view any part of their life in a positive way, particularly adversity, which their friends and family may also identify as being a negative or unfair occurrence. Resilience is a skill that you can start teaching yourself and work through over time, until it becomes more natural. You can even get someone to help you build your resilience, if you like.

Try making a list of a number of apparently negative things that have occurred in your life. If possible, pick things that happened more than a year ago. Now try to see if you can connect that experience of hardship with something new you have learned that has benefited you. For example, if you got into trouble with your credit card and built up a big debt, that may well have taught you to consider your decision to open a credit card account more carefully in the future. You may also have learned something useful about your capacity to pay back credit. If your adversity was that you had issues with an aggressive person, you may well have unknowingly used that experience to be more wary of people and not trust everyone – quite a useful skill for people on the autism spectrum and those with mental illness. If you have a friend or family member helping you with this exercise, ask them to look at your life in light of these events and negative experiences, and gain a more objective view of how you learned from the experience.

They can feed back to you things you have learned that you may not have realised.

Viewing adversity in this manner is also a good way of building positive thinking and skills for reframing negative thoughts. One of the ways that you can do this is through a SWOT analysis. SWOT stands for:

Strengths: your personal characteristics, knowledge and/or skills that are helpful.

Weaknesses: things within you that are currently barriers to achieving/ succeeding and/or living well.

Opportunities: external factors that can be used positively to help you achieve/succeed/live well.

Threats: external factors that have the potential to be barriers to success.

Sometimes people draw this or write lists of things in each area, which can be a very useful way to work through the situation and to think about how to best succeed or overcome those particular challenges:

	Positive	Negative
Internal	Strengths 1. 2. 3.	Weaknesses 1. 2. 3.
External	Opportunities 1. 2. 3.	Threats 1. 2. 3.

Once you have identified your strengths and opportunities, it can be much easier to manage your weaknesses and threats, as you know that you have some knowledge or skills and personal characteristics that are both useful and helpful in your life.

What follows is a SWOT analysis for Adam, when he and his family were trying to work out how to manage the next step in Adam's independence, which was to get a bus to school.

Adam's SWOT analysis around getting a bus to school

	Positive	Negative
Internal	Strengths 1. I know the bus timetable off by heart. 2. I know where to get the bus. 3. I know where to get off the bus.	Weaknesses 1. I am not yet very good with understanding how to use money. 2. I don't like the smell or sound of lots of people. 3. I am anxious about going on the bus by myself.
External	Opportunities 1. I can get a bus pass instead of using money. 2. My friend goes on the same bus I will go on (two stops after me). 3. I want to be able to get the bus to the movies on the weekends.	Threats 1. Some people on the bus might be mean. 2. The bus might not stop for me. 3. The bus might break down.

After we did this plan, mum said she would go on the bus with me until I was okay going by myself. She said she would take me to get a bus pass, and I could learn to use money another time, as the bus pass was cheaper. I told mum not to sit with me on the bus, but to sit where I could see her, so I would know when to get off, even if I got really anxious. Mum said that people might smell or be noisy, but I could use the same strategies I used for assembly – I wear headphones and have some essential oil on my shirt sleeves, so I can sniff that and it is nice. We talked about what I could do if people were mean, but if I wear my headphones and listen to my music, I can't really notice them anyway. Mum went on the bus with me for about three weeks, and then she just came to the bus stop with me for another week, while I got more confident that the bus would stop for me when I put my arm out towards the road. Now I can use the bus by myself. I can even get the bus to different places now, like the cinema. I was really anxious, but when I saw the SWOT analysis I realised how much I wanted to do this and how many skills I already had.

Life is generally easier for resilient people. This is not because they have less difficult things to deal with; rather it is because they have confidence that when something difficult arises, they will be able to cope with it. They also may have a resilient attitude, which means that instead of being afraid of hardship, they take life as it comes, and deal with issues that may arise.

Some qualities often demonstrated by resilient people include:

- having a better ability to cope with change

- viewing hardships as an obstacle to overcome rather than something to be defeated by

- setting goals to work towards in order to solve problems

- working to overcome difficulties and challenges that life presents

- having a greater level of self-awareness, including the ability to seek help when required

- having more realistic expectations from life

- having a greater ability to develop insight into their mental illness and/or autism

- being better able to identify their strengths and weaknesses

- learning from mistakes.

Being resilient and independent is a great thing to aspire to. It may grow incrementally over time without you even noticing.

Some tips for practising resilience and independence are as follows:

- Choose to challenge yourself a little with a task or activity. Make it manageable but something a little out of your 'comfort zone'.

- Cultivate a more positive attitude. This might sound hard – and it can be. Start with some basic reframing exercises, such as writing down three positive things that happen each day or three things to be grateful for. You could ask a friend or family member to tell you when you speak about yourself in a negative way or put yourself down in a conversation. Sometimes people are unaware of how negatively they view themselves – and as a consequence how negatively they speak about themselves. Being aware of this can be a good point to start reframing your approach to a more positive one.

- Start to view adversity as a teacher. Try to identify what you have learned from difficult experiences in the past.

- Learn about people with autism and/or mental illness who are independent and who have achieved great things, such as Temple Grandin, John Elder Robison, Susan Boyle or Dan Ackroyd. It doesn't even have to be a famous person. If you have an inspirational friend or family member with autism, use them as encouragement for your own life journey. When you find somebody who inspires you, use them as an example to help you master difficulties in your own life. You can meet people in autism/Asperger's groups online as well as or instead of in real life.

- Try practising independence. This could mean learning to take public transport, getting a part-time job, meeting up with people, taking on responsibilities you may not have done in the past (managing money etc.). If you physically require assistance to do these things, it is still being independent, it is about you deciding to try and do new things or see new places.

- Use your supports to build independence. If you have a mental health worker, ask them to help you do some act of independence that you might not be able to do without help.

From an autistic point of view, it is very interesting that links have been found between perfectionism, anxiety and low levels of resilience. Many people with autism are also perfectionists, and the internal drive to achieve perfection can create very high levels of anxiety. This constant anxiety and lack of acceptance of anything less than perfect makes it hard to be resilient. Perfectionism has also been linked to depression and has been described as a destructive characteristic that has to be reduced in order to increase resilience (Flett and Hewitt 2014).

LYNNE'S STORY: Learning to make mistakes

I used to be a perfectionist. I would spend hours trying to make sure my handwriting was perfect. Perfect for me meant beautiful tiny letters in an HB pencil. I wrote longer stories than anyone in class, because I was so focused. One day my teacher refused to grade my story, he said I was supposed to write in pen not pencil, and he couldn't read my tiny writing. I was devastated. I cried and screamed and yelled. From that moment on I stopped being a perfectionist. I just realised that no one else wanted perfection, they wanted what I call 'good enough'. Good enough means it does what it is supposed to, for example, when I wash the dishes they are clean enough to use again but not sparkling and shiny or anything. Sometimes my good enough annoys people, but being happy with good enough has prevented so much anxiety and stress. I think it is one of the main reasons I am so resilient, because it is okay to make a mistake and fix it up 'ish'.

SUMMARY OF STRATEGIES TO AID MENTAL HEALTH AND WELLBEING

Living well, when you live with a mental illness, can be a lifelong journey. You may do better at some times than others. 'Mental illness is a very powerful thing. If it is with you it is probably going to be there until the day you die. I am trying so hard to break mine, but it is not easy. It is my toughest fight ever' (Bruno, nd). Staying well and maintaining your mental health is very important. Here is a list of things that may assist:

- Take responsibility for your own life and health – nobody else can change your life for you. Positive change can only happen from the moment at which you decide you need to improve your life.

- There are strategies and treatments for all kinds of mental health issues.

- You are not alone – many other people will be experiencing similar things to you.

- Seek help for mental ill health, especially during a crisis.

- Learn the triggers and early warning signs for a crisis.

- Identify and use what strategies work for you in dealing with crises and meltdowns. A crisis usually only lasts for less than an hour. Use strategies such as distraction to help get through a crisis – find different activities that work for you.

- Build insight by getting to know yourself and your mind.

- Build resilience by using adversity and hardship to increase your understanding around how to overcome difficulties.

- Surround yourself with positive sensory experiences for when you are having a hard time. Things such as stim toys can be invaluable.

- When life is very difficult, remind yourself that 'this, too, will pass'.

- Learn to reward yourself for achievement or improvement.

- Try to maintain good relationships with family, close friends, your partner and/or your children.

- Recognise that autistic people and neurotypical people tend to communicate differently. This doesn't mean that one or other style is 'right' – each style is valid. But be aware of this when dealing with mental health clinicians, as they may misinterpret what you say.

- Seeking help is a sign of strength.

- Independence does not mean doing everything by yourself. You can access support and be independent. Everyone needs help with something.

- Build meaning and purpose in your life. This could be achieved through interests, working, studying, family or community involvement.

- Take medication as prescribed.

- If you have one, see your psychiatrist and/or mental health case manager regularly.

- Learn to love yourself – challenge any negative thoughts or beliefs you have about yourself.

- Understand your diagnosis. Seek clarification or explanation of it from your doctor if need be. If you think your diagnosis is inappropriate or inaccurate, consider seeking a second opinion.

- If you use a psychologist or psychotherapist, be prepared to shop around to find one that works well for you. There are different therapy models, and some will be more effective than others.

- Medication is not a 'one size fits all'. It may take a few attempts to find the medication/s that work for you. Be patient because getting the right one usually provides some good results.

- Get involved in autism and/or mental health communities. This will help you to value and respect yourself as an autist and as a person with a mental illness as well as connecting with like-minded people.

- Maintain your physical health – exercise and see your doctor regularly.

- Avoid becoming dependent on either drugs or alcohol. Seek help if this is an issue for you.

- Make a list of relaxation techniques and practise them when required.

- Make a 'happy box' filled with things you love and positive affirmations about you. Look at it regularly.

- Practise acceptance. Let go of any blame or regret.

- Tell yourself you are amazing on a regular basis.

- Do what works for you.

RESOURCES

Autism support

There are a number of online and face-to-face support groups for parents of autistic children. These are often local and delivered through an autism support organisation. There are also a number of these groups online, in social media. A few examples are:

Yellow Ladybugs:

>   http://yellowladybugs.com.au

Autism Meetup (central point for support groups):

>   http://autism.meetup.com

Autism Parent Support Group:

>   www.autismparentssupport.org/index.html

United States

AWN Autism Women's Network:

>   http://autismwomensnetwork.org

US Asperger & Autism Association:

>   www.usautism.org

ASAN (Autism Self-Advocacy Network):

>   http://autisticadvocacy.org

United Kingdom

The National Autistic Society:

www.autism.org.uk

Autism Helpline:

Tel: 0845 070 4004 (open Monday–Friday, 10am–4pm)

Email: autismhelpline@nas.org.uk

Australia and New Zealand

Autism Spectrum Australia (Aspect):

www.autismspectrum.org.au

ASAN (Autism Self-Advocacy Network) Australia and New Zealand:

www.asan-au.org

Mental illness support

SANE Australia:

www.SANE.org

Mental Health Foundation:

www.mentalhealth.org.uk

Anxiety support

Anxiety UK:

www.anxietyuk.org.uk

Anxiety Disorders Association of Victoria (ADAVIC):

www.adavic.org.au

Dubin, N. (2009) *Asperger Syndrome and Anxiety.* London: Jessica Kingsley Publishers.

Depression support

beyondblue:

www.beyondblue.org.au

Black Dog Institute:

www.blackdoginstitute.org.au

Dubin, N. (2014) *The Autism Spectrum and Depression*. London: Jessica Kingsley Publishers.

Wilkinson, L.A. (2015) *Overcoming Anxiety and Depression on the Autism Spectrum*. London: Jessica Kingsley Publishers.

Psychosis support

Rethink Mental Illness, UK schizophrenia fellowship:

www.rethink.org

Jeffs, S. (2009) *Flying with Paper Wings*. Melbourne, VIC: Spinifex Press.

Eating disorders support

Beat (UK), Beating eating disorders:

www.b-eat.co.uk

Suicide – crisis and counselling helplines
USA

Suicide Prevention Lifeline:

Tel: 1-800-273-8255, available 24 hours a day, 365 days a year.

UK and Republic of Ireland

The Samaritans:

Tel: 08457 90 90 90 (UK)

Tel: 1850 60 90 90 (Republic of Ireland), available 24 hours a day, 365 days a year.

Australia

Lifeline:

Tel: 13 1114, available 24 hours a day, 365 days a year.

Mindfulness

The Happiness Trap:

www.thehappinesstrap.com

Mindfulness:

www.mindfulness.org.au

Mitchell, C. (2013) *Mindful Living with Asperger Syndrome.* London: Jessica Kingsley Publishers.

Psychology

American Psychological Association:

www.apa.org

Dialectical behaviour therapy

Linehan, M. (1993) *Skills Training Manual for Treating Borderline Personality Disorder.* New York: Guilford Press.

Cognitive behaviour therapy

MoodGym Training Progam, CBT-based online mental health course:

https://moodgym.anu.edu.au/welcome

Wilkinson, L.A. (2015) *Overcoming Anxiety and Depression on the Autism Spectrum – A Self-Help Guide Using CBT*. London: Jessica Kingsley Publishers.

Mental health 12-step/self-help groups

GROW (America):

www.growinamerica.org

GROW (Australia):

www.grow.org.au

Tel: 1800 558 268

Sleep resources

Aitken, K.J. (2014) *Sleep Well on the Autism Spectrum*. London: Jessica Kingsley Publishers.

Positive books about living with autism

Attwood, T. and Lesko, A. (2014) *Been There, Done That, Try This* (Edited by C. Evans). London: Jessica Kingsley Publishers.

Kim, C. (2014) *Nerdy, Shy and Socially Inappropriate*. London: Jessica Kingsley Publishers.

Lawson, W. (2000) *Life Behind Glass*. London: Jessica Kingsley Publishers.

Regan, T. (2014) *Shorts*. London: Jessica Kingsley Publishers.

Santomauro, J. (ed.) *Autism All-Stars*. London: Jessica Kingsley Publishers.

Autism in popular culture – films, books etc.

Film: *Temple Grandin*, directed by Mick Jackson 2010.

Film: *Mozart and the Whale*, directed by Petter Naess 2005.

Documentary: *Alone in a Crowded Room*, directed by Lucy Paplinska 2010.

Film: *The Imitation Game*, directed by Morten Tildum 2015.

Film: *Adam*, directed by Max Meyer 2009.

Haddon, M. (2004) *The Curious Incident of the Dog in the Nighttime*. London: Vintage.

Simsion, G. (2014) *The Rosie Project*. New York: Simon & Schuster.

Temple Grandin TED Talk, 'The world needs all kinds of minds', available at www.ted.com/talks/temple_grandin_the_world_needs_all_kinds_of_minds?language=en

Jeanette Purkis TEDx Talk, 'Disability, resilience and achieving the supposedly impossible', available at http://tedxtalks.ted.com/video/Disability-Resilience-and-Achie

Chris Varney TEDx Talk, 'Autism: How my unstoppable mother proved the experts wrong', available at http://tedxtalks.ted.com/video/Autism-how-my-unstoppable-mothe

Books for children around autism

Hames, A. and McCaffrey, M. (eds) (2003) *Special Brothers and Sisters*. London: Jessica Kingsley Publishers.
(For siblings of children with special needs or serious illness)

Hoopman, K. (2001) *Of Mice and Aliens*. London: Jessica Kingsley Publishers.

Hoopman, K. (2006) *All Cats have Asperger Syndrome*. London: Jessica Kingsley Publishers.

Whelton, J. (2003) *Can I Tell You about Asperger Syndrome?* London: Jessica Kingsley Publishers.

Therapy and assistance pets
United Kingdom

- Dogs for Good: www.dogsforthedisabled.org
- Psychological Assistance Dogs UK: http://padogsuk.org
- The Blue Dog: www.thebluedog.org/en/

Australia

- AWARE (Assisting, Wellbeing, Ability, Recovery & Empowerment) Dogs Australia Inc.: www.awaredogs.org.au/our_services/
- mindDog: http://minddog.org.au
- Righteous Pups Australia: www.righteouspups.org.au

United States of America

- Service Dog Central: http://servicedogcentral.org
- Healing Allies – Assistance Dogs: www.mentalhealthdogs.org
- 4 Paws for Ability: http://4pawsforability.org/autism-assistance-dog/
- Little Angels Service Dogs: www.littleangelsservicedogs.org/psychiatricservicedogs.html

Canada

- Canadian Service Dog Foundation: http://servicedog.ca/programs/emotional-support-animals
- The Canadian Foundation for Animal Assisted Support Services: www.cf4aass.org
- Autism Dog Services: www.autismdogservices.ca

New Zealand

- Assistance Dogs New Zealand Trust: www.assistancedogstrust. org.nz

- Perfect Partners Assistance Dogs Trust: www.ppadt.org.nz

Republic of Ireland

- Autism Assistance Dogs Ireland: www.autismassistance dog sireland.ie

GLOSSARY

Acceptance commitment therapy (ACT) – ACT is a therapy model that uses mindfulness techniques to help people stay in the present and let go of the past. The core message of ACT is for people to accept what is out of their control and then make a commitment to take action to improve their life. The aim of ACT is to increase people's ability to live a full and meaningful life.

Autism – In this book, the term 'autism' is used to describe the various conditions on the autism spectrum, including Asperger's syndrome, autism, PDD-NOS (pervasive developmental disorder not otherwise specified) and autistic spectrum condition. The phrase 'autistic spectrum disorder' is not used in this book due to its connotations of deficits and incompetence.

Autism/autistic spectrum – The word 'spectrum' describes the range of challenges that people with autism may experience, and the degree to which they may be affected.

Autistic person/person with autism – In this book person-first terminology ('person with autism') and identity-first terminology ('autistic person') are used interchangeably, reflecting the fact that there are preferences for both approaches within the autistic community.

Asperger's syndrome – This is a condition on the autism spectrum. It was included in the diagnostic taxonomy of DSM-IV, but was omitted from the latest iteration of the DSM, the DSM-V. Some people on the autism spectrum who gained a diagnosis of Asperger's syndrome identify with that diagnosis whilst others are comfortable identifying as autistic.

Clinician – This is a mental health worker, and could include a psychiatrist, psychologist, psychotherapist, mental health nurse, general practitioner, social worker or occupational therapist, or one of a number of other disciplines. In the context of this book, clinicians are those people providing treatment, support and assistance for mental health issues and/or concerns resulting from autism.

Cognitive behavioural therapy (CBT) – CBT is a therapy model that aims to help clients change their behaviour through changing their thinking. CBT comes from the viewpoint that psychological problems develop as a consequence of learnt ways of thinking and behaving, and that learning new ways of thinking and behaving will address the psychological issues. CBT is a widely-used therapy technique and is used for a large range of psychological and behaviour issues.

Dialectical behaviour therapy (DBT) – DBT is a type of psychotherapy that was originally developed by American psychologist, Marsha Linehan. It is based on CBT, and has been adapted to meet the needs of people who experience emotions so intensely it is problematic, including those who self-harm or have issues with eating disorders.

Mental illness – This is a condition that causes serious disorder in a person's behaviour or thinking. Mental illnesses include (but are not limited to) depression, anxiety disorders, psychotic disorders such as schizophrenia and bipolar disorder and eating disorders.

Neurotypical – This term is used to describe people who do not have a diagnosis of an autism spectrum condition, that is, a non-autistic person.

PECS – This stands for Picture Exchange Communication System. PECS was developed in 1985 as an augmentative/alternative communication system for individuals on the autism spectrum.

Psychotherapy – This describes a number of therapies designed to assist people to manage their mental health. These therapies include cognitive behaviour therapy (CBT), dialectical behaviour therapy (DBT), acceptance and commitment therapy (ACT), creative arts therapies and narrative therapy. Individuals tend to respond differently to each therapy, with some being more beneficial for one person and others for another person.

Solution-focused brief therapy (SFBT) – SFBT is a psychotherapy model which focuses on the desired outcome of therapy as a solution rather than focusing on the problems which resulted in the need for therapy. It works by the therapist encouraging the client to imagine their preferred future. They then work together to take steps which will lead to that future.

REFERENCES

Ackerman, S.J. and Hilsenroth, M.J. (2001) 'A review of therapist characteristics and techniques negatively impacting the therapeutic alliance.' *Psychotherapy: Theory, Research, Practice, Training 38*, 171–185.

Andrews, G. and Slade, T. (2001) 'Interpreting scores on the Kessler Psychological Distress Scale (k10).' *Australian and New Zealand Journal of Public Health 25*, 494–497.

Autism Society (no date) 'Siblings.' Available at www.autism-society.org/living-with-autism/family-issues/siblings/, accessed on 4 April 2015.

APA (American Psychiatric Association) (2013) *Diagnostic Criteria for Autism Spectrum Disorder: DSM-5*. Washington, DC: APA.

Attwood T. (1998) *Asperger's syndrome: A guide for parents and professionals.* London: Jessica Kingsley Publishers

Australian Human Rights Commission (no date) 'About disability rights.' Available at www.humanrights.gov.au/our-work/disability-rights/about-disability-rights, accessed on 26 January 2015.

Baron, M.G. (ed.) (2006) *Stress and Coping in Autism*. Oxford: Oxford University Press.

Bejerot, S., Eriksson, J.M. and Mörtberg, E. (2014) 'Social anxiety in adult autism spectrum disorder.' *Psychiatry Research 220*, 1–2, 705–707.

Burrows, K., C. Adams, J. Spiers, and S. Millman. (2008) 'Factors affecting behavior and welfare of service dogs for children with autism spectrum disorder.' *J. Appl. Anim. Welf. Sci. 11*, 42–62.

Cassell, E.J. (1978) *The Healer's Art*. Cambridge, Mass: M.I.T. Press.

Cassidy S., Bradley, P., Robinson, J., Allison, C., McHugh, M. and Baron-Cohen, S. (2014) 'Suicidal ideation and suicide plans or attempts in adults with Asperger's syndrome attending a specialist diagnostic clinic: a clinical cohort study.' *The Lancet Psychiatry 1*, 142–147.

CDC (Centers for Disease Control and Prevention) (no date, a) 'Diagnostic criteria for 299.00 Autism Spectrum Disorder.' Available at www.cdc.gov/ncbddd/autism/hcp-dsm.html, accessed on 21 October 2015.

CDC (Centers for Disease Control and Prevention) (no date, b) 'Autism spectrum disorder (ASD). Data & statistics.' Available at www.cdc.gov/ncbddd/autism/data.html, accessed on 28 March 2015.

Champ, S. (2002) 'Foreword.' In V. Carr and S. Halpin, *Stigma and Discrimination – A Bulletin of the Low Prevalence Disorders Study* (p.iv). Canberra, ACT: Australian Commonwealth Department of Health and Ageing. Available at www.health.gov.au/internet/main/publishing.nsf/Content/724D498F68ABC0ACCA257BF0001939A7/$File/Stigma.pdf, accessed on 23 October 2015.

Claxton G. (1990) *The Heart of Buddhism: Practical Wisdom for an Agitated World.* London: Crucible.

Clissold, E. (2012) *Suffering in Silence: Psychiatric Co-morbidities in Autistic Spectrum Disorder.* London: Royal College of Psychiatrists.

Davis, B., Nattrass K., O'Brien S., Patronek G. and MacCollin M. (2004). Anthrozoos 12(2):130–146.

Depp, C.A. and Jeste, D.V. (2006) 'Definitions and predictors of successful aging: A comprehensive review of larger quantitative studies.' *The American Journal of Geriatric Psychiatry 14*(1), 6–20.

Doidge, N. (2007). *The Brain That Changes Itself: Stories of Personal Triumph from the Frontiers of Brain Science.* New York: Viking. Print.

Doidge, N. (2010) *The Brain that Changes Itself: Stories of Personal Triumph from the Frontiers of Brain Science.* Carlton North, VIC: Scribe Publications.

Doidge, N. (2015). *The Brain's Way of Healing: Remarkable Discoveries and Recoveries from the Frontiers of Neuroplasticity.* London: Penguin. Print.

Flett, G.L. and Hewitt, P.L. (2014) 'A proposed framework for preventing perfectionism and promoting resilience and mental health among vulnerable children and adolescents.' *Psychology in the Schools 51*(9), 899–912.

Ghaziuddin, M. (2002) 'Depression in persons with autism: Implications for research and clinical care.' *Journal of Autism and Developmental Disorders 32*(4), 299–306.

Goodall, E. (2013) *Understanding and Facilitating the Achievement of Autistic Potential.* Christchurch: CreateSpace Independent Publishing Platform.

Gorman, D.A. and Abi-Jaoude, E. (2014) 'Obsessive-compulsive disorder.' *Canadian Medical Association Journal 186*, 11, 1.

Hargus, E., Crane, C., Barnhofer, T. and Williams, J.M. (2010) 'Effects of mindfulness on meta-awareness and specificity of describing prodromal symptoms in suicidal depression.' *Emotion 10*, 34–42.

Harris, R. (2006) 'Embracing your demons: An overview of acceptance and commitment therapy.' *Psychotherapy in Australia 12*, 4, 2–8. Available at www.actmindfully.com.au/upimages/Dr_Russ_Harris_-_A_Non-technical_Overview_of_ACT.pdf, accessed on 23 February 2015.

Hassed, C. (2011) 'The essence of mental health and mindfulness.' *Teacher Learning Network 18*, 2, 36–39.

Hassed, C. (2014) 'Opinion: Why attention matters'. *Incite*, 16. Available at search.informit.com.au/documentSummary;dn=184103572636881; res=IELHSS> ISSN: 0158-0876.

Hayes, S.C. (2004) 'Acceptance and commitment therapy, relational frame theory, and the third wave of behavior therapy.' *Behavior Therapy 35*, 639–665.

Hayes-Skelton, S.A., Roemer, L. and Orsillo, S.M. (2013) 'A randomized clinical trial comparing an acceptance-based behavior therapy to applied relaxation for generalized anxiety disorder.' *Journal of Consulting and Clinical Psychology 81*, 5, 761–773.

headspace (no date, a) 'Identifying risk factors and warning signs for suicide.' Available at http://headspace.org.au/schools/identifying-risk-factors-and-warning-signs-for-suicide/, accessed on 20 October 2015.

headspace (no date, b) 'Self harm mythbuster.' Available at www.headspace.org.au/media/101054/self_harm_mythbusterv2.pdf, accessed on 23 January 2015.

Hoermann, S., Zupanick, C. and Dombeck, M. (2013) 'Dialectical behaviour therapy for personality disorders.' 6 December. Available at www.mentalhelp.net/articles/dialectical-behavior-therapy-for-personality-disorders-dbt/, accessed on 22 October 2015.

Hofmann, S.G. (2014) *Social Anxiety Clinical, Developmental, and Social Perspectives*. Burlington, MA: Elsevier Science.

ICP (Institute of Clinical Psychologists) (no date) 'Solution focused therapy.' Available at http://icp.org.au/therapy_info/solution-therapy/, accessed on 24 February 2015.

ICD10Data.com (no date) 'Pervasive developmental disorders.' *ICD-10-CM Diagnosis Code F84*. Available at www.icd10data.com/ICD10CM/Codes/F01-F99/F80-F89/F84-/F84, accessed on 11 March 2015.

Kabat-Zinn, J. (1980) *Full Catastrophe Living. Using the Wisdom of Your Body and Mind to Face Stress, Pain, and Illness*. New York: Dell Publishing.

Kabat-Zinn, J. (2003) 'Mindfulness-based interventions in context: Past, present, and future.' *Clinical Psychology: Science and Practice 10*, 144–156.

Kerns, C.M. and Kendall, P.C. (2012) 'The presentation and classification of anxiety in autism spectrum disorder.' *Clinical Psychology: Science and Practice 19*, 4, 323–347.

Lavretsky, H. (2010) 'Geriatric psychiatry: Part 2: Resilience, stress, and the neurobiology of aging.' *Psychiatric Times 27*, 9, 10–14.

Linehan, M. (1993) *Skills Training Manual for Treating Borderline Personality Disorder: Diagnosis and Treatment of Mental Disorders*. New York: Guilford Press.

McConnell, A., Brown, C., Shoda, T., Stayton, L. and Martin, C. (2011) 'Friends with benefits: on the positive consequences of pet ownership.' *Journal of Personality & Social Psychology 101*(6). Summary available at www.apa.org/news/press/releases/2011/07/cats-dogs.aspx, accessed on 4 March 2013.

Malchiodi, C. (2005) *Expressive Therapies – History, Theory and Practice*. New York: Guilford Press.

Mallon, G.P. (1992) 'Utilization of animals as therapeutic adjuncts with children and youth: A review of the literature.' *Child and Youth Care Forum 21*, 1, 53–67.

Mann, M., Hosman, C., Schlaama, H. and DeVries, M. (2004) 'Self-esteem in a broad-spectrum approach for mental health promotion.' *Health Education Research: Theory and Practice 19*, 4, 357–372.

Martin, F. and Farnum, J. (2002). 'Animal-assisted therapies for children with pervasive developmental disorders.' *Western Journal of Nursing Research 24*, 6, 657–670.

Morrison, M.L. (2007) 'Health benefits of animal-assisted interventions.' *Complementary Health Practice Review 12*, 51–62.

Myles, B.S., Trautman M. and Schelvan. R.L. (2004). *The Hidden Curriculum: Practical Solutions for Understanding Unstated Rules in Social Situations*. Shawnee Mission, KS: Autism Asperger Pub. Print.

National Autistic Society, The (no date, a) 'Genetics of autism spectrum disorders.' Available at www.autism.org.uk/24984, accessed on 28 March 2015.

National Autistic Society, The (no date, b) 'Working with people with autism: health.' Available at www.autism.org.uk/working-with/health/mental-health-and-asperger-syndrome.aspx, accessed on 10 August 2014.

National Autistic Society (2015). Available at www.autism.org.uk/24984, accessed July 2015.

National Institute of Child Health and Human Development (NICHD) (2013). Available at www.nichd.nih.gov/health/topics/autism/conditioninfo/Pages/treatments.aspx.

Nepps, P., Stewart, C.N. and Bruckno, S.R. (2014) 'Animal-assisted activity.' *Journal of Evidence-Based Complementary & Alternative Medicine 19*, 3, 211–215.

O'Haire, M.E. (2013) 'Animal-assisted intervention for autism spectrum disorder: a systematic literature review.' *Journal of Autism and Developmental Disorders 43*, 1606–1622.

Patrick, R.P. and Ames, B.N. (2015) 'Vitamin D and the omega-3 fatty acids control serotonin synthesis and action, part 2: relevance for ADHD, bipolar, schizophrenia, and impulsive behavior.' *The FASEB Journal 29*, 6, 2207–2222.

Pescosolido, B.A., Monahan, J., Link, B.G., Stueve, A. and Kikuzawa, S. (1999) 'The public's view of the competence, dangerousness, and need for legal coercion of persons with mental health problems.' *American Journal of Public Health 89*, 9, 1339–1345.

Pierce, K., Müller, R.-A., Ambrose, J., Allen, G. and Courchesne, E. (2001) 'Face processing occurs outside the fusiform 'face area' in autism: evidence from functional MRI.' *Brain 124*, 2059–2073.

Pigeon, W.R., Carr, M., Gorman, C. and Perlis, M.L. (2010) 'Effects of a tart cherry juice beverage on the sleep of older adults with insomnia: A pilot study.' *Journal of Medicinal Food 13*, 3, 579–583.

Raes, F., Dewulf, D., van Heeringen, C. and Williams, J.M. (2009) 'Mindfulness and reduced cognitive reactivity to sad mood: Evidence from a correlational study and a non-randomized waiting list controlled study.' *Behaviour Research and Therapy 47*, 623–627.

Research Autism (no date) 'Cognitive and behavioural therapies and autism.' Available at www.researchautism.net/autism-interventions/types/psychological-interventions/cognitive-and-behavioural-therapies, accessed on 22 February 2015.

Reynolds, A. (2012) 'The benefits of companion animals for children with autism.' *Research Focus, The SCAS Journal*, Autumn.

Robertson, G. (2015) 'Managing stress through mindfulness.' Presented at the Asperger Services Australia Conference, Brisbane, February.

Rodgers, J., Glod, M., Connolly, B. and McConachie, H. (2012) 'The relationship between anxiety and repetitive behaviours in autism spectrum disorder.' *Journal of Autism and Developmental Disorders 42*, 11, 2404–2409.

Rossetti, J. and King, C. (2010) 'Use of animal-assisted therapy with psychiatric patients.' *Journal of Psychosocial Nursing & Mental Health Services 48*, 11, 44–48.

Ruini, C. and Fava, G.A. (2009) 'Well-being therapy for generalized anxiety disorder.' *Journal of Clinical Psychology 65*, 5, 510–519.

SANE Australia (no date) 'Anxiety disorder.' *Mental Health & Illness. Facts & Guides*. Melbourne, VIC: SANE Australia. Available at www.sane.org/mental-health-and-illness/facts-and-guides/anxiety-disorder, accessed on 25 July 2015.

Sasson, N.J., Lam, K.S.L., Parlier, M., Daniels, J.L. and Pive, J. (2013) 'Autism and the broad autism phenotype: familial patterns and intergenerational transmission.' *Journal of Neurodevelopmental Disorders 5*, 1, 11.

Sebat, J. et al. (2007) 'Strong Association of De Novo Copy Number Mutations with Autism.' *Science 20*, 5823, 445–449.

Segal, Z.V., Williams, J.M. and Teasdale, J.D. (2002) *Mindfulness-based Cognitive Therapy for Depression: A New Approach to Preventing Relapse*. New York: Guilford Press.

selfharmUK (no date, a) 'The myths: Attention please.' Available at www.selfharm.co.uk/get/myths/attention_please, accessed on 21 January 2015.

selfharmUK (no date, b) 'The facts: Recovering from self-harm.' Available at www.selfharm.co.uk/get/facts/recovering_from_self-harm, accessed on 23 January 2015.

Singh, N.N., Lancioni, G.E., Manikam, R., Winton, A.S.W., Singh, A.N., Singh, J. and Singh, A.D. (2011) 'A mindfulness-based strategy for self-management of aggressive behavior in adolescents with autism.' *Research in Autism Spectrum Disorders 5*, 3, 1153–1158.

Spek, A.A., van Ham, N.C. and Nyklicek, I. (2013) 'Mindfulness-based therapy in adults with an autism spectrum disorder: A randomized controlled trial.' *Research in Developmental Disabilities: A Multidisciplinary Journal 34*, 1, 246–253.

Taylor, G.J., Bagby, M.R. and Parker, J.D.A. (1999) *Disorders of Affect Regulation: Alexithymia in Medical and Psychiatric Illness.* Cambridge: Cambridge University Press.

Tsai, L. (2007) 'Asperger syndrome and medication treatment.' *Focus on Autism and Other Developmental Disabilities 22*, 3, 138–148.

Wing L. (1986). 'Clarification on Asperger's syndrome.' *Journal of Autism and Developmental Disorders 16*, 4, 513–15.

ABOUT THE AUTHORS

One of the book's authors, Jeanette Purkis, is a successful civil servant, author, public speaker and autism advocate with a lived experience of autism and mental illness. Dr Jane Nugent is a psychiatric career medical officer, general practitioner (GP) and lecturer in pharmacology who has both a professional interest in psychopharmacology and a personal interest in and understanding of the autism spectrum. Dr Emma Goodall has Asperger's. She has managed a regional mental health organisation as well as being an autism spectrum consultant, lecturer and early career researcher in the area of autism.

The unique perspectives of psychiatrist, educator and lived experience expert are brought together in this book to provide a holistic overview of living well with autism and mental health issues for individuals, families, clinicians and health professionals.

INDEX